Whence They Came

Whence They Came

Deportation from Canada 1900-1935

Barbara Roberts
Foreword by Irving Abella

University of Ottawa Press

 UNIVERSITÉ D'OTTAWA
UNIVERSITY OF OTTAWA

Canadian Cataloguing in Publication Data

Roberts, Barbara Ann
Whence they came: deportation from Canada, 1900-1935

Bibliography: p.
ISBN 0-7766-0163-6

1. Deportation—Canada—History. 2. Canada—Emigration and immigration—Government
policy—History. I. Title.

JV7253.R62 1988   364.6'8   C88-090318-X

Typeset in Caxton Book by Nancy Poirier Typesetting Limited
Printed and bound by D.W. Friesen, Altona, Manitoba
Design by Chris Jackson, Ottawa

This book has been published with the help of a grant from the Canadian Federation for
the Humanities, using funds provided by the Social Sciences and Humanities Research
Council of Canada.

CONTENTS

FOREWORD   vii

ACKNOWLEDGEMENTS   xi

1
The Functions of Deportation   1

2
The Law and Deportation   11

3
Incidence and Patterns of Deportation   37

4
Developing the System, 1890s-1920   53

5
The Alien Bolshevik Menace, 1910-1920s   71

6
The Bureaucracy Matures, 1920s-1935   99

7
Troublemakers and Communists, 1930-1935   125

8
''Shovelling Out'' the Redundant, 1930-1935   159

9
''Purely Administrative Proceedings''   195

NOTES   203

APPENDIX
Ministers Responsible for Immigration, 1867-1936   235

BIBLIOGRAPHY   237

FOREWORD

Canada is a peculiar nation. Peopled by immigrants, it is a country, paradoxically, which hates immigration. Every single public opinion survey over the past fifty years indicates that most Canadians – including by the way, most immigrants themselves – do not want any substantial increase in the number of people admitted to this country. This attitude may surprise Canadians, but historically it should not.

It is one of our great national myths that Canada has a long history of welcoming refugees and dissidents, of always being in the forefront in accepting the world's oppressed and dispossessed, of being receptive and hospitable to wave after wave of immigrants.

We Canadians like to think that racism and bigotry are European or American in origin and play little part in our history, tradition or psyche. We see our's as a country of vast open space and of limitless potential which has always been open and available to the proverbial huddled masses yearning to be free.

Yet as the recent literature in Canadian history has shown, the Canadian record is one of which we ought not be proud. Our treatment of our native people as well as our abysmal history in admitting blacks, Chinese, Japanese, Indians and, during the 1930s and 1940s Jews, should lay to rest the myth of our liberalism and enlightenment on matters of race and immigration.

Let us face fact. For most of our history Canadian immigration laws were racist and exclusionary. We knew precisely what kind of people we wanted, and how to keep out those we didn't. Until the 1960s our immigration policies divided the world into two – the ''preferred'' races who were always welcome in Canada and the ''non-preferred'' who rarely were. The former were of British and European stock; the latter included almost everybody else.

The central problem of Canadian immigration policy is that for most of our history we did not have one. Since 1867 the country has had precisely four immigration acts. Nor has there ever been in Canada – neither now nor in the past – any clearly articulated national consensus about what immigration should be or what it would do. Except for one constant – its discriminatory aspects – our policies have had little consistency.

There is good reason for our lack of a grand public vision: immigration is an issue that divides Canadians far more than it unites them. It has been a political hot potato that no one in Ottawa wanted to touch. Indeed not until 1952, fully eighty-five years after we became a nation, and after the country had absorbed millions of newcomers, did we finally feel it was time to create an independent Department of Immigration with its own minister. Until then immigration was so little thought of that its responsibilities were passed back and forth amongst various reluctant departments – clearly an indication of how little respect, or thought, was given to immigration policy. At one time or another it came under the responsibility of the Departments of the Interior, Agriculture, Mines and Natural Resources.

As a result, until recently, immigration policy was largely in the hands of a small number of bureaucrats. Throughout most of our history this tiny group, almost by default, orchestrated our immigration policies. Their role, as they saw it, was not to find ways to bring people to Canada, but rather to devise restrictions to keep them out. They were our country's gatekeepers, yet they were determined to open the gates as little and as narrowly as possible.

And for the greater part of our history they succeeded. It was only in the past twenty-five years that Canada abandoned her discriminatory policies and opened herself to immigrants from places never before recognized as potential sources of immigrants – the Caribbean, India, Pakistan, South-East Asia, and the Middle East.

It is this small group of government officials who strove so desperately to fend off "offensive" peoples that is the subject of this fascinating book. Indeed, as Barbara Roberts shows, not only did they succeed in keeping our doors closed, but they also managed to find a way to get rid of some of those who managed to break through their carefully erected restrictive barriers. Her story of the repugnant deportation practices in Canada between 1900 and 1935 is a powerful indictment of Canadian immigration policy. Using a remarkable array of sources, Dr. Roberts brings to light for the first time, the murky activities of government officials who used deportation to dispose of a wide variety of unwanted immigrants.

For thirty-five years immigration officials – on their own, usually without consulting Parliament or their ministers – not only decided who could come to Canada, but how to get rid of those already here they did not want. This handful of bureaucrafts were *de facto* judges and juries on all immigration matters. Their decisions on whom to deport, as Roberts makes clear, were not only arbitrary, they were often illegal. For years immigration authorities broke the law with impunity in order to protect Canada from those they deemed "undesirable", Canada's record in deporting immigrants was by far the worst in the entire British Commonwealth.

This is an important book. Roberts carefully and dispassionately describes the behaviour of a Department of Immigration which seemed to be, on occasion, the rogue elephant of the Canadian bureaucracy. Yet it is important to note that the activities of these officials – illegal and bizarre as they often were – raised scarcely a ripple of protest in Parliament or in the country at large. After all, most Canadians, and certainly all politicians in this period, approved of what the bureaucrats were doing – ridding Canada of the poor and the unemployed as well as those who might be politically unacceptable.

Canada has come a long way since the 1930s. And certainly over the past three or four decades we have become a haven for millions of immigrants and refugees looking for salvation and freedom. But there are still a number of Canadians – too many – who resent what is happening to this country, who wish to turn the immigration clock back fifty years, who feel that Canada is beginning to look like the United Nations with so many black, brown, and yellow faces on their streets and subways.

For them as well as for all Canadians, *Whence They Came* is a timely reminder of the cruelty and inequity of an earlier immigration policy. If we err in the future, as we likely will, let it be, for once, on the side of humanity.

IRVING ABELLA
Toronto, August 1988

ACKNOWLEDGEMENTS

Earlier parts of my research on deportation were aided by grants from the Social Sciences and Humanities Research Council, Secretary of State Multiculturalism Programme, and the University of Winnipeg.

I am grateful for ideas, insights, and various other kinds of material and moral support at various stages, from Cornelius Jaenen, Alison Griffith, Marguerite Cassin, Leslie Laczko, and too many other colleagues, friends, and family members to name here. I particularly want to acknowledge the love and help I have received from my feminist friends who sustain and inspire me. Over the years required to complete this book, David Millar has provided much in the way of domestic services, enthusiasm for the project, and recurring good humour. I have benefitted especially from his expertise and generosity as a researcher, historian, and teacher. I am also indebted to various patient souls who have helped make my writing more readable, most recently my editor, Wendy Duschenes.

My interest in deportation arose partly from my own experiences as an immigrant to Canada. Immigration is part of our family history: my maternal grandfather came to Canada from England in 1911; my mother married an American in the 1930s and left to live in the United States, where I grew up. I came to Canada in 1970, one of thousands of self-imposed political exiles from the U.S., believing I had found a more just and humane homeland.

This book is dedicated to the deports. It could have been me.

1

The Functions of Deportation

This book is a study of deportation of immigrants from Canada to the countries whence they had come, between 1900 and 1935. The first chapter considers the part that deportation played in managing the labour supply and maintaining the social order. The next chapter provides an overview of the legal framework for deportation, looking also at factors that influenced the timing and specific provisions of the pertinent sections of the legislation. Chapter 3 offers a critical look at the official statistics on deportation, and explores some of the misleading conclusions suggested by the official reports of the Department of Immigration. The fourth chapter outlines the early years of deportation, identifying the patterns developed in those years that would be significant in subsequent decades. Chapter 5 examines in more detail one of these patterns: the systematic deportation of radicals and dissidents in the period immediately before and after the First World War. Next, Chapter 6 describes the deportation practices of the mature bureaucracy between 1920 and 1935. Chapter 7 returns to the theme of political deportation to explore the use of deportation to control those who resisted the social and economic conditions of the Great Depression of the 1930s. The wholesale deportation of the unemployed (denied by the government) from Canada during that same period is described in Chapter 8. Finally, Chapter 9 considers the arbitrary and unjust manner (and often illegal) in which deportation has been carried out.

Although deportation played a crucial part in immigration policy, and was from time to time the subject of controversy, it has been little studied by historians. Perhaps this lack of interest is due to the general impression, carefully cultivated by officials and politicians responsible for its management, that deportation was an exceptional and infrequent occurrence, caused by the failing or malfeasance of individual immigrants. As this book will show, nothing could be further from the truth. It is only through careful examination of behind-the-scenes evidence that the fallacy of this blame-the-victim explanation can be seen. The sources upon which this book is based include internal records of the Department of Immigration, as well as those of municipal and provincial governments and other federal departments; oral history interviews; first-hand accounts of victims and their supporters; contemporary and historical legal and other documents, and scholarly studies.

The responsibility for deportation – and immigration – has moved from one ministry to another over the years, and operated under various names. (For the sake of consistency, I have referred to ''the Department of Immigration'' throughout.) At Confederation, immigration and quarantine matters were dealt with by the Department of Agriculture. In 1892, immigration matters were moved to the Department of the Interior, which dealt with land settlement; a separate Immigration Branch was set up as part of Interior in 1893. (Quarantine services remained under Agriculture until 1918, when they, along with immigration medical inspection services, moved to the newly created Department of Health.) An independent Department of Immigration and Colonization was established in 1917; this arrangement endured until 1936.

Although the period after that date is beyond the scope of this study, readers may wish to know the recent history of the Department. From 1936 to 1950, Immigration was reduced to a branch of the Department of Mines and Resources. The Department of Citizenship and Immigration was formed in 1950 from the Immigration Branch of Mines and Resources and the Citizenship and Citizenship Registration Branch of the Secretary of State; this was replaced by the Department of Manpower and Immigration in 1966, which became the Canada Employment and Immigration Commission in 1977, now part of the Ministry of Employment and Immigration. Since 1967 deportation has been the responsibility of the Immigration Appeal Board. Although certain features of the law, policy, and procedures have been changed, the essentials have remained consistent to the present day.

Canada's deportation practices were among the most arbitrary in the Commonwealth. Parliament and the courts were neither well informed about, nor had significant control over, the policies and practices of the Department of Immigration, whose bureaucrats carried out a clandestine and illegal immigrant selection process, and deported immigrants according to their own informal and extralegal system of justice. Immigration officials misrepresented and concealed their activities. "Deports" had fewer rights than criminals; they were not entitled to due process, to know the precise nature of charges against them, to confront their accusers, or to be tried by a jury of their peers. They were presumed guilty and their hearings took place at closed administrative tribunals.

Deportation helped to relieve employers, municipalities, and the state from the burdens of poverty, unemployment, and political unrest. Deportation helped the municipalities to "shovel out" some of their poor in much the same way as emigration had helped English parishes in the early nineteenth century, and reduced relief and other maintenance costs. Deportation removed workers when they became useless, surplus, or obstreperous. It helped the state to reduce maintenance costs for some of its non-producing members, by deferring these costs to the economies of the sending countries. It also served some function of social and political control by eliminating social protesters. Deportation was a necessary part of immigration, the equivalent of the sewage system of cities. It was the drain through which our immigration refuse was directed, in order to assure that "the river of our national life" would not be "polluted by the turbid streams"[1] of the immigrant unfit, unemployed, and unprofitable.

Deportation of the economically unfit is a practice going back to the early days of English poor relief. Eligibility for poor relief (welfare) was based on the right of "settlement", akin to domicile or citizenship. Settlement was acquired through birth; women took their husband's settlement upon marriage. By the mid-nineteenth century, settlement could be gained in some circumstances by five years' residence. Parishes could rid themselves of paupers or prospective paupers who did not have settlement by a process called "removal".[2] Legal removal was carried out by an overseer of the removing parish, and took place from the parish where the person lived but did not have settlement, to the parish of settlement. When done legally, it was a costly process. Less expensive alternatives were popular. One was to have the person arrested for vagrancy. This was so common as to lead one scholar to comment that vagrancy laws were ''the penal side of the poor law.'' The vagrant could simply be sent through parishes by cart from constable to constable until he or she reached the home parish. The minimal costs were paid by the parishes through which the vagrant moved. In some cases the vagrant was punished by whipping or imprisonment, or both, before being sent away. Another cheap method was used against pregnant women who did not have settlement. Even non-pauper pregnant women represented a potential cost to the parish. If their child was born in a given parish, there it would have settlement. Single women, and married women who may have been settled by birth, but lost their own settlement when they married a man from another parish, were vulnerable to such removals. Sometimes parishes tried to smuggle women over the line into the next parish, quite late in their pregnancy. Substantial numbers of pregnant women became vagrants because they were expelled from parishes. The practices employed were often ''bereft of both humanity and decency.''[3]

The powers of the parish to remove were increased by the Act of Settlement of 1662, which defined categories of removables. As long as people did not apply for relief, they might be left alone unless it seemed likely that they would become public charges. If they did apply for relief, however, their removal was likely. The 1834 Poor Law Report recommended some reform in this area, notably that the practice of removing pregnant women cease, and that a child born outside of marriage take its mother's settlement, regardless of where it was born.[4]

The parallels between British poor law removal in the eighteenth and nineteenth centuries and deportation from Canada in the late nineteenth and early twentieth are striking. In most instances, persons were safe from expulsion if they had settlement or domicile. Expulsion was usually contingent upon becoming a public charge. Persons who did not apply for relief were generally untouched. Legal removal or deportation was used to pass paupers and their relief costs back to their home parish or country of origin, where they could not be deferred or refused. To follow the legal procedures laid out in the legislation was costly to the removing parish or to the federal government. Attempts were frequently made to cut down the expenses: by sending vagrants away in carts and having the in-transit parishes pay costs, in the one case, or forcing the transportation companies to pay, in the other.

Deportation was intimately connected to poor relief in late nineteenth and early twentieth century Canada. The Department of Immigration stated on numerous occasions (and the law confirmed it) that deportation was a relief to the municipalities and provinces. Canadian transportation companies seem to have concurred in this view, as a Canadian Pacific Railway (CPR) Passenger Agent made clear in his complaint that the CPR was being asked by Immigration to help municipalities ''shovel out'' their paupers: ''Municipalities should take care of their own poor,'' he said; ''there is no reason that I can see why private corporations should participate in a matter of this kind anymore than any other tax payer.''[5] Deputy Minister of Agriculture J. C. Taché testified in 1877 that

> All countries which receive large numbers of immigrants naturally adopt a rule of this nature; I notice in the report of the New York Immigration Commissioners, very considerable sums for a service of this kind, even in prosperous years.[6]

States often ''repatriated'' foreign paupers. New York State alone removed 1,672 public charges between 1923 and 1928, removed 177 insane immigrants in 1928, and 197 in 1929. This was in addition to the bulk of legal deportation, which was carried out by the U.S. federal government.[7] Canada too ''repatriated'' immigrants; this is shown by the Department's internal statistics on problems with British female domestics in the 1920s and 1930s. ''Repatriation'', whether by federal or local government, constituted an informal and extralegal system of deportation. Both informal and legal systems of deportation played an important role in Canadian immigration policy.

The stated ideal of Canadian immigration policy was to attract a permanent agricultural population. Behind this ideal, thinly concealed and little denied, lay a more-or-less Wakefieldian system.[8] These permanent settlers would often be forced into wage labour, either in the short term to accumulate the capital to start farming their own land (''cash stake''), or in the long term to supplement inadequate farm earnings.[9] Hidden behind that bitter but still palatable modification of the ideal lay yet another reality: a massive system of importing industrial workers who could hardly claim to be farmers, even potentially. As Donald Avery has shown, Canada's immigration policy promoted the recruitment of a large body of unskilled industrial workers who would function (and likely remain) as an industrial proletariat.[10] Yet whether the immigrants were thought to go straight to their Prairie homesteads, to detour briefly or intermittently into wage labour, or to be permanently absorbed into the industrial sector of the economy, one thing was clear: Canada claimed to expect these immigrants to become Canadians.

Even the severest critics of Canadian immigration policy accepted the claim that Canada was trying to attract a permanent population. Attempts by corporate interests to import large numbers of contract workers for short-term jobs were refused by the government. As Avery points out, Immigration officials "time after time refused to allow industrial workers into the country on temporary permits."[11] If industrial workers entered Canada, they came on the same legal terms as the highly prized legitimate agriculturalists on whose work of building the nation it was much more politically sound to focus: as landed immigrants who were eligible for citizenship after three years. (After 1919 the period was extended to five years.)

The federal government was uncomfortable about what they recognized to be the reality of the immigrant industrial proletariat lying behind the myth of the immigrant independent agricultural producer. But this "reality" was little more than another myth that disguised a politically devastating truth: "many of the Europeans who came to Canada were in effect guest workers, who met the needs of Canadian industry and agriculture and then went home."[12] In fact, by 1920 the federal government systematically determined how many harvesters would be needed, and encouraged and sometimes directly supervised their importation from the U.S. and the British Isles. Although harvesters came in as landed immigrants, "the Annual harvest migrations to the Prairie Provinces led to no considerable permanent movements of population," George Haythorne (later Assistant Deputy Minister of Labour) explained in 1933.[13]

Agriculture's seasonality makes it easy to detect this stream of migrant labour thinly concealed within the flow of would-be permanent settlers. Yet other industries were equally if not more dependent upon this type of work force. This was particularly true of lumbering, mining, and railway construction. The Department was not particularly pleased about this. As Avery points out, "by 1913, Immigration officials were concerned that Canada was becoming increasingly committed to a guest-worker form of immigration." But there was little that the Department could do. These industries wanted "an expendable labour force [that] takes its problems away when it is re-exported," as the American Dillingham Commission on Immigration put it in 1910. The Department could only refuse to issue temporary work permits.[14] This did not matter to the employers: as long as there was a flow of cheap immigrant labour, it made little difference whether they were legally guest workers or landed immigrants. In fact, the latter status offered a number of advantages to the employer, in part because it was unregulated.

Canada's concealed guest worker system offered significant economic and political advantages to employers and the state. A migrant work force displays certain characteristics. As Michael Burawoy has pointed out, the functions of maintenance and reproduction of the migrant work force invariably take place in different locations. In a migrant labour system, the costs of renewing the work force are passed on completely or partially to the sending economy or state. The employer of migrant labour is "neither responsible politically nor accountable financially to the external political and economic systems," that is, to the sending countries.[15] The receiving, or employing, country has greatly reduced costs for social services partly because the families of workers remain in the sending country, where the costs of educational, medical, and other social services are paid. These reproductive costs (of family formation, child rearing, and labour market training) are thus of no concern to the receiving employers or government. Migrant labour is cheap not only in terms of lower wages paid to the migrant worker, but in terms of other maintenance costs of the work force. Migrant workers can be kept in camps, fed en masse, and provided with minimal welfare services. Moreover, if these workers are injured, incapacitated, or incapable, neither the employer nor the state is obliged to take care of them in the long term. Since, under this system, these workers have no claim on the resources of the receiving country or the employer, they can be sent back "home" when their usefulness is at an end. In some instances, migrant workers may end up becoming domestic workers as long-term residents or citizens, and change from migrant to immigrant with a consequent improvement in status in terms of political if not economic rights.

The situations of South African migrant miners and California farm workers have much in common with those of immigrant industrial workers in Canada earlier this century. South African mine tasks were allotted according to race, workers were housed in barracks in isolated camps, and paid enough to keep themselves going and send a bit home, but not to save a large enough amount to stop wage work. In Canada there was also a system of occupational segregation and subordination based on ethnicity; many workers were housed and fed in isolated camps, often at very low standards. Sojourners who came to Canada in boom times may have realised their dream of returning home rich but, for many – or possibly the majority, in times of economic depression – suddenly the dream could turn to ashes. The pre-First World War railway workers are a case in point: thousands were trapped by the depression, imprisoned in internment camps during the war, and released to the big companies when the demand for their labour again became acute.

The alternatives for many of these immigrants, if not the majority, were: to continue working in Canada, taking (or hoping to take) long visits back home; to become an agricultural settler, often on land so marginal or so expensive to put into production that continued seasonal wage work was necessary; or to join the permanent industrial proletariat. Deciding to remain permanently in Canada was no guarantee that they would be permitted to do so. Unless immigrants lived here continuously long enough to attain domicile and, ideally, citizenship, they could be deported if they got into trouble or ceased to be productive workers. This deportation could take place legally and formally, under the auspices of the Department, or it could take place informally, outside the legal framework. For instance, an immigrant thrown out of work might apply to a municipality for some form of poor relief; the municipality would then report the immigrant to the Department and set in motion the legal deportation process. Alternatively, the municipality could refuse to grant relief. In many cases, this would leave the immigrant little alternative but to effect his or her own do-it-yourself "deportation". This method was even cheaper for the municipality and the federal government, and was favoured in times of economic distress.[16]

There was much less incentive to give poor relief to immigrants in Canada than in some other places. In the British Isles in the eighteenth century, in parts of the U.S. in the twentieth, poor relief was given to agricultural and other workers to retain them until their labour was needed, at which time the relief was cut off and they were forced to take the available jobs. In Canada it was not necessary to use poor relief to maintain a readily available supply of cheap labour; immigration provided this, particularly after the First World War when inflow was directly adjusted to the labour requirements of certain large employers.

Deportation was one of the mechanisms that maintained a balance between the need for cheap labour in times of economic expansion, and the desire to cut welfare costs in times of economic contraction. Those who were superfluous to demand or useless to production, and those who upset or threatened the system could be removed, if they were immigrants – and they often were. Deportation deferred some of the costs of maintaining and reproducing the labour force onto the sending country and economy. Deportation was an unheralded but important way not only to keep the stream of immigration pure, but, more to the point, to keep profits high and problems few. An industrial economy needs a large supply of mobile labour. Canadian immigration policy made sure that acquiring that labour supply was not a problem. Deportation helped to assure that removing it was not a problem either. Deportation, both formal and informal, helped to create a hidden system of migrant labour that functioned much like a "guest worker" system, even though stated policy was that immigrants were to be permanent settlers.[17] It was a concealed but necessary regulator of the balance between labour demand and labour supply, which was in itself a critical determinant of Canadian immigration policy and practice between 1900 and 1935.

2

The Law and Deportation

The legal bases for the actions of the Department of Immigration were the Immigration Acts and amendments passed by Parliament, supplemented by various Orders-in-Council. Departmental policies, regulations, and practice were mandated to conform to the decisions of Parliament which, with Cabinet, was responsible for determining and overseeing the Department's activities; such was the continuing judgement of law courts. Although Parliament passed the laws that governed the Department, most Members of Parliament were quite ignorant about the powers and practices of the Department, particularly insofar as deportation was concerned. Parliament's control was tenuous and illusory. Most of the legislation related to deportation was passed at the instigation of the Department itself. Information given to the Minister and to Parliament was carefully selected by functionaries in the Department. Legislative change was as likely to legalize existing practices as to set in motion new procedures. From 1906 onwards, laws reflected the increasingly arbitrary practices of the Department. Fundamentals of British justice, such as the right to trial by jury, had no legal place in the deportation process. As long as the Department followed the laws in the Immigration Act, it was free to utilise the most arbitrary methods. The courts were specifically prohibited from interfering as long as no illegalities were discernible. Because deportation was defined as an administrative proceeding, it was not subject to public scrutiny. Parliament had no way of knowing, and seemed to take little interest in, the details of the normal day-to-day operations of deportation. Thus, there were few effective checks on the Department.

Deportation of legal immigrants was not officially permitted before the 1906 Immigration Act was passed. Nevertheless, there had been laws since 1869 to restrict certain kinds of immigration, and since 1889 certain classes could be sent back whence they came. The Department of Immigration followed ''a general line of action'' whereby immigrants insane, disabled, or destitute in Canada were required to be shipped back at the transportation companies' expense, much as if they had never gained admission. The 1906 Act allowed the Department to deport immigrants within two years of entry for many of the same causes specified as grounds for exclusion.[1] The deportation powers lay in several clauses of the Act. Section 28 provided that

> any person landed in Canada who, within two years thereafter, has become a charge upon the public funds, whether municipal, provincial, or federal, or an inmate of or a charge upon any charitable institution, may be deported and returned to the port or place whence such immigrant came or sailed for Canada.

Section 32 stipulated that those bringing in immigrants would, under certain circumstances, be responsible for transporting them out of Canada:

> All railway or transportation companies or other persons bringing immigrants from any country into Canada shall, on the demand of the Superintendent of Immigration, deport to the country whence he was brought, any immigrant prohibited by this Act or any order in council or regulation made thereunder, from being landed in Canada who was brought in by such railway, transportation company or other person into Canada within a period of two years prior to the date of such demand.

Prohibited immigrants under the 1906 Act included the diseased, infirm, disabled, handicapped and destitute. The Governor General in Council had the right to prohibit others:[2]

> Whenever in Canada an immigrant has within two years of his landing in Canada committed a crime involving moral turpitude, or become an inmate of a jail or hospital or other charitable institution, it shall be the duty of the clerk or secretary of the municipality to forthwith notify the Minister thereof, giving full particulars. On receipt of such

information the Minister may, on investigating the facts, order the deportation of such immigrant at the cost and charges of such immigrant if he is able to pay, and if not then at the cost of the municipality wherein he has last been regularly resident, if so ordered by the Minister, and if he is a vagrant or tramp, or there is no such municipality, then at the cost of the Department of Interior.[3]

The Act of 1910 added provisions for deportation on the grounds of moral and political unsuitability. The moral grounds were covered in Section 3, which listed the prohibited classes; subsections (e) and (f) were an expansion of the 1906 provisions against prostitution and related offences, to which now [sexual] immorality was added:

> (e) prostitutes and women and girls coming to Canada for any immoral purpose and pimps or persons living on the avails of prostitution;
> (f) persons who procure or attempt to bring into Canada prostitutes or women or girls for the purpose of prostitution or other immoral purpose;

The political provisions were found in Section 41:

> Whenever any person other than a Canadian citizen advocates in Canada the overthrow by force or violence of the government of Great Britain or Canada, or other British dominion, colony, possession or dependency, or the overthrow by force or violence of constituted law and authority, or the assassination of any official of the government of Great Britain or Canada or other British dominion, colony, possession or dependency, or of any foreign government, or shall by word or act create or attempt to create riot or public disorder in Canada, or shall by common repute belong to or be suspected of belonging to any secret society or organization which extorts money from, or in any way attempts to control, any resident of Canada by force or threat of bodily harm, or by blackmail; such persons for the purposes of this Act shall be considered and classed as an undesirable immigrant, and it shall be the duty of any officer becoming cognizant thereof, and the duty of the clerk, secretary or other official of any municipality in Canada wherein such a person may be, to forthwith send a written complaint thereof to the Minister or Superintendent of Immigration, giving full particulars.

Any immigrant in Canada contrary to the provisions of the Act was subject to investigation by the Department, and if suspected of belonging to the prohibited or undesirable classes, could be detained for examination by a Board of Inquiry composed of officials of the Department. If, after investigation, the person were found to be a member of the prohibited or undesirable classes as specified by the Act, they would be deported, subject to right of appeal to the Minister.[4]

The provision for deportation for certain conditions or types of offence under the 1910 Act established the legal framework for deportation that was to remain substantially unchanged until well after the Second World War (and in some respects until the present day). Subsequent legislation refined procedures; specified the steps in the processes by which deportations were to be carried out; increased the numbers and types of immigrants technically deportable; and expanded the already considerable powers of the Department to act arbitrarily, as long as it adhered to the complicated regulations. The main features of deportation, and the main legal causes given by the Department to account for its deportations, were established with the passage of the 1910 Act.

American practice was perhaps the single most important influence in shaping the 1910 Canadian legislation. This influence was particularly evident in the clauses that excluded immigrants on account of their immorality or their political beliefs. The U.S. Act of 1903 to regulate the immigration of aliens into the United States was "prohibitive in character," according to a study done by a Canadian immigration official, and unlike Canadian legislation, contained almost no provisions for the protection of immigrants on the voyage or at landing.

Among the prohibited classes in the U.S. law of 1903 were:

> anarchists, or persons who believe in or advocate the overthrow by force or violence of the Government of the United States, or of all government, or of all forms of law, or the assassination of public officials.

This was the first time in either country that immigrants were prohibited on account of their political beliefs.[5]

The U.S. prohibition of anarchists marked the crest of anti-anarchist hysteria following the 1901 assassination of President McKinley. It was almost completely unnecessary because there were virtually no immigrant anarchists to exclude or expel. Canada had even less reason to fear this group, but nonetheless Canada followed the American example and by 1910 included anarchists in its prohibited classes.[6]

Although there were few alien anarchists in the U.S., there were other kinds of radicals considered dangerous, such as the Industrial

Workers of the World (IWW) and other labour "agitators" (particularly the new industrial unionists). To U.S. immigration authorities, they were all dangerous "anarchists". Tensions between the conservatives and vested interests, on the one hand, and the reformers, progressives, and radicals, on the other, were high in the U.S. Tightening up on immigration legislation, especially concerning the exclusion and expulsion of "undesirables", was one of the responses to this tension. The situation in Canada and the official response to it were similar to those in the United States, so far as the Department of Immigration was concerned.

Canadian preoccupation with U.S. immigration law is on record at least as early as 1900, when Canadian immigration authorities noted with interest the sections on exclusion and expulsion in the U.S. Treasury Department Digest of Immigration Laws and Decisions of 1899. In 1904 Canadian Minister of Immigration Clifford Sifton requested a comparison between Canadian and U.S. laws, to be used in amending the Canadian legislation. In subsequent years, the U.S. Act was again seen as a model by various Canadian immigration officials concerned with revising Canadian laws. These officials used as a point of reference the U.S. Act's definitions of terms, of classes prohibited, classes deportable, deportation procedures, and length of time during which immigrants could be deported. Although it was not necessarily their intent to always have Canadian legislation copy U.S. law, Immigration officials regarded U.S. legislation as a model and wanted to incorporate certain of the U.S. provisions into the Canadian Act.[7]

Sifton had supported this view when he was Minister from 1896 to 1905. So did his successor, Frank Oliver, although it is not clear whether he came into office with this view or was converted to it by his staff. The galley proofs of Oliver's proposed 1906 Bill compared in detail the provisions of the new Canadian legislation with the existing law, explaining the defects of the latter and the merits of the former by comparison to U.S. legislation. Subsequent discussion in Parliament was based on this material. Oliver also ordered the Department to make a clause-by-clause comparison between the proposed 1906 Canadian legislation, and the existing U.S. Act. In the new Canadian Act of 1910, there were some departures from U.S. legislation. While the prohibited classes were essentially the same, the Canadian Act did not bar anarchists from entry; instead, it provided for their post-entry deportation. There was also a difference in the statute of limitation for deportation, i.e., the period after landing within which an immigrant could be deported. In Canada it had been two years; in the U.S., three. The Canadian period later became the same.[8]

The debt owed to the U.S. legislation was acknowledged by Canadian officials. In the Commons, Oliver explained,

> while we have taken advantage of a good deal of the work that has been done in the drafting of the United States Act we have not found it advantageous to follow it in all its particulars.

The most compelling reason for not following it exactly seemed to be that certain sections of the U.S. Act were not clearly worded, or did not address Canadian conditions. Other sections were applicable in their entirety, and were reproduced verbatim. When U.S. officials were shown the Canadian Bill and asked to comment, the U.S. Commissioner of Immigration at Ellis Island wrote to the Canadian Chief Medical Officer that he was gratified indeed "to note how closely together the two Governments are working on immigration lines."[9]

How U.S. laws found their way into the Canadian Immigration Acts can be seen in the insertion into the Canadian Act of 1910 of "immorality" as grounds for exclusion or expulsion. Before this, deportations for immorality had taken place, but they were not legal deportations and officials were concerned about repercussions. In a 1907 case the Winnipeg Commissioner of Immigration Obed Smith wrote to his superior, Superintendent of Immigration Scott, about a Swedish man "carrying on immoral practices to the detriment of public welfare," who had been deported very rapidly when he threatened to fight the order. Safer methods were needed. If the immigrant could be convicted of a crime involving moral turpitude (never clearly or satisfactorily defined), they could be deported as a criminal; there could be no appeal and no "problem". The Commissioner suggested an amendment to the Immigration Act: an immigrant who was "guilty of immoral practices" or who "seems to be unable to discriminate between right and wrong," or who "is a moral pervert in the opinion of the Department, shall be declared an undesirable." Without such an amendment, it was risky for the Department to illegally deport an immigrant "who plainly was an undesirable, yet [as the Commissioner himself admitted] *scarcely* came within the exact wording of the Act."[10]

By 1908 the Department realized that laws must be passed to legalize its current practices. The Department had been brought to court for its illegalities, and had been forced to release several "deports", as they were called. Early that year, the Department wrote to a variety of officials, agents, medical officers and the like, soliciting suggestions for amendments. T.R.E. McInnes, a lawyer who had done intelligence-gathering and policy-advising immigration work for Laurier, was hired by the Department to draft a new Act. McInnes worked directly with Minister Oliver to respond to pressures from within and outside the Department for various amendments. In McInnes' original draft of December 1909, there was no immorality clause. The later draft that became law included immorality as a ground for exclusion and deportation.[11] McInnes had been strongly opposed to such a provision. Superintendent Scott was strongly in favour.

Scott had become preoccupied with the problem of "eloping couples". In March 1909 he had complained that under the provisions of the existing legislation he could not prevent eloping couples from immigrating to Canada, and he wanted the power to stop them. Canada debarred only prostitutes and those living off the revenue of prostitution. Unless "elopers" were connected with prostitution, they could not be legally excluded or expelled.[12]

Scott wanted the Canadian law to use the same language as that of the United States. McInnes strongly disagreed with this suggestion. He had deliberately left out the phrase referring to immorality from his draft of the Act, believing that as long as it fell short of prostitution, immorality was not "any business of an Immigration officer or of a Government." Prostitution was a crime; immorality was not. Adultery, for instance, although a crime in some of the American states, was not criminal according to British or Canadian law. As well, McInnes decried the U.S. "tendencies to meddle in purely personal and private affairs." Immigration officers were "not intended to be general custodians of the morals of passengers to Canada, nor are they qualified to regulate the exercise of natural functions," he argued. Further, McInnes believed that it was a mistake to keep out "elopers". On the contrary, he thought "the more of them the better" because they usually settled in agrarian districts and "if they have the spunk enough to elope, they must have the makings of citizens in them." But he told Scott that he would "as in duty bound . . . lay your suggestion before the Minister." The issue languished on the Minister's desk for nine months. Scott revived it by sending the Minister a list of all of the suggested amendments to the Act. The new Canadian Act, which received assent 4 May 1910, followed U.S. practice and language in making immorality grounds for exclusion and expulsion.[13]

Political exclusion and deportation provisions of the Canadian Act were also virtual copies of U.S. legislation. Until 1910, the Amendments to the Immigration Act were generally concerned with clarifying definitions; outlining duties of immigration officials; increasing and specifying the responsibilities of the transportation companies for delivering healthy acceptable immigrants; providing for more widespread and thorough civil and medical inspections; increasing the power of the Governor General or the Minister to prohibit or control certain aspects of immigration; and prohibiting or expelling particular types of immigrants. Before 1910, potential immigrants had been prohibited from entering Canada when they were deemed to have physical or mental defects; when they had already become, or would in future likely become a public charge; or when they were criminals. Prohibition was based on personal undesirability. As individuals, these immigrants might constitute a danger to the public health, the public safety, or the public purse. Immoral immigrants were also individually undesirable, in effect a danger to public morals. The politically undesirable were another category altogether. They were not necessarily undesirable on physical, mental, or moral grounds, as individuals. Their undesirability as a class sprang from the view of the government that they were "directly a menace to the state."[14]

This "dangerous" class was covered under Section 41 of the 1910 Act. According to the explanatory notes on the Bill to Amend the Act, which was first introduced as Bill 17 in 1909, and passed as Bill 102 on 22 March 1910, Section 41 was based on Section 2 of the American Act. The note explained the danger of this group and justified the measures taken by the U.S. government to deal with the problem. In Washington, a special bureau dealt with anarchists, who were increasingly seen as a danger to society. This section of the Canadian Act, the note said, was intended to prevent similar types of people from becoming a menace in Canada. The wording of the Canadian Act was similar to that of the American Act.[15]

Similar parallels exist between the U.S. legislation of 1917 and 1918, and the Canadian amendments of 1919. Departmental correspondence shows that these parallels were deliberate. Scott wanted to include two points in the new legislation: "certain prohibited classes", and a limit of five years for deportations instead of three. The five-year limit for deportations applied generally in the U.S., except in the case of immigrants who were political offenders. For them, there was no limit; under the U.S. Act of 1917, they could be deported at any time after entry. This Act was originally passed by the U.S. Congress and vetoed by the President in 1913, and again in 1915. President Wilson was concerned about the difficulty of distinguishing between political exiles and anarchistic property-destroying radicals. In February 1917 Congress overrode Wilson's second veto and the Act became law. Thus, aliens deemed to conform to its provisions could be deported ''at any time'' after legal entry. This provision was unchanged in the 1918 U.S. Act upon which certain clauses in the Canadian legislation of 1919 were to be based.[16]

The 1919 Canadian Bill to amend the Immigration Act explained its debt to U.S. legislation. A U.S. Public Health Service definition of ''constitutional psychopathic inferiority'' was used, for example. Yet more noteworthy were the similarities of the last-minute amendment rushed through both Houses on 5 June 1919 and assented to 6 June 1919, which made it possible for the government to deport a naturalized citizen, or almost anyone not Canadian-born, on account of their political beliefs or actions, no matter how long they had been in Canada. This measure passed through the Commons with no debate, in something like seven-and-a-half minutes, and through the Senate in perhaps ten minutes.[17]

The 6 June 1919 amendment affected only Section 41 of the Act. As amended, the section read:

(1) Every person who by word or act in Canada seeks to overthrow by force or violence the government of or constituted law and authority in the United Kingdom of Great Britain and Ireland, or Canada, or any of the provinces of Canada, or the government of any other of His Majesty's dominions, colonies, possessions or dependencies, or advocates the assassination of any official of any of the said governments or of any foreign government, or who in Canada defends or suggests the unlawful destruction of property or by word or act creates or attempts to create any riot or public disorder in Canada, or who without lawful authority assumes any powers of government in Canada or in any part thereof, or who by common repute belongs to or is suspected of belonging to any secret society or organization which extorts money from or in any way attempts to blackmail, or who is a member of or affiliated with any organization entertaining or teaching disbelief in or opposition to organized government shall, for the purposes of this Act, be deemed to belong to the prohibited or undesirable classes, and shall be liable to deportation in the manner provided by this Act, and it shall be the duty of any officer becoming cognizant thereof and of the clerk, secretary, or other official of any municipality

to send a written complaint to the Minister, giving full particulars:
Provided, that this section shall not apply to any person who is a
British subject, either by reason of birth in Canada, or by reason of
naturalization in Canada.

(2) Proof that any person belonged to or was within the description
of any of the prohibited or undesirable classes within the meaning of
this section at any time since the fourth day of May, one thousand
nine hundred and ten, shall for all the purposes of this Act, be deemed
to establish prima facie that he still belongs to such prohibited or
undesirable class or classes.[18]

The 6 June amendment was aimed at the British-born leaders of the
Winnipeg General Strike[19] as well as at radicals who were not deportable
under the previous law.

Although the amendment was precipitated by the Winnipeg General
Strike, its roots lay in events in Canadian society as a whole, and in what
was becoming a habit by the officials of the Department of Immigration
of following American precedent in their shaping of Canadian immigration law. By early 1919, Canada was in a state of political uproar. The
powers-that-be feared class warfare. There was much discontent among
ordinary working people because of high inflation. There had been a series
of union recognition and cost-of-living strikes during 1918 and 1919,
some of them quite serious, such as those among municipal and railway
employees. Union membership exploded as unskilled and ethnic workers
joined industrial unions in numbers not equalled again until 1943.
Organizing drives were beginning to reach mining, logging, and harvesting
workers and railroad navvies, as well as workers in the non-primary
sectors. Arthur Meighen spoke for those who feared where this would
lead when he said that radical industrial unionism simply could not be
permitted because it would line up all of the employed against their
employers, and they would be ''fighting it out for supremacy.''[20]

Discontent had political sources as well. Since the ''conscription
election'' of 1917, there had been angry complaints about profiteering
(which was even more distasteful in view of the rate of inflation), and
about conscription, which was seen as an ''unequal sacrifice''; that is,
the rich should be required to sacrifice money if ordinary people were
to be required to sacrifice their lives. The government was understand-
ably nervous about this situation and attempted to crack down on its critics
through a series of Orders-in-Council in September 1918 designed to
suppress radicals of all kinds. Order-in-Council PC2384 was aimed mostly

at the IWW and the Russian Social Democratic Party, but also proscribed a number of organizations desiring to bring about economic, political, governmental, industrial, or social change in Canada by force, violence, or injury to any person or property. PC2786 added more names to the list of proscribed organizations. PC2381 banned publications and literature using Finnish, Russian, Ukrainian, Hungarian, and German, for example.[21]

The effect of this crackdown was to label ethnic organizations as radical and to drive ethnics to the left. The unity among radicals that the government had feared was in fact increased. In the face of this unity, the Borden government appointed the Mathers Commission (Royal Commission on Industrial Unrest), and hoped to stifle the radicals by passing a series of reforms which were essentially meaningless. John Bruce, the chief organizer in Canada of the American Federation of Labour, and Tom Moore of the Trades and Labour Council (TLC), were representatives on the Commission. The Commission travelled the country for the first four months of 1919, and listened to stories of discontent even from those who described themselves as conservative.

By the week of 6 June 1919, events had reached a crisis in the Winnipeg General Strike. At that time, the government told Bruce and Moore that they were to sit down and write their recommendations for the Royal Commission. They were assured that no panic action would be taken against the strikers; rather, some measure of reform would be effected, based on their recommendations. "They double crossed us," said Bruce.[22]

The betrayal took the form of Bill 03, an additional amendment to the original 1919 amendments to the Immigration Act. The originally proposed 1919 amendments would have left Section 41 substantially unchanged, but the new amendment was draconian, at least by Canadian standards. Significance lay in two provisions. The original 1919 Bill had modified Section 2 (d) of the Immigration Act, to prevent the attainment of domicile and to assure that domicile already gained was lost "by any person belonging to the prohibited or undesirable classes within the meaning of Section 41 of this Act." Thus, domicile was no protection against politically motivated deportation. The stated intent of this amendment was to allow the Department to deport anarchists and other Section 41 undesirables even after five years' residence. This would have been impossible under the old provision which allowed deportation on political grounds only if an immigrant were an anarchist at entry, or became so before five years had elapsed.[23]

This was drastic enough, but the 6 June amendment provided also that anyone who was not a Canadian-born or naturalized citizen could be deported for political offences. Here was a provision obviously aimed at the British-born Winnipeg General Strike leaders. British subjects born outside Canada gained Canadian citizenship automatically after acquiring domicile, rather than by naturalization. A final provision made Section 41 retroactive; that is, if someone had fallen "within the description" of the prohibited and undesirable classes within the meaning of Section 41 "at anytime" since 4 May 1910, that person was still a member of that group and by definition deportable under these provisions. Citizens by naturalization were not safe either. Under the 1919 Amendment to the Naturalization Act, if someone were shown to be "disaffected" or "disloyal", their naturalization could be revoked; they would then fall under Section 41 and could then be deported.[24]

At the same time, the Criminal Code was amended by Order-in-Council. The new sections, 97A and 97B, were the most directly equivalent to Section 41 of the Immigration Act. Section 97A dealt with any organization that aimed to "bring about any government, industrial, or economic change" in Canada by acts or threats of force, violence, or injury to person or property, or to advocate these for the purpose of bringing about such changes "or for any other purpose." Such a group was an "unlawful association". The property of such an association or its officers could be seized under the authority of the Dominion Police or the RCMP, and forfeited to the Crown. Anyone displaying anything (such as insignia or literature) suggesting any connection with such an unlawful organization was by definition guilty and liable for up to twenty years' imprisonment. In the absence of proof to the contrary, anyone going to meetings, speaking publicly, or in any way acting on behalf of an organization, was considered a member. Anyone permitting such a meeting to take place could be fined or jailed (up to $5,000 or five years, or both). Judges could issue warrants to search for and seize any documents or other evidence of membership in, or affiliation or sympathy with, such an unlawful association. Section 97B dealt with publications, literature and advertising connected with these organizations, providing for prison sentences of up to twenty years for anyone publishing, selling, circulating, or importing any such materials. It also made it the duty of any Canadian official to seize such materials found in any vehicle, or vessel, or on docks, in stations, post offices, or otherwise being shipped or distributed.

These sections, later known as Section 98, were added to the Criminal Code to widen categories of political offences, acts, thoughts, or affiliations considered seditious.[25] Earlier, such offences had been covered mainly by Sections 132 and 133 of the Criminal Code. Section 133 had said that certain activities were not seditious if undertaken with the proper intent (with the idea that his Majesty was mistaken or misled in something, or if the offender were merely pointing out defects in governments or institutions in order for these to be lawfully changed and improved), as opposed to intentions of illegal or violent overthrow or destruction.[26] Section 133 was repealed and replaced with Sections 97A and 97B. Because these latter provided that association with unlawful or seditious organizations or persons was itself seditious, and did not provide for innocent intent, they were in every way more severe and less judicious than the Section 133 they replaced.

Much has been made of the 1919 emergency amendments. It is undeniable that they were rushed through Parliament by the Meighenite hard liners (left in charge while Borden was off in France signing the peace treaty), in order to use deportation to deal with the Winnipeg General Strike leaders who could not be dealt with by the Criminal Code as it then stood. Deportation – an essentially arbitrary, closed, administrative proceeding – was particularly attractive in the circumstances. Although they did not in fact succeed in deporting the British-born strike leaders, Minister of Labour Gideon Robertson later claimed that this legislation was used to deport "a substantial number of men in different parts of Canada" although "most . . . were not British subjects."[27]

The Department's subsequent claim that no British subjects were deported under this amendment, or, alternatively, that no deportations were made under the legislation has been accepted by historians of the left, as well as politicians. On the other hand Gideon Robertson claimed in 1920 that the retroactive subsection (2) had been so effective in cleaning out all of the undesirables that it was no longer needed a year after it had been passed.[28] There is no indication in the files of the Department that anyone was upset by Robertson's statement, or felt compelled to correct, challenge, or deny it. At the very least, Robertson's claims made in the Senate debates (which extended over a period of two sessions) throw into question the validity of the Department's assertion that deportations were not made under the 6 June 1919 amendment.

Parliament took less than an hour to augment Section 41 of the Immigration Act with tremendously broadened and arbitrary powers to deport immigrants for political offences. But it was to take nine full years to remove these added powers and return this Section to the form in which it entered the Act in 1910.[29] The delay was occasioned not by the attempts of the Department to retain these powers (for in fact whatever their private feelings, Immigration officials drew up several Bills for repeal) but rather by the intransigence of the Senate, which refused on five separate occasions to pass liberalizing or revoking measures.

The 6 June 1919 amendments to Section 41 displeased the left, and to a certain extent some of the right. What little protest there was from the latter, as from the mainstream, emphasized the discrimination against British-born subjects under the amendment: aliens who had become naturalized citizens were safe from deportation (unless of course they had their certificates revoked), while British-born immigrants here for the same length of time could be deported because their Canadian citizenship was not based on naturalization. In effect, the amendment legalized the deportation of a class of Canadian citizens. The Quebec branch of the Great War Veterans Association protested, but not against the deportation of undesirable immigrants regardless of how long they had been in Canada – that was all to the good, as far as they were concerned. Rather, they were upset that British-born subjects who had citizenship by domicile were subject to such deportation.[30]

Labour protested the 6 June amendment. Within a week, Tom Moore of the TLC, and other union representatives met with Premier Borden and Minister of Immigration James Calder, to demand that the amendment be removed. Moore wanted to return to Section 41 as it had been in 1910, arguing that it was unfair and illegal to have different standards for deportation for political offences than for other offences under the Immigration Act. Further, Moore argued that if a British subject got into political trouble, he or she should "be dealt with under the Criminal Code and be made to suffer the penalty of the law in Canada rather than be deported therefrom." Moore was not convinced by the Department's claim that the discrimination against political offenders was based on the fact that they were as a class "directly a menace to the state."[31]

The strong showing of the Progressives in the 1921 election helped labour and other groups attempting to create pressure for changes in repressive laws. This was certainly an important factor in attempts to repeal the 6 June amendment, and probably explains much about the ultimate achievement of this goal. The first such attempt had been made in April 1920, however, before the Progressive federal sweep (Ontario and Manitoba provincial elections showed changing public opinion earlier). The government introduced a Bill to eliminate "right away" the provision in Section 41 for the "deportation of a British subject for sedition, conspiracy, etc." The phrase near the end of the first clause in Section 41 that kept British-born Canadians liable would be eliminated, and instead the phrase "every person other than a Canadian citizen" would be substituted.[32]

What constituted Canadian citizenship had been defined in section 2 (f) of the 1910 Immigration Act. A Canadian citizen was (1) a person born in Canada who had not become an alien (for example, by marrying an alien, in the case of Canadian-born women, or by taking another citizenship); (2) a British subject who had acquired Canadian domicile (three years' residence in 1910; five years' in 1919); or (3) a person naturalized as a citizen under Canadian law (after the same residence requirements for domicile) who had not become an alien (by marriage, for women) or lost Canadian domicile (by living out of the country for a certain period, for example). Anyone who was not a British subject was an alien. These definitions set forth in the 1910 Immigration Act were unchanged in 1919 or thereafter.[33]

According to the Department, the changes to Section 41 proposed in 1920 would place British subjects born outside Canada on an equal footing with all other immigrants, and would remove subsection 2, which had been very controversial. The Department's memo to Minister Calder, to brief him for his presentation in Parliament, argues that this subsection was "unfair" legislation because it was retroactive to 1910. The Department reiterated its claim that it had not used the legislation, but wanted nonetheless to "save considerable hard feeling" by revoking it.[34]

In the Senate, Minister of Labour Gideon Robertson argued on several grounds in favour of removing the broad powers given to Section 41 in the 1919 amendment. The first reason was that the emergency that gave rise to the need for such special powers was over. Secondly, Robertson said, labour had pointed out that it was "unfair and un-British . . . to say that a British subject should be deported without a trial." This essentially unarguable point, he said, made the legislation a red flag in the face of which labour would be even harder to control. As for the claim that removing the special powers was an act of weakness, he thought this almost absurd. The government claimed that the amendment had been necessary in the first place because the Criminal Code was inadequate, but subsequent amendments to the Criminal Code, passed in June 1919, had rendered it quite adequate to deal with subversives. Thus, the 1919 Immigration Act amendments were legally superfluous, argued Robertson.

Thus far, Robertson's arguments echoed the Department's brief used by Calder in the Commons. But flatly contradicting the Minister and the Department of Immigration, Robertson went on to boast that the 1919 amendments were not only legally but also practically superfluous – not because they had never been used to deport anyone, but rather because the government had already successfully and thoroughly used the legislation to rid themselves of all of the subversives and other undesirables. Robertson claimed that there was nobody left in Canada whom the government wanted to deport who could not be dealt with under Section 41, as it had stood before the 6 June 1919 amendment:

> Citizens of foreign countries who came to Canada and were guilty of seditious acts and utterances merited deportation, even though these utterances or acts were committed prior to the time the legislation was passed [6 June 1919]. We dealt with a substantial number. Now, that having been done, and more than a year having gone by during which that work has been carried out and concluded, there is no necessity for continuing on our statute books a law that will permit an officer of the Immigration Department to cause to be deported a British subject, who has been in this country more than five years.[35]

The Senators were not convinced. Alarmed by the same stirrings that were to change the House of Commons, they believed that the unrest of the previous year still existed. To the Senators, to remove the amendment would be to announce to people like the Winnipeg strikers that they were free to carry out their ''nefarious'' activities. Removing the special powers from Section 41 was ''well calculated to encourage agitators all over Canada . . . a confession of weakness on the part of the Government,'' and would be seen as bowing to pressure from labour organizations.[36] The Bill was soundly defeated.

The second attempt to remove the 1919 amendment took place at the end of 1921 when the government introduced Bill 139 in the House of Commons. The provisions concerning Section 41 were much as the year before; that is, repealing subsection 2 and replacing the excepting phrase in the end of Section 1 with the clause ''except for Canadian citizens.'' Yet another clause in the Bill revealed more clearly the King government's strategy of concessions to the mainstream of labour, while opposing more radical (industrial) unionism: representatives from international labour organizations were to be given easier temporary entry as was already given to commercial travellers or professionals. This was a concession for which the American Federation of Labor had long been pushing. That part of the amending Bill was no problem, but the provision to amend Section 41 remained controversial. The Bill passed in the Commons but was defeated in the Senate.[37]

Labour MP Woodsworth's private member's bill was the only attempt made to change the Immigration Act during the 1922 session. The Woodsworth bill provided for trial by jury for political offences committed in Canada, before deportation for those offences. Woodsworth also proposed repealing subsection 2, the retroactive clause in Section 41, and objected as well to the provision that the mere suspicion of belonging to any secret organization of a proscribed type was grounds for deportation. Woodsworth characterized the 6 June amendment as "absolutely vicious in character." Minister of Immigration Charles Stewart countered that the Woodsworth bill would "throw the gates very wide open." Meighen, architect of the 1919 repressive measures, claimed that his amendments "had never been used arbitrarily." Woodsworth's bill was eventually defeated by a wide margin. In fact, it never had a chance: deportation without trial by jury was a fundamental part of Canadian immigration law, a point which Woodsworth and other progressives never completely understood. Until the Department worked out alternative strategies, jury trials were unacceptable. Nonetheless, a special committee appointed to study the bill proposed, and the Commons agreed, that the sections permitting the deportation of non-Canadian-born British subjects who had acquired domicile be removed from the Act in the next session.[38]

Bill 136, the third attempt by the government to eliminate the 1919 amendments to Section 41, passed the Commons 11 May 1923. It provided that "any alien in Canada" (that is, any non-British non-citizen, domiciled or not) who came under the list of offences outlined in the sections should be deported. The 1923 bill clarified the language of Section 41, repealed the section concerned with assuming the powers of government (the phrase that had been aimed at the Strike Committee), the phrases that included offences against government or legally constituted authority (the narrow anarchist clause), and also repealed subsection 2 and eliminated the clause permitting the deportation of domiciled British subjects.[39] The Bill did not pass in the Senate.

Essentially the same process took place in 1924, with Bill 195 given first reading in the House 24 June. The Department claimed again that it had never deported anyone under the "extended authority" of the 6 June 1919 amendment. The bill got through the House, but the amendments to Section 41 were defeated for the fourth time in the Senate by a vote of about twenty-five to seven, leaving the Immigration Act unchanged.[40] The fifth, almost annual, attempt to remove the 1919 amendments began early in 1926 in more or less the same fashion as its predecessors. The bill sent to the Commons in March was the 1924 version of the amendments to Section 41.

The labour members of the House, dissatisfied with the bill, wanted more thorough amendments and in 1926 were in a position to attain them, as the King minority government needed labour support to stay in power. Labour's objections to Section 41 were two-fold: it allowed deportation for political offences after a hearing by a Board of Inquiry rather than a court conviction based on a trial by jury; it discriminated against the British-born because they could be deported while domiciled, while an alien naturalized as a Canadian citizen could not be deported. Bill 91 introduced in March 1926 restored Section 41 to what it had been before the 6 June amendment. This satisfied labour's second objection but not the first. Woodsworth demanded amendments to provide for court trials in political deportation cases, as well as to end the discrimination against domiciled British-born immigrants. Woodsworth did not necessarily intend to put up a battle to prevent deportation after domicile, but was determined to end deportations for Section 41 offences "unless there has been a conviction" in a court of law.[41]

In response to Woodsworth's criticism, the Department prepared two other versions of Bill 91. The first alternative would altogether repeal Section 41 and make political deportations possible only following criminal convictions. They thought this version would be easier to pass, and would avoid claims that the Department was trying to increase its power. At the same time it would satisfy the labour members. But the Department preferred the second version, which would repeal Section 41 and at the same time modify Section 40. Section 40, the main provision for deportation in the Immigration Act, set out various grounds for deportation, such as becoming a public charge, becoming an inmate of a hospital for the insane or other public or charitable institution, or becoming convicted of a criminal charge. These provisions, as a rule, did not apply to persons who had been in Canada for more than five years and who thus had domicile. (For certain causes persons here more than five years could be deported, mainly if they had not legally entered or had been at entry a member of the prohibited classes and thus were by definition incapable of acquiring domicile no matter how long they were here.) The Department proposed to change Section 40 so that any alien regardless of domicile, and any Briton who had not yet obtained domicile, could be deported under Section 40. Thus the Department could deport domiciled aliens who had become inmates of institutions after they had lived in Canada more than five years. "We might not get this through, but it would strengthen our hands if we could," wrote Acting Deputy Minister Frederick Blair.[42]

The Department recognized that there might be some objection to strengthening its powers under Section 40 by removing the exemption against deportation for domiciled aliens, but it did not think these objections could be upheld. "I cannot see there is any reason why we should recognize the right of an alien to exemption from deportation after living in the country for five years if he is an undesirable within the meaning of Section 40," said Blair. Becoming a public charge, inmate of a public or charitable institution, hospital for the insane and so on, or "conviction for any political or other criminal offence *at any time* while he resides in Canada would make him subject to deportation." Under this bill, the only safety for aliens in Canada would be naturalization as a Canadian citizen. "If an alien wants to remain an alien and yet be protected against deportation, he can do so by behaving himself in Canada."[43]

In order for this strategy to work, the Criminal Code would have to be amended to "save as much of Section 41 as possible" so that offences under Section 41 would become offences under the Criminal Code. Under the proposed scheme, a political offence would result in arrest, court trial, and if conviction resulted, a Board of Inquiry would merely determine that such a conviction had taken place and deportation would be automatic. In fact, said Blair, "it would simplify matters for the Department, if deportation for a political offence were dependent upon a conviction in Canada."[44]

Blair believed that the existing provisions of Part II of the Criminal Code were relatively adequate to replace Section 41. In a memo to the Deputy Minister, Blair explained that Part II of the Criminal Code contained Sections 73-141 which covered offences against public order and external security. Blair thought that the offences listed in Part II were roughly equivalent to the offences covered in Section 41 of the Immigration Act.[45]

At the same time that labour members had been successfully pressuring the Liberal minority government to try to amend Section 41 of the Immigration Act, they were similarly pushing for amendments to the Criminal Code. What Blair had not known while he was devising his scheme to extend the powers of the Department by amending Sections 40 and 41 was that a Bill to amend the Criminal Code, by repealing Section 97A and 97B and reinstating Section 133, was about to be introduced. The Department of Immigration was not happy about this event. If Section 41 were repealed and deportation made contingent upon criminal conviction under the Criminal Code *minus* Sections 97A and B, it would be harder to get rid of immigrants for political reasons. Blair concluded that "there appears to be little left in the way of political offences for which an immigrant may be convicted."[46] The Department had no objection to political deportations requiring a court conviction rather than a Departmental hearing, as long as tough provisions for seditious or subversive offences were left in the Criminal Code.

Yet even without the help of the Criminal Code, all would not be lost. The Department had a variety of other legal categories within which to deport "undesirables", which also could be used to deport political undesirables. As well, persons in trouble for political offences were likely to have legal, economic, or social problems: loss of job, arrest on technically correct but spurious charges (such as vagrancy, riot, unlawful assembly, incitement to riot, assault, resisting arrest). These problems were likely to bring such persons "within reach of the Department," as officials often phrased it, and thus easily deportable for some violation of the Immigration Act such as having become a public charge or having been convicted of a crime. Further, the Department expected that the increase in its deportation powers under a strengthened Section 40 would make up for the loss of power if Section 41 were repealed.

In the original Bill 91 of 1926, Section 41 used the phrase, "whenever any alien [advocates in Canada the overthrow by force etc.]"; that is, British subjects, domiciled or not, and naturalized Canadian citizens, could not be deported under Section 41. The 1919 Section 41 had provided that "every person" was liable for deportation on these grounds, except for Canadian citizens by birth or naturalization.[47]

It was Blair's version of the 1926 Bill that was passed by the House; non-citizens convicted of certain criminal (political) offences were deportable under the revised Section 40, regardless of domicile. This was the Bill that was introduced to the Senate. Liberal Senator Raoul Dandurand, who introduced it, explained its merits almost word-for-word from a memo prepared for the occasion by Blair. He repeated once again the arguments of the past five years: the "emergency" was long past; the 1919 amendment put too much power in the hands of a Board of Inquiry which might consist of just one Immigration officer with little or no legal training; and British justice and the public interest demanded that Courts of Justice deal with political offences. The proposed amendment would leave the country ample protection against undesirables under Section 40 because Part II of the Criminal Code covered political offences equivalent to those covered in Section 41 of the Immigration Act. Finally, and surprisingly, he argued that the 1919 amendment should be repealed because it had never been used, so there would be no loss in being rid of it.[48]

No one challenged Dandurand's assertion that the 1919 powers had never been used. Senators Tanner and Griesbach asked if there had been no deportations; Dandurand replied that there had been none. No one referred to Gideon Robertson's emphatic and detailed claims in the 1920 debate. Even more extraordinarily, Dandurand claimed that Section 41 in the 1910 version had never been utilised.[49]

The Senators were unpersuaded. Winnipeg Tory Senator Lindrum McMeans' comments were typical. The "Red menace" had grown, he said: "today the country is honeycombed with people who are preaching these doctrines even in the Sunday Schools." The government could now get rid of a political undesirable without "the expense of charging him with a crime or keeping him in the penitentiary." Why should the government "charge [political agitators] with a crime and . . . try them, when you have not any evidence to convict them? Do you think anyone of good character would be accused of sedition and deported?" he asked. Several Senators felt that the anti-sedition sections of the Criminal Code were not adequate replacements for Section 41, particularly if Section 133 were reinstated and Sections 97A and B and were repealed, as proposed. It is interesting to note that Dandurand repeated the claims of the Department of Justice that there had been "no prosecutions before our courts anywhere in the country under these sections."[50]

One of the few Senators who demurred was Sir Allen Aylesworth, a Toronto Liberal and a constitutional lawyer. Aylesworth recalled his involvement as an MP in the 1910 Commons debates on the initial addition of Section 41 to the Immigration Act. He argued that political deportation should not be a matter for a tribunal, but rather for the courts: "I thought in 1910 that it was a most dangerous thing to deny any

British subject the right to have his case investigated in court by judge or jury . . . I still think so." The Section was too arbitrary, took away "British liberty" and the right of habeas corpus, and violated the Magna Carta. Dandurand's view was similar: he characterized political deportation by tribunal as "an arbitrary autocratic act." Liberal Senator Napoléan-Antoine Belcourt went further, suggesting Section 40 should be repealed, "on stronger grounds than 41," because it permitted deportation without court trial. Other Senators were skeptical or indifferent.[51]

James Calder, former Minister of Immigration, poured scorn on such sentiments. Pointing out that the right to a court trial for political offences had been negated by law "for a long period of years", and that there was little essential difference between the 1919 and 1910 versions of Section 41, he argued that the Canadian government, like its South African, Australian, and American counterparts who simply rounded up and deported such "undesirable persons", must have strong powers to deal with radicals. But such powers would never be abused, he claimed:

> In practice that would never take place at all. When the law was changed in 1919 I was Minister of Immigration, and there were those who at the time desired to have one of our immigration officers try certain people and decide whether they should be deported or not. I as Minister and the Government as well, would not allow that at all. We said, "In those particular cases let the question go to the courts." It did go to the courts . . . there has never been a case in which any hardship has occurred under this law, either under the 1910 provision or under the amendment of 1919. There is in the law a power that the government, through its officers, can exercise if it chooses, but I am quite certain that in the administration of this law no Minister of Immigration, or no government would ever allow one, two or three immigration officers to deport a man without the full knowledge and sanction of the government itself – not only the Minister, but of the entire government – for deportation is a serious matter.[52]

Of course this was patent nonsense. And Calder was better informed than many of the Senators, most of whom did not realize that court trials had no place in deportation. Most understood little or nothing of the Immigration Act or the workings of the Department of Immigration. Apparently they had little interest in the issue, for they failed to challenge inconsistencies, and willingly accepted conflicting and illogical claims. Ultimately they defeated a motion to take the bill to second reading, with a margin of nearly two to one.

Senators not involved in the affairs of the Department had little routine access to information about its practices. But Calder's astonishing misrepresentations are another matter. It is difficult to believe that he simply did not know or understand that his underlings routinely used arbitrary star chamber tactics in closed hearings, in violation of British traditions of justice (although consistent with immigration law), or even acted illegally on occasion.[53]

Acting Deputy Minister Blair explained to Bruce Walker, senior Canadian Immigration official in London, "No doubt Mr. Calder had reference to what was done in Winnipeg in 1919 when a special Board of Inquiry was created and the Police Magistrate, if I remember correctly, was made a member" of the Board that tried and deported several non-British Winnipeg Strike activists. Blair seems to imply by this that such an appointment created a Board less arbitrary (albeit less legal) than one composed only of Department officials. Nevertheless, said Blair, Calder's statement was "absolutely incorrect as a matter of law and the Section as it stands does just exactly what Mr. Calder said no Government would do, viz., put into the hands of any Board of Inquiry, even if one person, the power to order deportation."[54] And such had been the case since Section 41 was first introduced in 1910.

It was in 1928, on the sixth try, that the special powers of political deportation given the Department by the 6 June 1919 amendment to Section 41 were finally removed. This time the government took a different approach, initiating the process through an Order-in-Council, then moving to the Commons. The Commons Bill 187, which removed Section 41 and strengthened Section 40, was introduced by Minister of Immigration Fowke, who explained that the approach through the Order-in-Council had been taken because the same measure had been passed the previous session by the House but turned down by the Senate. It is not clear if his intent was to avoid debate or merely to expedite. Because the same bill had been approved before, it moved through the House quickly, with little debate and few questions. The government reiterated its argument that Section 41 was unnecessary, as political deportations could be carried out through Section 40 of the Immigration Act and Part II of the Criminal Code.

The bill passed easily. In the Senate, however, it hit another snag. The debate repeated the familiar arguments that removing the 1919 powers from Section 41 would be "bowing to the Reds." Finally the bill was referred to a special committee. The committee amended the bill;

they eliminated all reference to deportation by trial by jury for political offences listed in the Criminal Code, and instead returned Section 41 to more or less what it had been in 1910. The Section after the 1928 amendment was passed read, ''whenever any person other than a Canadian citizen advocates in Canada . . . .'' Subsection 2 was gone, along with the clause that permitted the deportation of domiciled British subjects. All of the 1919 amendments were done away with. The 1928 Act met all of the labour objections to the provisions under which political deportation was carried out, except for the most important: trial by jury.[55]

The position of the Immigration Department remained relatively unchanged. Deportation had always had as little to do with the courts as possible. The Department was not accountable to the courts or to Parliament as long as it stayed within the law. Despite the fact that they still could, and did, deport people quite routinely for political activities or reasons, overt political charges were usually unnecessary because there were so many other labels that could be used. Thus the Department was not unwilling to eliminate its unusual powers and normalize Section 41. The Department did not overstate the case when it said that it did not need emergency powers; normal ones were quite sufficient. As long as deportation remained a purely administrative proceeding, and as long as the Department acted within the law that gave it such a broad scope, arbitrary decisions could continue to be the norm.

In the ensuing years, all attempts to curb the Department's powers were stymied, including one proposal by Woodsworth and his labour colleagues to abolish the Department of Immigration and Colonization, as it was by then named. In 1931, Woodsworth's Bill 44 attempted to ensure that someone resident in Canada for ten continuous years could not be deported. The Department argued that this would make it impossible to deport undesirables such as mental defectives, epileptics, and criminals. In 1933 and 1934 Woodsworth attempted to amend the Act to redefine ''public charge'' to exclude people receiving unemployment relief. Again, the Department pointed out the inconvenience and expense that would result if the Act were passed. The amendment, it claimed, was clumsily worded and its purpose was unclear. In 1934, CCF-Labour MP Abraham Heaps tried to amend Section 40 so that municipalities would not have to notify the Department about immigrants who had become public charges. The Department argued that municipalities had never considered this anything but optional.[56] The issue in the 1930s was not the law governing deportation, but rather the way in which the Department acted under the provisions of the law.

The Department could deport people under three broad headings: for something they had done, or for some condition, prior to entry; for something in their manner of entry; or for something done, or some condition, after entry. The provisions concerned with the first category could be found mostly in Section 3 of the Act which listed prohibited immigrants. Prohibitions were concerned with medical conditions, with political beliefs or activities, economic situation, criminal record, or morals, as well as a catch-all category of those entering or remaining in Canada contrary to the provisions of the Immigration Act. All that was necessary was to show that an immigrant belonged to a prohibited class, and therefore could not, by definition, legally enter Canada and obtain domicile. Deportation of someone in the prohibited classes was very much like refusing to admit them at the port of entry, and in effect, claimed the Department, was just such a retroactive refusal to admit. Deportation for membership in the prohibited classes was not limited by period of residence. Theoretically an immigrant could be deported after decades of Canadian residence. Some were.

Deportation for something connected with the manner of entry was also fairly simple to carry out. Section 33 of the Act set out the requirement to submit to inspection upon entry, and to submit to questions put by an Immigration official as part of the examination for entry. If it could be shown that someone had entered without being inspected and legally admitted, or someone had obtained entry by misrepresentation or fraud (by lying about or concealing some information that might have placed them in the prohibited classes), then such a person was not in Canada legally and could be deported automatically once that fact were established. This too was represented as retroactive refusal at the port of entry.

Deportation for causes arising subsequent to legal entry into Canada was less simple. The Act set out in Sections 40 and 41 most of the major causes for deportation under this third heading. Section 40 provided for the deportation of persons who had become public charges, or who had been convicted of crimes. Many of the reasons for deportation set out in Section 40 were similar to those in Section 3 detailing the prohibited classes; the main difference was the element of time. Under Section 40, municipal officials were responsible for sending to the Department a written complaint that an immigrant had become a public charge or inmate. After ascertaining that this was indeed the case, the Department could effect deportation of an insane or feebleminded inmate of a hospital, either under Section 3 or Section 40. Deportations under Section 40 were usually limited to within five years after legal entry (after 1919; before that date, the limit was three years). The Department found it easier to deport a domiciled immigrant under Section 3, or even under Section 33. Time spent as an inmate as described by Section 40, however, did not count towards getting domicile.

Deportation was an administrative, not a judicial matter; therefore prospective deports did not have the rights that they would have had in a judicial process. The administrative proceeding was based on a hearing in front of a panel of officers of the Department who were appointed by the Minister. In some cases one officer of the Department could constitute the hearing body. There was provision under the Act for warning the deport of his or her rights, however limited they were. Theoretically they included the right to be represented by legal counsel, although very few immigrants could afford it, and the Department was not enthusiastic about interference by lawyers. The single operative right, as far as most cases were concerned, was the right to appeal the decision of the Board of Inquiry to the Minister of Immigration. If the hearing had been carried out according to the regulations, following the procedures outlined in the Act, the proper forms filled out, the proper phrasing used, and the evidence adduced in standardized ways according to directives issued by the Department, then there would seldom be a basis for overturning the decision. In some instances cases went beyond the Department of Immigration. The Deputy Minister might ask the Department of Justice for an opinion on a legal technicality – usually some question about the meaning of a phrase in the Act, or whether some evidence would be construed as supporting a particular conclusion or line of action.

The deportation process was overturned by the courts only when the Department got caught being sloppy in its procedures, exceeded its legal authority under the Act (which was not easy to do, since its authority was so broad) or, occasionally, when some flaw in the Act was discovered. The Department tried to carry out its procedures so that they would stand up to court examination if necessary. When a court decision went against it, the Department would try to amend the Act, or issue orders to follow procedures that would be less vulnerable to interference. The Immigration Act gave officials of the Department the power to determine and administer deportation, with virtually no interference from the courts or Parliament.[57]

3

Incidence and Patterns of Deportation

The obvious place to look for information about the extent and causes of deportation is in the published annual reports of the Department of Immigration (under its various names over the years). Each annual report gives the number of people deported, and the causes for which they were deported. Yet these seemingly straightforward statistics are at best misleading, and at times deliberately deceptive. For example, in the annual report for 1933-34, the Department pointed out that in the thirty years from 1901-02 to 1933-34, deportations amounted to only one per cent of total immigration.[1] What the Department was not so eager to discuss was the fact that the rate of deportation was not constant, but rather had shown a consistent increase, from .052 per cent in 1901-02, to 36.47 per cent in 1933-34. Individual years showed a great deal of variation.

These tedious figures, innocuous at first glance, are puzzling when more closely examined. For instance, the statistics indicate marked increases and decreases in deportation. The first significant peak in the rate of deportation was in the fiscal year 1908-09, when deportation reached the rate of 1.18 per cent of immigration. The rate fell the next year to below 1 per cent, and did not exceed this rate until 1914-15. The following year the rate of deportation rose to 2.5 per cent, then fell until 1921-22, when it rose again to more than 2 per cent. During the mid-1920s, deportation remained above 1 per cent of immigration, and in 1929-30 it climbed again to above 2 per cent. The next few years saw an unprecedented boom in deportation relative to immigration: for every 100 immigrants entering Canada during those years, between 27 and 36 were officially deported. The rate of deportation fell to a still high 9 per cent in 1934-35, the last year considered in this study.

TABLE I[2]

FISCAL YEAR ENDING	NUMBER OF IMMIGRANTS	NUMBER OF DEPORTS	DEPORTS AS % IMMIGRANTS
1903	128,364	67	0.05
1904	130,331	85	0.06
1905	146,266	86	0.05
1906	189,064	137	0.07
1907	124,667	201	0.16
1908	262,469	825	0.31
1909	146,908	1,748	1.18
1910	208,794	734	0.35
1911	311,084	784	0.25
1912	354,237	959	0.27
1913	402,432	1,281	0.31
1914	384,878	1,834	0.47
1915	144,789	1,734	1.19
1916	48,537	1,243	2.56
1917	75,374	605	0.80
1918	79,074	527	0.66
1919	57,702	454	0.78
1920	117,336	655	0.55
1921	148,477	1,044	0.70
1922	89,999	2,046	2.27
1923	72,887	1,632	2.23
1924	148,560	2,106	1.41
1925	111,362	1,686	1.51
1926	96,064	1,716	1.78
1927	143,991	1,585	1.10
1928	151,597	1,866	1.23
1929	167,722	1,964	1.17
1930	163,288	3,963	2.42
1931	88,223	4,376	4.96
1932	25,752	7,025	27.27
1933	19,782	7,131	36.04
1934	13,903	4,474	32.18
1935	12,136	1,128	9.29

Increased rates of deportation may simply mean that the numbers coming into Canada decreased while the numbers being deported remained the same. Yet the increase in rates of deportation relative to immigration was matched fairly consistently by an increase in the absolute numbers deported, beginning with 67 in 1902-03, and peaking at 7,131 in 1932-33. Generally speaking, deportation was higher in numbers in years when large numbers of immigrants entered.

There were certain important exceptions to this trend. In 1907-08 there were 262,469 entrants, and 825 deports. In 1908-09, however, there were slightly more than half the number of entrants (146,908), but more than twice the number of deports (1,748). In 1913-14, there were 384,878 immigrants admitted, and 1,834 deported. The following year, entrants dropped to 144,789, while deportations remained at 1,734. In 1918-19, immigration remained low at 57,702, with deportation correspondingly low at 454. But in 1919-20, the number of immigrants more than doubled to 117,336, while the number of deportations increased by not quite a third to 655. For 1920-21, immigration was 148,477, and deportation 1,044, while the next year immigration fell to 89,999 while deportation almost doubled to reach 2,046. Similarly, a striking disjuncture between the numbers of immigrants versus deportations appeared in 1928-29 and 1929-30, with 167,722 and 163,288 immigrants respectively, compared to 1,964 and 3,963 deportations. The following year immigrants dwindled to 88,224 while deportations rose to 4,376. The sharpest contrast was between the 19,782 immigrants and the 7,131 deportations of 1933-34. This year represents the high and the low points of the deportation-immigration work of the Department. These relationships are clear in the following graphic.

We cannot trace a simple direct relationship between large numbers of immigrants and large numbers of deports by fiscal year. Months or years may have elapsed between the entrance and deportation of an individual. In order to take this into account, it is useful to recalculate the numbers entering over longer periods than the fiscal year in question. Table II shows this recalculation. It gives the percentage of those deported in relation to a moving average of those admitted. For the years before 1919-20, a three-year moving average has been used (because three years was the length of time necessary to establish domicile, after which most immigrants could not be deported). For 1909, then, the calculation represents the numbers actually entering in 1908-09, 1907-08, and 1906-07, divided by three. The figures used for the years after 1919-20 are based on a five-year moving average (the time to establish domicile having been increased to five years by the amendments to the Immigration Act in 1919), so the rate for 1927-28, for instance, is based on the average of that year and the four previous fiscal years, including 1923-24.[4]

This smoothing out of irregularities is clearer in Graph II.

The rates of deportation measured against the moving averages of immigration differ in some respects from the rates of deportation compared to crude immigration figures by individual fiscal year. For example, Table II shows that the rate of deportation did not exceed 1 per cent until fiscal 1920-21, although it did rise near to 1 per cent in 1908-09. Yet the rates of deportation for the 1920s remain as high

GRAPH I[3]

Immigration And Deportation By Fiscal Year

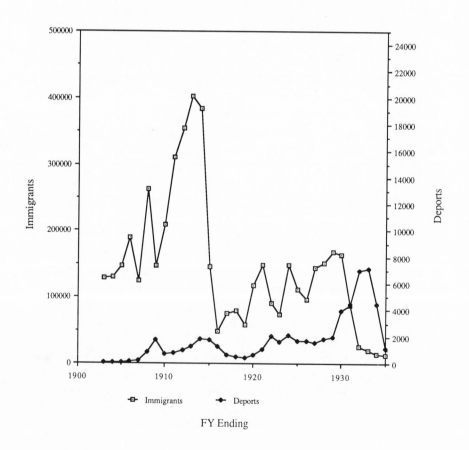

FY Ending

TABLE II

FISCAL YEAR ENDING	DEPORTS % BY IMMIGRANTS (MOVING AVERAGES)
1903	0.08
1904	0.07
1905	0.06
1906	0.08
1907	0.13
1908	0.42
1909	0.98
1910	0.35
1911	0.35
1912	0.32
1913	0.35
1914	0.48
1915	0.55
1916	0.64
1917	0.67
1918	0.77
1919	0.64
1920	0.86
1921	1.09
1922	2.07
1923	1.67
1924	1.82
1925	1.47
1926	1.65
1927	1.38
1928	1.43
1929	1.46
1930	2.74
1931	3.06
1932	5.88
1933	7.67
1934	7.19
1935	3.52

as, and sometimes exceed, the crude rates shown in Table I. Table II deportation rates for the 1930s, however, are as much as five times lower than the crude rates for those years.

These tables show the proportion of deportations to immigration (crude numbers or moving averages), while the graph below compares the numbers of people deported to the moving averages of immigration. This permits other comparisons. For example, the increase in deportation in 1907-08 is far sharper than the increase in immigration. Deportations fall after 1908-09, hit a low in 1909-10, and then climb again to the level of 1908-09; but during that period, immigration was increasing

GRAPH II

Immigration Moving Averages

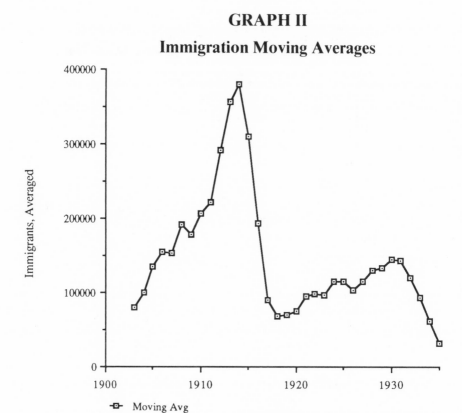

(moving-averaged). Here again, there seem to be anomalies in the relationship between the numbers of people coming in and the numbers being deported. There is a tremendous decline in entrants during the First World War, together with a decline in numbers deported, but it was immigration that declined more sharply. After the fiscal year 1917-18, the number of entrants rose gradually for two years, and then climbed to the postwar normal flow. During this same period, deportation fell gradually for a year, then climbed far more sharply than immigration, reaching a peak in 1921-22. During the 1920s, moving-averaged immigration increased steadily, while deportation showed more peaks and valleys. In 1928-29, the two streams diverged sharply: deportation soared while moving-averaged immigration plummetted after 1930-31.

GRAPH III

Immigration (moving average) and Deportation

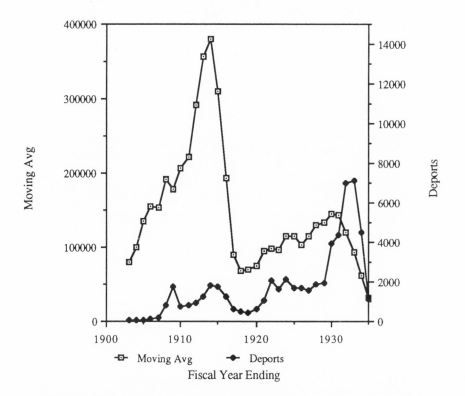

Fiscal Year Ending

Clearly, deportation did not depend directly on the rate of immigration. It is insufficient to look at rates of deportation, or at absolute numbers deported. Causes of deportation need to be considered.

The Department of Immigration included information on the causes of deportation in its statistical reports each year. The five categories under which causes were listed were: "medical causes", "public charge", "criminality", "other civil causes", and "accompanying" (nondeportable members of deports' families, such as Canadian-born children). Table III shows deportations reported by cause for each fiscal year. The same information is depicted in Graph IV.

Table IV shows causes of deportation as a percentage of all deportations within a given year. For instance, in 1923-24 the Department listed 36 per cent of all deportations under the category of public charge.

According to statistics published by the Department, the single most important cause of deportation for the whole period was becoming a public charge. Their figures show a peak in public charge deportations in 1908-09, a plateau from 1913-14 to 1915-16 and, in 1921-22, another

TABLE III
NUMBERS DEPORTED, BY CAUSE

FISCAL YEAR ENDING	MEDICAL CAUSES	PUBLIC CHARGE	CRIMINAL-ITY	OTHER CIVIL CAUSES	ACCOM-PANYING
1903	49	14	0	0	4
1904	61	19	1	1	3
1905	58	19	8	0	1
1906	110	18	1	4	4
1907	126	28	12	0	35
1908	392	309	68	30	26
1909	467	1,074	115	71	21
1910	212	348	130	44	0
1911	222	289	172	83	18
1912	229	343	242	128	17
1913	370	392	334	169	16
1914	570	715	376	163	10
1915	379	789	404	128	34
1916	206	635	329	68	5
1917	98	161	277	60	9
1918	39	91	274	84	39
1919	70	103	236	35	10
1920	123	158	334	22	18
1921	133	236	586	52	37
1922	313	950	630	105	48
1923	282	679	543	76	52
1924	649	775	511	93	78
1925	420	543	520	58	145
1926	410	506	453	189	158
1927	470	354	447	149	165
1928	519	430	426	257	254
1929	650	444	441	194	235
1930	600	2,106	591	107	559
1931	789	2,245	868	200	274
1932	697	4,507	1,006	270	545
1933	476	4,916	836	277	626
1934	301	2,991	493	250	439
1935	144	464	267	172	81

GRAPH IV

Numbers Deported, By Cause

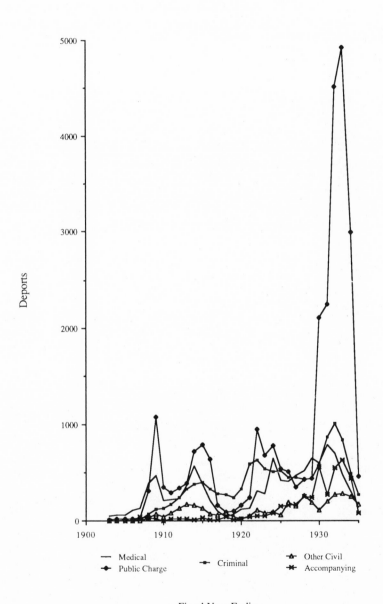

Fiscal Year Ending

peak nearly as high as that resulting from the 1908 depression. From 1928-29 to 1929-30, public charge deportations increased five-fold (more than twice the total in the 1908 depression), and doubled in the following year. Public charge deportations peaked in 1932-33, and fell to pre-

TABLE IV
CAUSES AS A PERCENTAGE OF TOTAL DEPORTATION BY
FISCAL YEAR (rounded nearest per cent)

FISCAL YEAR ENDING	MEDICAL CAUSES	PUBLIC CHARGE	CRIMINAL-ITY	OTHER CIVIL CAUSES	ACCOM-PANYING
1903	73	21	00	00	06
1904	72	22	01	01	03
1905	67	22	09	00	01
1906	80	13	00	03	03
1907	63	13	06	00	17
1908	47	37	08	03	03
1909	27	61	06	04	01
1910	29	47	17	05	00
1911	28	37	22	10	01
1912	24	36	25	13	01
1913	29	31	26	13	01
1914	31	39	20	09	00
1915	22	45	23	07	02
1916	16	51	26	05	00
1917	16	26	46	10	01
1918	07	17	52	16	07
1919	15	23	52	08	02
1920	19	24	51	03	03
1921	13	23	56	05	04
1922	15	46	31	05	02
1923	17	42	33	05	03
1924	31	36	34	04	04
1925	25	32	30	03	09
1926	24	29	26	03	09
1927	30	22	28	09	10
1928	27	23	22	14	13
1929	33	23	22	10	12
1930	15	53	15	03	14
1931	18	51	20	04	06
1932	10	64	14	04	08
1933	07	69	12	04	09
1934	06	67	11	05	10
1935	13	41	24	15	07
TOTAL 1903-35	18	50	21	06	07

Great Depression levels two years later. More than 50 per cent of all of the deportations in the entire thirty-three-year period were listed under the heading "public charge".

By contrast, over the entire period criminality accounted for 21 per cent of total deportations, medical causes for 18 per cent, accompanying for 7 per cent, and other civil causes for 6 per cent. In the early years, nearly all of the reported deportations were for medical causes, until 1907-08 when public charge was invoked to deport more than one-third of the cases of that year. Medical deportations did not again exceed those for public charge until 1926-27; for the three years following that date medical deportations increased.

Criminality did not emerge as an important cause for deportation until 1908-09, when it almost doubled and then continued to increase sharply for the next seven years. In the four years leading up to 1920-21, criminality accounted for more than half of all deportations. By 1920-21, it was the most significant single cause for deportation. Thereafter it was superseded by other categories, although it continued to account for substantial numbers of deportations. Less important, but waxing and waning in small percentages that reflected the general intensity of all deportation, were the categories, other civil causes, and accompanying. All of the causes of deportation show gradual increases over the period, and in a number of cases they rise even when the level of immigration is falling.

The Department's statistics raise a number of troublesome questions. For instance, the Department's published claim, that it had deported only 1 per cent of the total number of immigrants entering Canada, came at a very strange time. The Department was expelling immigrants (by no means all of them recently arrived) at an embarrassing rate, and being lambasted on that account in the Canadian and British press and elsewhere. The Department's 1 per cent figure was a weak attempt to distract attention from the unprecedented high rate of deportation of the unemployed during the Great Depression. Furthermore, this figure concealed, behind an innocuous average, several previous heights in deportation – each one of which was followed by a plateau higher than the previous norm, even in the relatively prosperous 1920s. In this sense, the Department's use of the average was a classic example of lying with statistics.

Another question is raised by the discrepancy between the peaks in numbers expelled and numbers entering. There were four periods of tremendous increases in deportation: 1908-09, 1913-14, 1921-24, and 1929-30. These peaks in deportation do not correlate to peaks in immigration. For instance, from 1907-08, deportation more than doubled while immigration was almost halved. The discrepancy between these rates widened in the later periods. It is necessary to look beyond the sheer numbers of immigrants, and the ''bad apples in the barrel'' theory for an explanation of the marked fluctuations in deportation. What is striking about these four periods is that they coincide with periods of severe economic depression in Canada. Moreover, the Department's own statistics show that the high numbers expelled at these times were largely composed of those who had become public charges. In other words, those immigrants who were deported in the peak depression periods were those who had become pauperized in Canada as a result of general economic depression. This conjuncture reveals as nonsense another common sense assumption: that deportation was the result of individual failure for which the immigrants themselves were responsible. In fact, during the Great Depression, deportation was an officially sanctioned alternative to unemployment relief for immigrants. In times of low demand, Canada was able to export, by legal and other forms of deportation, some of its surplus labour force.

Economic factors alone lie behind the majority of deportations as reported by the Department. Ostensibly non-economic causes are more difficult to explain when they show sudden rises or declines. Medical deportations, for example, also show fluctuations different from those of the immigrant stream itself. How can we explain the high numbers deported for medical causes during the 1920s, when the rates were up to three times those of prewar medical deportations? It is absurd to assume that the state of health or physical condition of immigrants admitted to Canada in the 1920s was much worse than in earlier decades, especially when we recall that medical inspection became ever more stringent and restrictive. This too suggests that deportation cannot be ascribed solely or chiefly to the qualities of the immigrants themselves.

Perhaps the most perplexing and provoking questions are raised by the criminality category. On the surface, it seems clear cut: conviction for a criminal offence was grounds for deportation. Yet in the nine-year period after 1916, criminality accounted for one-third to one-half of all deportations. There are marked variations in a rate that, by common sense standards, should remain fairly constant. The statistics suggest recurring crime waves among immigrants. Or is the apparent crime wave a creation of the reporting procedure? Instead of an increasing propensity on the part of immigrants to commit criminal acts, there may well have been an increasing propensity on the part of the authorities to convict immigrants of crimes such as vagrancy, watching and besetting (picketing), being a nuisance or obstruction to the police, as well as a number of "enemy alien" infractions invented during the First World War.

The use of the criminality category to effect deportation for "crimes" that were essentially political in nature, was a form of political repression that continued for many years. Crime is not merely a legal, but a socio-economic and political category.[5] Criminality deportations rose sharply in periods of political repression, for instance during the official crackdown against the Industrial Workers of the World and other radical industrial unionists around the First World War, and against political protestors of the early 1930s. The Department's public statistics do not specify the type of criminal activity for which immigrants were deported: political crimes are lumped in with theft and assault. Moreover, ostensibly clear cut violations of law may have political implications. The drug laws are an example: supposedly intended to combat the drug traffic, the laws were concerned with the consumption of opium by Chinese workers in British Columbia, while ignoring the far more significant consumption of opium by the white population (in pharmaceutical products). The Chinese at that time were welcomed by employers as a cheap labour force; hated by white workers who saw them as competitors; and a political hot potato for the provincial government. Singling out the Chinese as drug offenders made it easy to dispose of them, and to define labour issues in racial rather than class terms. The racist focus of the drug laws also supported the view that outsiders and aliens caused unrest[6] – a claim which underlay the use of the law to control and deport immigrants.[7]

Research has suggested that criminality statistics are a better reflection of social control than of real crime.[8] One must question the source for the categories used to develop criminality statistics. One must also ask who is convicted, what are the circumstances, and which actions do, and which do not, lead to convictions.[9] Authorities have at times created criminality categories to control certain elements of the population.[10] Some social historians suggest that neither the crime statistics nor the historical statistics and other data from which crime indicators are derived can be reliably used for such a purpose.[11] Other studies have identified the use of the criminal justice system to control surplus population which cannot be absorbed into the economy (or the polity).[12]

The Department's statistics can be manipulated to reveal as well as conceal. Measuring deportation by cause against three- and five-year moving averages of immigration produces an index with which to measure the use of the various causes to effect and explain deportation.

These index numbers do not add up to 100 per cent, across each line. They are, however, strictly comparable to each other in a given year, or over the entire period – a comparability which is lacking in the year-to-year percentages in the "percentage by causes" table (Table IV). For instance, compare public charge for the years ending 1912 and 1924. The percentage for both years is 9 per cent, but the *intensity* has increased sixfold from .11 to .67.

Several striking tendencies appear on this index. Public charge remains the leading factor through most of the period, but its intensity varies from three to almost ten times normal up to the 1920s. In this decade it never falls below its pre-war peak, and in the 1930s it increases eighteenfold, dwarfing all other causes. Nevertheless, during the First World War, criminality rises to unprecedented heights, for a time far exceeding the public charge category as the favoured device for deportation. In four years, from fiscal year 1906-07 to fiscal year 1910-11, deportation changed from a one-cause system to a multiple-category system, in which several lesser-used causes reinforced and occasionally supplanted the favoured devices. The use of a multiple-cause system raised the incidence of deportation as a whole to progressively higher levels, whichever cause predominated.

This change in complexity reflected not only economic crises and legislative actions, but also increasing bureaucratic sophistication and utilization of the enforcement structures. The result of this was that an increasing proportion of immigrants were expelled before they had completed residency requirements, despite the fact that they had immigrated under higher entrance standards. The intensity of deportation for all causes increased from previous normal levels in the prosperous years, such as 1909-10 to 1913-14, to a still higher level between 1922-23 and 1928-29. Each prosperous, or, rather, "normal" period marks an increased intensity in deportation.

The conclusion to be drawn is that while deportation was most certainly a means of removing the unemployed and useless, it was something else as well. As the population rose, the flow of immigration (even in the good years) could be filtered more carefully to ensure that the classes Canada kept were the classes Canada wanted. The increasing intensity of deportation suggests that this is not merely a myth: an immigrant of the 1920s was three or four times as likely to be deported for any cause

TABLE V
INDEX OF INTENSITY:
% OF DEPORTATION BY CAUSE AGAINST AVERAGED IMMIGRATION

FISCAL YEAR ENDING	MEDICAL CAUSES	PUBLIC CHARGE	CRIMINAL- ITY	OTHER CIVIL CAUSES	ACCOM- PANYING
1903	0.06	0.01	0.00	0.00	0.00
1904	0.05	0.01	0.00	0.00	0.00
1905	0.04	0.01	0.00	0.00	0.00
1906	0.07	0.01	0.00	0.00	0.00
1907	0.08	0.01	0.00	0.00	0.02
1908	0.20	0.16	0.03	0.01	0.01
1909	0.26	0.60	0.06	0.03	0.01
1910	0.10	0.16	0.06	0.02	0.00
1911	0.09	0.13	0.07	0.03	0.00
1912	0.07	0.11	0.08	0.04	0.00
1913	0.10	0.11	0.09	0.04	0.00
1914	0.14	0.18	0.09	0.04	0.00
1915	0.12	0.25	0.13	0.04	0.01
1916	0.10	0.32	0.17	0.03	0.00
1917	0.10	0.17	0.30	0.06	0.01
1918	0.05	0.13	0.40	0.12	0.05
1919	0.09	0.14	0.33	0.04	0.01
1920	0.16	0.20	0.44	0.02	0.02
1921	0.13	0.24	0.61	0.05	0.03
1922	0.31	0.96	0.63	0.10	0.04
1923	0.28	0.69	0.55	0.07	0.05
1924	0.56	0.67	0.44	0.08	0.06
1925	0.36	0.47	0.45	0.05	0.12
1926	0.39	0.48	0.43	0.18	0.15
1927	0.41	0.30	0.39	0.13	0.14
1928	0.39	0.32	0.32	0.19	0.19
1929	0.48	0.33	0.32	0.14	0.17
1930	0.41	1.45	0.40	0.07	0.38
1931	0.55	1.57	0.60	0.13	0.19
1932	0.58	3.77	0.84	0.22	0.45
1933	0.51	5.28	0.89	0.29	0.67
1934	0.48	4.80	0.79	0.40	0.70
1935	0.45	1.45	0.83	0.53	0.25

than was his or her predecessor of the 1910s. This meaningful comparison from period to period is only possible with this intensity index.

Two other anomalies emerge strongly from this index. First, criminality almost quadruples in intensity in the last three years of the First World War, and becomes more intensely used than medical reasons, for most of the ensuing period. This reflects a change in deportation devices which had important repercussions within the immigration bureaucracy itself. Secondly, the increase in the use of all deportation causes in the early 1930s epitomizes the more sophisticated shell game in which a variety of ostensible causes concealed the real economic functions of deportation. For instance, ''other civil causes'', that catch-all category, increased two and a half times above any previous peak of intensity, in the 1930s. By the 1920s, the process for ''throwing the book'' at potential deports had been well established: any cause that would stick, would do.

The annual reports of the Department do not suggest the practices revealed by internal documents. Some of the real reasons for deportation were concealed behind the legal causes promulgated by the Department. In order to understand why immigrants were deported, it is necessary to go beyond what the Department told the public, and to examine what the officials said to each other when they were not under scrutiny.

4

Developing the System, 1890s-1920

Deportation practices of Immigration officials between the early 1890s and the early 1920s can be readily seen to fall into three fairly distinct periods: 1890s-1906; 1906-1914; 1914-1920. During the first period, the Department was deporting so informally and unofficially (and extra-legally) that little can be known beyond the bare outlines of the practices of the time. Some trends are nonetheless clear. Deportations were made on an ad hoc basis when individual immigrants came to the notice of the Department, usually because of a real or perceived incapacity to support themselves. Most of these instances of inability to earn a living were due to some kind of physical incapacity, because of illness or injury or some kind of defect or condition. Often these people were casualties of industrial accidents. Sometimes the inability was related to moral rather than physical "disability"; this was a real and serious liability for women domestic servants at this time, as they were judged fit to work in their employers' homes not only on the basis of their physical but also their moral condition. These early deports were judged and deemed unfit on an individual basis and treated as individual cases.

Although the Department did not have the legal power to deport immigrants before 1906, statistics show deportations did take place from 1902 onwards. As early as the 1890s the federal government had a firmly established policy of sending back unwanted immigrants, that amounted to deportation. A system for shipping the deports had been developed so that helpless, ill, feebleminded, or insane immigrants were taken care of by immigration agents, railroad conductors, and other official and semi-official persons during their journeys of deportation.[1] After the 1902 Immigration Act gave government the power to set up a system (in effect after 1903) to exclude or send back "undesirables", the same informal methods of deportation continued for the following few years.

Correspondence of the Department of the Interior (at that time responsible for immigration matters) for 1895 shows that there was a "long standing rule" that immigrants who had become "unable to earn a living because of illness or bodily infirmity," accident, or other reason, would be deported. The Department reported, "it is the practice to send them back, as the simplest and cheapest mode of dealing with them." Sometimes this procedure was referred to as the return of "failed" immigrants. Often these people had been in Canada for less than a year, but departmental files describe deportations of immigrants who had been here four years or as many as ten years. The government often asked transportation companies to reduce fares or issue passes; the government sometimes paid all or part of the cost, depending on the financial resources of the immigrant. The government accepted some measure of responsibility for new arrivals in their first year, in accord with a policy established in 1878,[2] although this sense of responsibility seemed most pronounced when the government was considering deporting the immigrant.

The government did not automatically ship out people who had fallen upon hard times. Immigration buildings were sometimes used to shelter immigrants who were temporarily penniless, and Immigration agents tried to help them find employment. On rare occasions they acted contrary to policy by advancing funds to a particularly deserving family.[3]

Often immigrants fell on hard times through no fault of their own. Immigrants who were disabled at work received no compensation from their employers, and were sent home by the government at public expense. For example, Johan Altmeir came out from Austro-Hungary in 1893 and worked near Winnipeg for the Canadian Pacific Railway. He was wounded through the heart by a piece of metal and although he recovered and wanted to work, he was thereafter unable to do heavy work. The Department decided that he should be sent home to Europe to his wife and child. The CPR sent him free from Winnipeg to Quebec, the Intercolonial from Quebec to Halifax. As he was unable to pay the reduced Atlantic passage so kindly granted by the Allan Line, the Department tried to arrange for him to work his passage home.[4] This could not be done and the government paid.

In a somewhat similar instance, a young Dane could no longer work after he lost a hand in an accident at a planing mill near Limbank, Ontario. He had been working there for six months to learn English and save some money to go out farming in the Northwest. Because his wages were low he had not been able to save much in such a short period, and could not pay the costs of his own deportation after his release from hospital. The Department paid the costs of his maintenance and deportation, the Intercolonial gave him a pass between Saint John and Halifax. The CPR did not want to become involved in such cases and feared that "its acts of charity" in giving such passes would set a precedent. The CPR agent explained:

> Many towns in Canada have their poor that they want to send to many places, and we have in the past been repeatedly asked to assist, but we have declined, feeling that municipalities should take care of their own poor. There is no reason that I can see why private corporations should participate in a matter of this kind anymore than any other tax payer.[5]

Some immigrants were deported on "mental" grounds because they offended contemporary sensibilities and mores. A twenty-five-year old British immigrant was deported from Winnipeg via Montreal because he was "addicted to masturbation" which officials believed surely "will end in insanity". The case of a twenty-four-year old Swedish woman who had come to Canada as a domestic servant illuminates the thinking of the Department (as well as contemporary standards) in this somewhat delicate area. She had come with a party of domestics imported by Mrs. Haglin of Montreal. Mrs. Haglin complained to Montreal Immigration Agent Hoolahan that the young woman had a bad reputation and loose morals. Hoolahan was told by three young fellow domestics that the woman in question had "conducted herself like a prostitute" in her hometown in Sweden. She set a bad example for the others, Mrs. Haglin complained; she kept late hours, and got fired from her "situation". Mrs. Haglin requested that the Department deport the woman; Hoolahan agreed. No substantive evidence was brought forth. The woman was deported on the basis of these interviews, with no further hearing, for possessing a bad reputation and setting a bad example.[6]

Some immigrants were deported because they violated class norms. Mrs. Austin and her two young children had been deserted in Canada by her husband; soon after they had emigrated from England, he returned home, leaving her penniless. She stayed at the St. George Society's Montreal centre for British immigrants while the Department debated her case. The medical inspector in Montreal had ordered her deported. Immigration officials at Ottawa queried the order: it did not seem to be based on medical grounds, and they did not understand why she should be deported. The Montreal Charity Organization Society had requested it, so that she would not become a charity case in the city. The Department suggested that the children could be boarded and Mrs. Austin, who seemed healthy and willing, could work. The Montreal Immigration office countered that the inspector had ordered the deportation of this woman because he did not think that she was the "type" to do domestic work. Since other work for women was hard to find and would not pay enough to support herself, let alone children, Mrs. Austin would probably become a public charge. She and her children were deported.[7]

Two trends were established in this early period. The most significant was the practice of shipping out those unable to work, because of mental or physical illness or condition, or an injury received at work or otherwise in Canada. In the case of a work injury, immigrants could expect no compensation from the employer. Immigrants who were rendered helpless were shipped back "home".

The Department also shipped back those who did not fit in well in other ways, such as the British masturbator and the immoral Swedish domestic servant. Female immigrants were particularly vulnerable to the consequences of sexual or social deviance. This was in part because of economic factors such as the job market for female workers. Domestic service was the largest single paid female occupation in Canada, and an occupation for which the government and a variety of interest groups consistently and vigorously sought immigrants. The moral character of a domestic servant was a job qualification which she must demonstrate by producing a certificate of character from a previous employer or responsible person.[8]

The female immigrant, especially the domestic (and nearly all single women coming to Canada were domestics) could lose her ability to earn a living at her normal occupation because of an injury to her moral reputation, as well as because of physical disabilities which a male immigrant might also suffer. Moreover, if she had indeed engaged in sexual relations outside marriage, by choice or by force, and had become pregnant, she would be subject to deportation on these grounds. The birth of an illegitimate child was proof of immorality. As well, it often forced women to become public charges, because they could not support themselves before and after the birth, or because they could not pay the costs of confinement and thus were listed by a hospital or other institution as "public" patients. Domestics usually earned little, and their workplace was also their home. They could not save enough to pay for another home between the time they might be fired from one job for noticeable pregnancy, and the time they might hope to find another – a hope that was usually without foundation. Most jobs for women did not pay enough to support an adult.[9] Understanding the relationship between morality and work for female domestics is necessary for putting into context many of the deportations of single women from Canada in the early decades of the twentieth century.

The early period of deportations between the 1890s and 1906 had been characterized by a particular type, techniques and targets. Deportation was under-reported, informal and ad hoc. The role of government was essentially passive. Deportation was aimed at individuals who had come to the attention of the government as undesirables. The nominal reasons for deportation concerned the unfitness of the injured, incapable, and immoral.

The second period, from 1906 to the beginning of the First World War, marked the introduction of modern deportation practices. The Department's work became specified in law and regulation, became systematized, and rationalized. The Department adopted a more aggressive approach. It energetically constructed and operated a whole series of systems to search out, take into custody, and deport not only individuals but also members of undesirable social groups: the insane, infected, diseased, mentally defective, and the unemployed. Technically, the period was characterized by statistically accurate reporting of those deported for specific causes, cases actively sought out by the Department. Although the reporting of the work was modernized, the information beyond bare numbers was not available to the public.

Deportations became more numerous and more systematic after the 1906 Act went into effect. In fact, records of the Department suggest that the increased systematization of deportation was an important factor in the absolute and proportional increase in the numbers deported. Deportations continued to be attributed to more or less the same causes as before 1906. Now, however, the Department began to seek prospective deports instead of waiting to have problem immigrants brought to its attention. In October 1906, Chief Medical Officer Peter Bryce took the first step in this campaign of searching for deports, by notifying virtually all insane asylums and like institutions in Canada to send names of alien inmates, going back five years, so that they could be considered for deportation. The original impetus for this request had come from a decision by the United States to empty its asylums of Canadian inmates. By gathering names of American citizens in Canadian asylums and other institutions, Canadian officials hoped to show the American authorities that "they will suffer more than we" in any exchange.[10]

Chief Medical Officer Bryce extended the search to prisons shortly thereafter. At the same time, the Department hired Alfred Blanchet to work in the Province of Quebec to implement the Department's wish to "clear the country of undesirables who have come in . . . or who may . . . hereafter . . . succeed in gaining admission." Blanchet, formerly of the Grand Trunk Railway, was recommended by a cabinet minister and hired by Laurier, then acting as his own Minister of the Interior. Wardens of prisons and directors of institutions were told to assist Blanchet in his search for the unfit. In other provinces the "searching out" was done by mail. In Ontario, directors of asylums were eager to expel immigrant inmates. Deportation was under the direction of the medical officers of the Department, and seen as a medical problem. The medical officers were almost obsessively concerned with insanity and other forms of mental or physical degeneracy. Eligible cases were not likely to escape notice.[11]

This new thoroughness in the methods of the Department was largely due to the Department's new ability to deport legally. Anything done before the 1906 Act "really was not sanctioned by any special law," as Superintendent Scott explained to an Ontario provincial official. The Department continued to prefer deportations (especially of insane persons) to take place quietly, even though they were now quite legal, "since experience in New York has shown that the speculative lawyer may by habeas corpus proceedings give a good deal of trouble before the case has been gotten out of the country." With prison and insane asylum deportations, the emphasis was on increased searching out and secrecy. The Department wanted to make the arrangements "without exciting . . . suspicion," in order to avoid controversy or upset. Deportation of immigrants who were inmates of penal institutions could be arranged automatically no matter how trivial or serious the crime. A third area in which the work of the Department became more systematic was the deportation of immigrants who had become public charges. Mayors or clerks of municipalities could rid themselves of these immigrants by sending a written report to Immigration authorities in Ottawa.[12]

The Department enlisted the co-operation of a variety of public officials to help in the campaign "to weed out undesirables" and "to assist the Department as much as possible in keeping the stream of immigration coming in as pure as may be." It became increasingly important to the Department that this assistance come from the public rather than the private sector. By 1908 the Department was insisting that referrals of public charge cases come from municipal officials, as provided in the Immigration Act, rather than from charitable organizations or private individuals. The Department explained this shift in policy by claiming that private referrals might have been acceptable earlier because there had been little doubt about the deportability of the immigrants in question. But the Department had begun to receive requests for deportation of the impoverished "from so many different sources, some of them at the moment from some of the undesirables themselves, that it is felt to be only reasonable deportation papers being at least signed by the proper municipal authorities." It was because of these "innumerable" requests from other sources that the Department decided to "follow the law more closely."[13]

But the timing of this decision to funnel deportation requests through municipal officials was due to criticisms of the Department, by the Home Authorities in Britain, for sending back immigrants who had never "previously shown any such obnoxious characteristics as were attributed to them" by those requesting their deportation in Canada. It was to avoid such criticisms that the Department wanted a more official sanction for deportations, and insisted that responsible municipal officials "at least endorse" the various requests for deportation "originating in their various municipalities."[14] It was not solely in order to sidestep criticism from Britain that Ottawa was anxious to have requests for deportation originate from public and official sources. The Department wanted to be sure that there could be no question about the legality of the deportations. The aim of the process was to show that the deports were unfit, and had been of bad quality originally.

In the 1908 depression a myth appeared that was to enjoy significant publicity in the ensuing decades: the immigrant caused his/her own deportability by being lazy or unwilling to work. This convenient claim reappeared in 1913-14, and persisted like a deeply rooted weed in the 1930s. The necessity for the myth can be seen in the cost argument; that is, the Department had to argue that they were receiving flawed immigrants from the transportation companies in order to force the companies to pay deportation costs.

> No encouragement should be given to strong able bodied immigrants, well able to work, that they will be returned home free of expense simply because they are too lazy to apply themselves or happen to be suffering from temporary homesickness. It is intended that only the criminally inclined, mentally or physically incapable, and moral degenerates should be deported.[15]

Indiscriminate deportation of people who had become public charges would encourage ''idle and indolent habits.'' Local municipal authorities should make ''every effort . . . to induce strong and able bodied immigrants to work for their living if such is obtainable.''[16] The Department required municipal officials to send detailed information in their deportation requests. ''Reasons for inability to secure work'' had to be detailed in the complaint, ''as well as what if any efforts have been made either on their behalf or by the immigrants themselves'' to secure work. If the reasons for unemployment were sickness or incapability, then a medical certificate to that effect should be included in the request for deportation. The Department did not want it thought that unemployment and deportation were automatically linked. ''You will easily understand the necessity for discouraging the impression that deportation may be resorted to solely'' because immigrants were destitute and unable to find work, Scott wrote. Testimony from responsible authorities was needed about the capacity or willingnesss of the immigrant to work, and about the availability of work. ''Lack of work and liability to become a public charge are not satisfactory reasons for deportation'' under the Immigration Act. An immigrant must actually have become a public charge to be deported as such.[17]

By November 1908 Scott's tone had become exceedingly moralistic and sometimes verged on the hysterical. ''Lazy immigrants should not be encouraged in this idea'' that they can give up and go home, or escape without paying any penalty for their failures in Canada, Scott urged. ''If they will not work, and are physically fit for employment, they should be properly punished before resorting to deportation.'' Scott reiterated this punitive policy to numerous municipal officials: ''All physically capable immigrants who refuse to work when work is available should be made to understand that they will be severely punished for their neglect before being sent away.''[18]

This attitude, often expressed by nineteenth and twentieth century poor relief and welfare workers, would reappear in subsequent periods of high unemployment when the Department was embarrassed by increased public charge deportations. Deportation of the unemployed was not supposed to be automatic. It was necessary to identify lazy failed immigrants and to assure that they did not get away with anything. Inmates of asylums or prisons were clearly deportable (and perhaps sufficiently punished) by their very presence in these institutions. But the public charge cases were more ambiguous, and had to be treated differently.

> The deportation of misfits and indigents generally should be closely supervised by the local authorities and care should be exercised in order that none may be deported who are not thoroughly undesirable and incapable of reform; lazy or homesick immigrants should be made to understand distinctly that they are expected to accept whatever employment may be available, failing which they will be dealt with the same as any other citizen of Canada before any attempt is made to secure their deportation.[19]

Victorian attitudes about poverty and unemployment certainly played a part in this approach. More significant was the question of who was going to pay the costs of deportation.

Under the provisions of the 1906 Act (and earlier legislation and custom dating back to at least the 1880s) transportation companies who brought in immigrants who were defective, or in some other way contravened immigration laws, were responsible for taking these immigrants back again. The companies had never been particularly eager to do this, but usually could do little but comply. They did examine each individual case for a loophole. When deportations increased because of the 1908 depression, the costs to the companies rose. So too did their scrutiny of the deportation cases for which they were expected to pay. That this was a problem for the Department can be seen in its internal documents and correspondence. In March 1908, after the impact of the depression had been felt strongly, Scott cautioned that because the transportation companies were examining each case carefully, it was necessary to make sure that all cases did ''come clearly within the provisions of the Immigration

Act.'' In order to make sure that the companies paid the costs, it was important to distinguish between those immigrants who were ''public charges more the result of some temporary hardship readily overcome in the course of time,'' for which the transportation companies would probably refuse to pay, and ''those of a hopeless or irreclaimable nature'' for which the companies must pay. The same caution appeared in numerous warnings later that same year: the transportation companies could not be expected to accept responsibility willingly for deportations caused by the laziness, selfishness, and irresponsibility of wilfully unemployed immigrants, therefore municipalities must not automatically send forward such cases.[20]

This immediate dilemma was resolved by the Minister of the Interior who ordered: ''If the Mayor recommends deportation and it is within the law, deport.''[21] The emphasis on the importance of demonstrating that proper procedure had been followed in these cases lasted as long as the serious economic problems that created large numbers of unemployed for the Department to deport.

Proper documentation of the legal case for deportation was essential. As Scott explained to the head of a relief organization in Montreal, ''while pauperism may result in an immigrant becoming a public charge,'' pauperism alone ''is not considered a proper cause for deportation under the Act.'' It was necessary to show that a person had actually become legally liable to deportation. ''It is very desirable that in every case the evidence should be complete and in proper form before being finally submitted to the transportation companies concerned.'' Even after the Minister ordered that deportation, if within the law, should be automatically carried out at the request of the Mayors of municipalities, Scott continued to urge caution in deportation solely due to unemployment, because the transportation companies would refuse to pay the costs if they could argue that the immigrants were not defective when they arrived.[22]

The suggestion that deportation might be an easy way out for the irresponsible immigrant had been couched in moralistic terms, although the Department claimed that it was a question of law and justice. Neither of these was the real issue. The Department claimed repeatedly that it did not deport solely on the basis of unemployment. Its files show that this was not true; it routinely deported those who had become public charges solely because of unemployment. The Department was caught between the transportation companies and the municipalities. The Department wanted to make sure that the transportation companies paid the costs of these deportations, but the companies could claim that, because nothing was inherently wrong with such immigrants, there was no legal obligation to ship them back whence they had come.

On the other hand, the Department was pressured by the municipalities (and sometimes by agencies like the Charity Organization Society of Montreal which acted as a Protestant Relief Department for the City of Montreal) to remove unemployed immigrants who had become a charge on the municipalities. The Department tried to perform a precarious balancing act. It attempted to discourage the municipalities from using deportation to ship out their immigrant poor, and insisted that the municipalities' deportation complaints be in proper legal form. The former would cut down the flood of public charge deportations for which the transportation companies were asked to pay, and the latter would make it more difficult for the companies to evade payment. At the same time the Department tried to reassure the transportation companies that the deports with whom they were being presented were not the wicked, lazy, or unlucky, but rather the unfit. The undeserving poor were supposedly winnowed out. The Department attempted to dupe the transportation companies into paying for what amounted to a national system of immigrant poor relief through deportation.

There were limits to the timing and methods of deportation. Before the 1906 Act, for a one-year period the government assumed a small measure of responsibility for the immigrant, a responsibility sometimes discharged by arranging his or her deportation as a last resort. After the 1906 Act, the Department legally could deport within two years of arrival. This limit was relaxed by the Department of Justice: "there is no limit to the time in which he may be deported." The Department advised its agents to obtain written consent to their deportation from immigrants who had arrived prior to 13 July 1906 (when the new Act was effective); both the immigrants' consent and a "reasonable prospect" of reception in the home country were necessary to assure that deportation would go smoothly. The deportation period was extended to three years and further defined by the 1910 Amendment to the Immigration Act. Time spent as an inmate of a mental hospital, charitable, penal, or other public institution did not count as part of the three-year period. Anyone becoming a public charge within three years of landing was deportable. Earlier, there had been some question about the legality of a deportation when a long time had elapsed since the commission of the deportable offence, but the Department of Justice had ruled that the Department of Immigration was "empowered to act after the expiration of sentence or after the immediate cause for deportation had ceased to exist." Technically, this meant too that if an immigrant became a public charge at any time within three years of landing, even for just a brief period (for instance due to illness or unemployment), that immigrant was deportable. Insane immigrants were deportable at any time, if they had been insane within the five-year period previous to entering Canada.[23]

As a rule, the Department adhered to the statute of limitation rules on deportation. It did not always follow the rules on what were deportable offences, however. For instance, immoral immigrants, by which was usually meant a woman who lived with a man to whom she was not married, were an ambiguous group. "Immorality" was not clearly defined in the law. Deputy Minister of the Interior William Cory ruled in 1913 that a woman who had come to Canada "to live with a man in adultery" was not to be confused with a woman who had come to practice prostitution. The former was not supposed to be deported for that reason alone. The correspondence of the Department, however, suggests that these distinctions were not often made in practice. Nor did the Department always adhere to the law concerning procedures to be followed in carrying out deportations. For instance, in 1911 the Vancouver Agent J. H. MacGill expressed his concern that deportations of persons convicted of crimes were being carried out by a letter from Superintendent Scott, rather than by an Order for Deportation issued by a Board of Inquiry, as provided in the Act. Although the transportation companies might accept this procedure, a letter was not a legal substitute for a Deportation Order. Scott replied that no one had objected to this before, and that while MacGill might follow the law if he chose and obtain Deportation Orders from Boards of Inquiry, Scott thought that "the Department may safely continue the present practice."[24]

In fact it could not. In March 1912, four Armenians prosecuted for entering without proper inspection were convicted, fined, and sentenced to jail in lieu of paying fines, and ordered deported by the presiding magistrate. The four were then ordered released on a writ of habeas corpus. The writ argued that deportation could be ordered only by a Board of Inquiry, and that inasmuch as there had been no Board of Inquiry, these deportations were not legal. The new Vancouver Immigration agent Malcolm Reid suggested that other such deportation cases might be stopped by the courts on the same grounds. The Department had ordered the Vancouver office to follow legal procedures by holding Boards of Inquiry only when it was felt necessary or judicious to do so. Scott still thought that the Department could follow its informal (albeit extralegal) practice as before, since no transportation company or deportee had protested. Despite court cases unfavourable to the Department, it was to be left a matter for local discretion.[25]

There is much evidence that the Department did not always follow the law on deportation matters. When it began to follow certain parts of the law more closely, it was due as much to economic or political as to legal or moral factors. Although the period from 1906 to the First World War showed increased systematization and formalization of deportation procedures, the old ad hoc and sometimes illegal practices of the earlier period were still in evidence from time to time. Of course, as the provisions of the deportation laws became more comprehensive there would be less need to act outside the law. Each new law or regulation increased the powers allowed the Department.

The war period, from 1914 to the very early 1920s, was characterized first of all by a sharp curtailment in the numbers of deportations, and secondly by a sharp increase in the intensity of deportation work. Between these years the head office in Ottawa devoted a good deal of attention to instructing the local offices in how to build a tight case for each deportation, a case that could stand up to challenges from the courts, from the transportation companies, from foreign governments, and from interest groups in Canada. The war period offered a unique opportunity for the Department to learn how to conceal illegal or unfair practices behind the legal categories through which it reported its deportation work. The war also provided unique opportunities to ship out some residents who were not otherwise deportable because they had been here long enough to have domicile. As immigrants originating from enemy countries, they could be shipped out along with the internees. In fact, since one sure way to make someone deportable was to intern them, some politically troublesome people were interned for the express purpose of deportation after the war.[26] Although the major target groups remained the unfit and the unemployed, added to these were two new categories: enemy aliens, and agitators. Late in the war and just after, the deportation of agitators and radicals would become systematized, as the Department moved deliberately into the field of political deportations, based on wartime authority and experiences, but functioning to benefit interest groups such as large employers.

Shortly after the commencement of hostilities in 1914 the Minister of Immigration decided to deport to the British Isles only those immigrants who had friends there to receive and care for them. This was in part to avoid "adverse criticisms or comment in the Old Country." The Department told the municipalities that requests for deportation would be acknowledged but not necessarily carried out until conditions changed. This policy was developed in more detail in the fall of 1914. The Department told its agents to notify those requesting deportations that the Department "cannot consider the case while war conditions exist." The Department would continue to send away individual cases who could be cared for by friends. The local office had to send the Department a copy of the evidence because, as Scott explained, "I expect that sooner or later some objection will be raised against our sending forward some of these individual cases and I would like to be in a position to defend our action from correspondence on file before the deportation is ordered."[27]

Public charge deportations were delayed somewhat not only because of the concern that the transportation companies might refuse to pay the passage for those deported solely because of unemployment. The Department had the idea that by forcing the municipalities to support the unemployed, rather than shipping them back to the British Isles, it was helping with the war effort. The Canadian municipalities were not suffering as badly as Britain on account of the war, and keeping indigent immigrants was "one way by which we can help Great Britain and to my mind appears to be a patriotic duty," explained Scott.[28]

The Department continued to claim that it did not consider the fact of an immigrant becoming a public charge, solely on the basis of unemployment, as grounds for deportation. Scott explained to one annoyed city official that the steamship companies would say that the "Immigration Act was not drawn up to get rid of persons out of employment, but persons who are undesirable through sickness, feeblemindedness, inmates of gaols etc." If there were any sickness that contributed to an unemployment problem, or any contributing disease or perhaps feeblemindedness, Scott would ensure deportation.[29]

There was often another alternative. An unemployed immigrant could be arrested and convicted for vagrancy, and then easily deported. Sometimes the length of a vagrancy sentence was directly influenced by the wishes of the Department of Immigration. The sentence had to be long enough to permit the Department to arrange for the deportation, and short enough to save the municipality maintenance costs during the jail term. This sort of covert bargaining occurred with the blessing of the Department of Justice.[30] But the path from unemployment to deportation via vagrancy charges was not always smooth, and local agents turned to the Department for advice.

Scott might take the agent over the ground, step by step. Speaking of a specific case, he said: "We must find some ground for her deportation connected with 1) the manner of her entry, 2) her character before the entry showing she was a prohibited immigrant 3) something she may have done in Canada since her entry," explained Scott. It was not sufficient to be in jail on remand, she must actually have been sentenced in order to be deportable as a convicted criminal. The agent must examine her to find out if she was a prohibited immigrant under the Act. If there was something wrong with her entry, the applicable Sections were 33, and 7; if she were convicted of a crime (Section 40), she could be questioned as provided in Section 42 (which set out procedures for deportation examinations). Whether or not she could appeal depended on her being free from disease (Section 18). "Our action can be taken altogether separate and apart from that of the court, although if she is convicted then her deportation would naturally follow by the application of Sections 40 and 42." Fortunately, from the Department's point of view, this immigrant was convicted of vagrancy and thus easily deportable.[31] Once the Department had decided to deport someone, they worked methodically through each possibility until one was found. The decision to deport did not always follow upon the commission of some specific offence. Often, someone in the Department would decide that an immigrant should be deported, and the action followed the decision. The flexibility of the law provided much room for seeking the appropriate legal cause.

The deportation of "criminal immigrants (not enemies)" still proceeded more or less as usual except that it took much longer to carry out investigations for the first few months of the war. Despite the general difficulties of carrying out deportations, other than those to the United States, there was a bright spot. A ruling by the Americans permitted Canada to deport to the United States aliens who had resided in Canada less than three years, who had formerly long resided in the United States but who were not U.S. citizens. If Canada could show that, prior to their last entry into Canada, they had been rejected by a Canadian Immigration officer, these aliens could simply be deported to the U.S. instead of to their native countries. This would be much cheaper and much simpler. Therefore, the Department asked heads of all penal institutions, various city Relief and Department of Health Officers, and other public officials in most provinces to include questions about previous rejections by Canadian officials in their interrogations of these immigrants.[32]

Because the war affected available shipping, even the reduced numbers of deports were more difficult to transport across the Atlantic. By the winter of 1915, there were few sailings by Canadian lines, and those that sailed were full of troops. Before, in deport cases paid for by the government rather than by the transportation companies, the cost at a "charity rate" had been $15. During the war when it was necessary to ship via New York, the cost rose steeply to $50-$70. As conditions in Britain grew more "acute", deportation became a last resort.[33]

The slowdown on overseas deportations endured until after the end of the war. By 1918, the Department was frequently going through the deportation procedure, ordering the deportation, then simply holding the case (although not always holding the person) until deportation could be carried out. In the summer of 1919, an interoffice memo noted that "most of our deports at the present time go to the U.S.," the only type of deportation remaining unaffected by wartime conditions.[34]

Despite the fact that the war prevented the Department from eliminating numbers of the unemployed, it still gave the Department an unprecedented opportunity to lock up agitators and activists of enemy alien background, and to rid themselves of a raft of people whom they could never otherwise have deported because such deportations were illegal under the terms of the Immigration Act. Enemy aliens did not include prisoners of war, strictly speaking, although the lines between the two groups tended to blur. The government admitted to holding 8,579 internees in prison camps in Canada during the war, of which about 3,179 were real POWs; the remainder were civilians snatched up under the War Measures Act. Locking up civilians of enemy alien origin was part of a massive campaign of surveillance of enemy aliens in general and, ultimately, of harrassment of some aliens in particular: the radicals. Internees, like deports, were prisoners in fact, although not according to peacetime law. Under the Order-in-Council of 28 October 1914 internees were declared prisoners of war, thus had "no remedy in law." The management of internment camps during the war had its scandals and abuses, as well as its bungling and stupidities, although the camps were probably not much worse than some Department of Immigration detention facilities. By the end of 1915 there were nineteen internment sites in Canada, five of which were reception centres only. Originally the inmates were supposed to clear bush land for use by returned veterans after the war, but by the spring of 1916 some were released to do farm labour and industrial work. By the end of the war, there were still large numbers interned, and it was not until 27 February 1920 that the last batch of ninety men, nineteen women and children, left the camp at Kapuskasing to be "repatriated", as these deportations under the auspices of the Ministry of Justice were often called. In theory, the enemy aliens deported from the camps were POWs being repatriated. In practice, it was the "policy of the Government . . . to deport all interned enemy aliens who are considered undesirable" whether or not they were otherwise legally deportable.[35]

During the war, the Department did not want to send healthy enemy aliens "home", even if there were sailings, for this would help the enemy and "be a menace to our allies." There were other ways to deal with enemy aliens, as in one case involving an Ontario family: "If the party in question or her son-in-law are manifesting a pro-German attitude, and you will advise me, I will have the case looked into with a view to having them interned," Scott wrote to one "patriot". The Department was not interested in legitimate prisoners of war, except to know their names should they ever try to return to Canada. Prisoner of war deportations were sometimes handled more or less as rejections: some POWs were examined as if they had applied to enter as immigrants and had been turned down; then they could be sent back.[36] But this was not necessary in all cases. The Department wanted to send deportable enemy aliens back to Europe along with POWs. The original request came in 1918, after the armistice, but it took several months for shipments to be arranged. POW shipments did not begin on a large scale until February 1919, handled under the legal direction of the Minister of Justice, who had authority under the War Measures Act to remove, expel or deport enemy alien internees.[37]

The files of the Department show that whenever possible, ordinary deports, legal or not, were sent along with these "repatriatees". For instance, George Dowhy, Austrian, in Canada since 1909, was arrested in Winnipeg 4 March 1915, held at the internment camp at Kapuskasing, Ontario until November 1917, when he was released to do railroad work. In 1919, he was in Kingston Prison serving a five-year sentence; the Department considered him undesirable. Because he had been here since 1909 he was not legally deportable, but because he was of enemy alien origin, the Department was able to ship him out with the interned enemy aliens. An attempt to get rid of Clara Dubin, age 17 (an imbecile orphan

of German origin, imprisoned in an asylum since March 1914), failed
– not because she could not legally be deported, although that was true,
but because there were no other insane female prisoners of war. Thus,
the Internment Office refused to include her in their shipment. Tom
Taschuk's deportation was also arranged using this method: originally
an Austrian reservist but in Canada long enough to acquire domicile, he
was arrested in 1919 at Vegreville and interned at Vernon, British
Columbia; he was "not subject to deportation under the provisions of
the Immigration Act." Taschuk was a member of the IWW, a "socialist,
with Bolshevik tendencies, who has been actively engaged in endeavouring
to create discontent and rebellion in the foreign element in Canada." The
Department was eager to get rid of him.[38]

The Department also used the POW repatriation shipments to carry
out legal deportations. In September 1919 the internment camps at Vernon
and Kapuskasing were designated as immigrant stations to legalize their
use as detention centres for deports. By that fall, there were dozens of
enemy aliens being sent along with repatriatees, some legally deportable,
others not. An attempt by the Province of Quebec to clean out its asylums
failed only because the Department could not find space for the inmates
on the military-controlled sailings.[39]

The Department considered itself responsible for the protection of
the public purse, the public health, and the public morals. In order to
safeguard the country, the Department stretched, ignored, and sometimes
violated its own rules. As the laws and regulations became increasingly
complicated, deportation procedures were more minutely defined. In
numerous cases, the Department did not follow legal niceties. Its gradual
and piecemeal reforms were often due to painful, if infrequent, experiences
in the courts: losing deports on habeas corpus writs, and the like. The
common response of the Department was to tighten up the procedures
when it had to, and to try to have the law amended to legalize what it
had already been doing.

The Department's heightened sophistication in case building would
serve it well in the ensuing years. Wartime experience with the possibility
of deportation as a method of social and political control would be the
basis for overt and systematic political deportations until the mid-1920s,
and again in the 1930s, when they would reach another peak with the
prosecution of communists by the Department of Immigration.

5

The Alien Bolshevik Menace, 1910-1920s

The Canadian Department of Immigration moved into a new phase of deportation work in the latter stage of the First World War, with the deliberate and systematic deportation of agitators, activists and radicals. Some of these were people who had not done anything illegal, but who were considered undesirable on the basis of their political beliefs and activities. The threat they posed was not to the people of Canada, but to the vested interests such as big business, exploitative employers, and a government acting on behalf of interest groups. The radicals represented a new target group for deportation. Before, they had been removed on an individual basis, when possible. Now, they were to be dealt with as a group. Looking at the practices of the Department in this period gives insight into what the Department did when there was no legal basis for declaring such a group undesirable. It is important to understand that these people (to whom the Department tended to refer interchangeably as anarchists, agitators, IWW, Bolshevists, and, during the war, enemy aliens) were designated as undesirable not by legislation (as were, for example, immigrants with tuberculosis or venereal disease) but by employer blacklists and complaints, by the surveillance networks of the industrial and Dominion Police, the Royal Northwest Mounted Police (later the Royal Canadian Mounted Police), and U.S. intelligence, as well as by a certain anti-labour agitator tradition in immigration policy.

Much of the Department's activity tended to focus on the Industrial Workers of the World (IWW), in the early part of this period, making them a convenient illustration for this discussion. Before the Wobs, as they were called, were proscribed by an Order-in-Council passed under the War Measures Act, they were not an illegal organization in Canada. From 1918 to 1922 they were illegal, along with twenty other radical groups. After 1922, when the Justice Department ruled that there was nothing in the IWW constitution that was contrary to the provisions of the Immigration Act, they were declared legal again, insofar as immigration was concerned. In other words, before the period, 1918 to 1922, it was not legal to exclude or deport Wobblies simply because they were IWW members. It was not legal, but it was commonly done by the Department. In some cases there were clear illegalities in the actions of the Wobs, but in other cases, while the real reason for exclusion or deportation was being an IWW member, the nominal legal cause was criminality, for example, or becoming a public charge, or illegal entry. Thus in some cases the Department satisfied the letter, while violating the spirit of the law. In these circumstances, very careful attention was necessary in the preparation of cases. Thus, in order to justify what were shady and unfair, if not illegal, practices, the Department's documentation of its work became ever more complete and precise, and at the same time, more misleading. Legal reasons were sought that approximated the facts of the case, and the case was carefully made to fit the nominal legal causes for deportation. This active deportation work was carried out at a level of thoroughness that would not be exceeded until the police raids on communists in the early 1930s.

Although the Department had earlier tried to deport prominent radicals such as Emma Goldman in 1908, and it seems likely that some of the deportations of East Indians from British Columbia in this period were connected with alleged radical or seditious activity, the rise of Departmental concern over agitators parallels nicely the rise of organizing drives and strikes in Canada by IWW members and other labour radicals. References in the files to the problems of eliminating "agitators" appeared regularly by 1912. The Vancouver Immigration agent, for example, complained that some of these immigrants arrested by the Department (after local police had failed to convict them for vagrancy) were retaining lawyers and fighting deportation. It was in 1912 that the IWW led a major strike against British Columbia railway construction. The strike was multi-ethnic, well organized, and successful enough to upset, more than usual, employers and politicians who demanded that Wobblies and their ilk be deported on account of these activities.[1]

In theory this was not so difficult, as many of these Wobblies were from the United States. Labour organizers and strikers were notoriously liable to arrest on charges of vagrancy, rioting, or assault, because no matter what the law said, striking was regarded by employers and local interests, and often by local police as an activity that should be treated as if it were illegal, reprehensible, and immoral. Yet the actual illegality of the IWW, and of labour organizing, was not so much a fact as it was wishful thinking. For example, the Department of Justice ruled in 1913 that there was not ''anything in the Immigration Act which would justify refusing them admission to the country on the grounds of their being labour agitators.''[2]

These legal niceties crumbled under the wave of anti-radical hostility that became conveniently and inextricably mingled with anti-alien feeling by 1918. There were in effect three currents of repression that came together: attempts to suppress enemy aliens, who might threaten the war effort; attempts to suppress labour agitators, who were blamed for growing labour unrest and militancy as workers became angered by increased exploitation under the guise of the war effort; and finally, attempts to suppress foreign radicals, Bolsheviks, or whatever the current bogey was called. This is not to say that there were no real threats posed by the existence and activities of each group; there probably were. The point is that it was very convenient for employers and the government to see labour unrest, the growth of political and social radicalism, and the increase in militancy in general as an expression of the influence of dangerous aliens, rather than as a response of Canadians to Canadian conditions. From this, ''it was a simple step'' for those who believed that labour unrest was due to foreign agitation ''to proclaim that all strikes were treasonous.'' Harsh actions, however repressive, taken against the treasonous in wartime can be justified by the exigencies of national survival. Actions taken against the potentially treasonous were in the same category, justifiable in the hope of nipping treason in the bud before it flowered in a permissive atmosphere. As Laine has pointed out in connection with the Finns, ''the repressive measures and oppressive tactics of the Government . . . were designed to keep the Finnish radicals and their comrades in their place.'' Laine has commented that the government used tactics against socialists and other dissidents that would not have been tolerated if used against the general public. Yet the government had traditionally used similar tactics against one segment of that public: immigrants. What the government did to certain groups of immigrants during the war – to enemy aliens and dissenters, to paraphrase American historian William Preston's study of similar repression in the United States during this period – was different in degree rather than in kind, to what it had done to certain individual immigrants before the war.[3]

The question of what the general public would tolerate is a difficult one in connection with deportation. Because public charge deportations, statistically the most frequently cited legal cause, originated in complaints by municipal officials, it is clear that there was little resistance from such officials to the deportation of public charges as long as the procedures were properly carried out. Because deportation hearings were closed administrative affairs, the general public knew little of them anyway. Anyone asking would hear government propaganda from all save a few leftwing groups. Even to suppose that the general public might react negatively to deportation, especially deportation of dissenters, if it knew the whole story, is not sensible. What made it possible for the government to carry out its programme of repression was the "Red scare" climate based on anti-Red hysteria, stirred up by employers, government and the press, but shared by everyday people. If the "general public" refers to everybody except trade union activists, leftists and reformers, and most recent immigrants, then the general public seemed to care little about what the government did to the excluded.

Perhaps another factor in this question was the nature of the anti-Red repression in Canada. While in the United States there was a good deal of individual, private anti-radical action (by organizations like the Ku Klux Klan), in Canada

> the campaign against radicalism and Bolshevism was initiated, orchestrated, and executed by the federal government according to the laws on the books, or created especially for that purpose.[4]

Despite the fact that "very few of the groups kept under government surveillance were actually illegal," the claim has been made that the government "never exceeded its legal authority" in repressing the radicals, "because it did not have to." Even the Department of Immigration did not exceed its legal limits, according to this view, although admittedly certain parts of the Immigration Act were in "violation of the spirit of common justice."[5]

This impression, based on claims made by the Department itself, is false. The Department did indeed exceed its strict legal authority, despite its sweeping powers to act against aliens and radicals during the war.

Wartime anti-radical programmes of the Department of Immigration grew out of pre-war practices of dealing with labour agitators. Labour militance was not only a challenge to the establishment but, with the advent of the war and partly, but not entirely, because of its perceived foreign origins, a threat to the state, in the view of many military officials. Lieutenant Colonel R. W. Leonard's perspective was representative. He saw the IWW (synonymous with labour activism) as a subversive movement whose origins and purposes were alien to Canada. Its dangerous influence was widespread. In Northern Ontario, under the guise of the U.S.-proscribed Western Federation of Miners (now transmogrified into Mine, Mill and Smelter Workers) the IWW had successfully been recruiting not only the "foreign element" but English-speaking workers. There was no doubt that the IWW was foreign, full of "Finns, Polacks, Austrians and Hungarians and some Irish, and I believe it to be a thoroughly disloyal organization. This is borne out by some recent reports of labour troubles in Canada which have been fomented by enemy labourers."[6]

Anti-alien paranoia was further heightened by anticipation of anti-conscription activities, by late 1917. Brigadier General Henry Ruttan wrote from Winnipeg to Major General Willoughby G. Gwatkin, the Chief of General Staff, that there were many enemy aliens in the vicinity, "organized and fully under the control of Social Democratic Labor Leaders," who could quickly turn out 3-4,000 for demonstrations. If this group joined English- and French-speaking anti-conscriptionists under Social Democratic leadership, real problems could result. Ruttan advised increasing the supply of ammunition and maintaining troop levels until conscription was operating smoothly. Dissent from conscription was intolerable. Those who were "fond of talking and acting in a disloyal manner and who offer or incite resistance to conscription should be summarily dealt with." Similar conclusions were drawn by other military men. The Chief of Staff of the U.S. War Department warned the U.S. Military representative at the British Embassy in Washington that a Canadian IWW member in North Dakota was recruiting his fellows to go to Canada to start anti-conscription riots. His source of information was the U.S. Department of Justice.[7]

The Department of Immigration was important in the government's war against radicals. The Department responded to pleas from various sources to keep the IWW out of Canada, by patrolling usually isolated and unguarded border areas, and increasing and toughening up inspections of incoming immigrants in order to try to detect IWW members. The Department tried to reassure those requesting IWW alerts. Technically, it explained, the Immigration Act did not give it the legal authority to deal with IWW entry attempts, because the "fact that a man belongs to the IWW is not in itself sufficient" to exclude or deport him.

> However, there are usually other features connected with the majority of these cases which enable us to deal with them and you may rest assured that the Department is alive to the importance of the situation.

The Department was firmly on the side of those who opposed the Wobblies: "I have no sympathy with the IWW movement," explained Canadian Superintendent of Immigration Scott to an American anti-radical group.[8]

Requests for action against the IWW came from the private sector, and from within the government when officials acted in response to appeals from employers and employers' groups. For instance, the Minister of Labour forwarded letters from Canadian corporations requesting suppression of the IWW and asked Immigration to co-operate. Moreover, the Minister forwarded such appeals to Prime Minister Borden and asked him to instruct the RCMP to help out. The reply to this particular request reveals something about the duration of the anti-radical work of the Department, as well as something about its methods.

> For some time past – in fact for years – our officers have been alive to the danger of the IWW movement . . . . Although it may not always be possible to reject one of these men solely on the ground that he is a member of that organization, yet, there are usually other circumstances . . . and our inspectors are, as a rule, very careful to do this.[9]

In another instance Scott reassured the Minister of Labour, "I do not think any of our men would knowingly permit a member of the IWW to enter, if there is any way by which he can be rejected."[10]

From the U.S. authorities warnings came also. In one instance the Federal Bureau of Investigation (FBI) told the U.S. Immigration Inspector at an Idaho port to warn his Canadian counterpart of the entry into Canada of a German IWW leader, for the purpose of labour agitation, and perhaps for other reasons. The man was supposed to be German-born and a naturalized American citizen. "Although either of these statements may be wrong," said the FBI, "he is certainly of German extraction and is a good man to watch." The Department replied,

> I do not know whether it will be possible to reach Lintz under the Immigration Act but I would suggest a real effort in that direction. His name is in itself sufficient cause to pick him up for examination as a suspected enemy subject.[11]

Scott told the Canadian inspector to detain Lintz if he could not prove U.S. citizenship. The United States at that time regarded any male aged fourteen years or older who was not a naturalized citizen as an enemy subject, regardless of his other citizenship. "A similar interpretation on our part might be useful in a case like this," if it were possible, mused Scott. "However, there may be something connected with the manner of his entry, possibly under Subsection 10 of Section 33, which will enable you to deal with him," advised the Superintendent. The warning against Lintz set off a manhunt by the police, and Bruce Walker, the Commissioner of Immigration in Winnipeg, echoed the determination of his superiors in Ottawa in promising to deal with the man. "As soon as he has been located I shall doubtless find some means of sending him back whence he came." Unhappily for the forces of law and order, despite an intensive investigation that included the use of an undercover agent who tailed Lintz for several weeks and illegally opened Lintz's mail, nothing could be found against him before he left legally several months later. Lintz had been carefully shadowed, reported the Mounties, and although he was a "noisy and extreme socialist," there was no evidence that he was a member of the IWW, nor had he organized for the Wobblies in Canada.[12]

   This failure to "get" anything on a man considered undesirable for political reasons was irksome to the Department. There were other cases, often frustrating. The Immigration Commissioner at Winnipeg appealed for more power in August 1914. He wanted to be allowed to take some other course of action than the legal channels of deportation. He had already carried out several arrests, prosecutions, and deportations of Wobblies, and felt that, while normally deportation would be an adequate measure, it was not enough to deal with such "considerable numbers" as there were present in his region. He feared that several of these deports had written to invite all of their friends to come to Canada and make trouble. ''When they are known, it is easy of course to reject them,'' but the problem was that they could not always be spotted. The official in Winnipeg wanted simply to hand over to the U.S. authorities those Wobblies caught in Canada, without going through the legal procedures of deportation.[13]

Superintendent Scott refused to countenance such an arrangement, because there was no procedural machinery to ''order these deportations in a peremptory manner.'' Instead he suggested that the Winnipeg official continue to use the ''strongest endeavours'' to keep out the Wobblies, and failing that,

> to arrange for their arrest by our own officers or by the police of any admitted *who in any way* lay themselves open to arrest, even though their breaches of the law be technical rather than serious.[14]

This was more or less what the man in Winnipeg had been doing. Some cases were easier to arrange than others. For instance, the official described to his superiors in Ottawa one case involving the arrest of John Keeting, who had ''created an agitation and a disturbance by openly advocating the views of the IWW'' while riding on a train. ''I had this man arrested'' and tried for deportation under Section 41 of the Immigration Act, ''relying particularly on these words: 'shall by word or act create or attempt to create riot or public disorder in Canada'.'' The tactic was successful; Keeting was found guilty, fined and imprisoned, and then deported. This action was at least based on some case in law, however farfetched that law's interpretation. Others were even less substantial, although equally successful. RCMP and Department of Immigration officers arrested those members of the IWW who got into Canada, and the Department brought charges against them.

> While our legal action in these cases has not rested upon a very solid foundation, yet we have prevented any serious numbers of the members of this organization from entering . . . and so have been able to control the action of those who have succeeded in getting through.[15]

Other actions of the Department were at best questionable. In one instance, the Vancouver agent found two men and a woman, all Canadians, selling leftist literature and newspapers, including the IWW newspaper. The agent explained that because at the present time, such literature was ''coming in through the mails . . . and being sold on the newsstands'' quite legally, and because he could do nothing under the Immigration Act since all three were Canadians, he had let them go. But he informed local officials that these three agitators were coming, so that when they approached company towns by boat, they would not be permitted to land.[16]

In some cases the Department found itself unable to do anything to prevent agitation by particular individuals such as Ernest Lindberg. He had been arrested for vagrancy in Vancouver; the agent wanted to deport him, but Lindberg claimed to be legally landed and domiciled. This was indeed the case; Lindberg had been in Canada for eight years and could not be deported. The Vancouver Immigration office was deeply regretful that they could take no action. ''On account of this man's IWW activities, his deportation if it could have been effected would be very satisfactory to authorities here.''[17]

By 1918 increased complaints from employers blaming labour unrest on IWW agitation added to official alarm. The government identified the ''IWW menace'' with ''enemy conspiracies . . . against the war effort.'' The IWW were believed to be financed by enemy agents. The Dominion Police established an IWW section (a forerunner of the 1930s' Red Squads) and spy and police reports identified numbers of ''foreigners'' who were Wobblies. Although Commissioner Zachary Wood of the Dominion Police did not subscribe to the notion that the IWW posed a real danger, he was in the minority. Borden listened to the hardliners. When he asked Montreal conservative lawyer C. H. Cahan in May 1918 to study the problems of radical elements, Borden had already concluded that labour militancy was part of a Bolshevik conspiracy more dangerous to Canada than were the Germans. Since in Cahan's view Russians, Finns and Ukrainians should be treated like enemy aliens because they were ''bolshies'', he was not particularly troubled by questions of legality or logic.[18]

Cahan was the architect of most of the wartime Orders-in-Council squelching formerly legal activities long distasteful to the authorities. His proposal incorporated police (municipal, provincial, and federal) and private interest organizations into a vast central intelligence and enforcement network aimed at detecting and putting down dissent. He was commissioned by Minister Charles Doherty and Deputy Minister Edmund Newcombe of the Department of Justice (admittedly as a result of his own solicitations) to create just such an edifice.[19] Cahan's repressive proposals began to be passed as Orders-in-Council in mid-September 1918. By the end of the month he was installed as Director of Public Safety. (He remained in office until early 1919 when he resigned because his Orwellian measures were not enforced.)

Cahan's demand for draconian internal security measures was the logical outcome of official paranoia about links between foreign agitators, labour unrest, political dissent, and treason. Anti-agitator fears were running rampant in officialdom by the fall of 1918. They were fueled by domestic and foreign sources. The most important domestic sources may have been Mountie spy reports, complaints by employers about labour agitation, and rightwing pressure from men in high places. The foreign sources included diplomatic, military and internal security and intelligence officers of British, American, and other Allied governments. Their fears were exacerbated by the failure of the Allied invasion of Russia to put down the Russian Revolution. The view that labour agitators, IWW members or sympathisers and Bolsheviks were synonymous was strongly in evidence. For example the intelligence officer of the Allied Expeditionary Force in Siberia wrote to Washington that certain Russians leaving Vladivostok should be refused U.S. visas or Canadian entry because they were "under strong suspicion of being IWW or Bolshevik agents." In December 1918 and January 1919 the Canadian government was approaching academics to give anti-Bolshevik lectures as part of a systematic anti-radical campaign. Some members of the academy did not find the government's proposal acceptable. University of Toronto President Robert Falconer replied that working class discontent was caused by high prices and unemployment, and antiradical propaganda would simply do more harm. But the few liberal (or more sophisticated) holdouts appear to have been the exception. The popular view in government offices was that all of these tendencies were, in the context of the holy crusade of the war, immoral and should be illegal. And illegal they became. As Ian Angus puts it, "the government outlawed the left."[20] Criminalizing dissent made the Department of Immigration's political deportation work easier, in part because it made it more legitimate.

By comparison with some other government officials and bureaucrats, the Department of Immigration officials seem almost moderate. Nonetheless, they were frustrated by their inability to deal effectively with the increasing danger that they believed was posed by the IWW. Since the early fall of 1918 Superintendent Scott had been exploring various avenues to increase Immigration's power to act. Scott wanted to have some kind of regulation put into effect that would "give us a ready means of dealing with these people.'' He had written to the Department of Justice to ask for help. Scott had received reports from the Department of Defence and other sources, outlining the extent of IWW and other labour activities. He had seen evidence including ''correspondence (intercepted no doubt) between agents of the IWW in Chicago, and persons in Vancouver'' that indicated that the IWW was a nationwide problem in Canada. ''Judging by the names on the list, most of the members in British Columbia are of foreign birth or origin,'' he commented. He also compared the ''stringent measures being taken in the United States for the suppression of the IWW,'' in contrast to his own relative helplessness. There was an ''urgent need'' now for some regulation to deal with the IWW under the Immigration Act, Scott argued. At present he had no legal power to exclude the IWW from Canada except by rejecting them as persons liable to become public charges, ''which in many instances is rather far fetched.'' Scott pointed out that under Section 38 of the current Immigration Act the Governor General had the power to prohibit the landing of immigrants of any class. Scott asked the Department of Justice to rule on whether the IWW could properly be ''designated as a class.''[21]

In fact, the Department of Justice was at this time considering repressive legislation to take care of the IWW and ''people of this sort.'' Order-in-Council PC 2381 banning enemy alien languages was passed in September 1918; it was aimed at the suppression of union and radical literature. Another Order, PC 2384, passed 28 September 1918, outlawed fourteen radical groups (including a couple of Nationalist Chinese, that is, pro-Kuomintang organizations!) including the IWW, various ''revolutionary'' and social democratic groups most of whom were not English- or French-speaking. Subsequent Orders-in-Council went further: PC 2525, in effect from 11 October 1918 until 19 November 1919, banned strikes and lockouts and established fines and imprisonment for a variety of activities connected with industrial disputes. Copies of these Orders-in-Council were sent by the Chief of Dominion Police Arthur Sherwood to Scott, for distribution to all Immigration officials. These orders, Sherwood explained, were for the purpose of ''stamping out unlawful associations . . . putting a stop to the seditious ravings of members of these Organizations'' and excluding their ''vile seditious literature.'' PC 2384 was rescinded by Order-in-Council 2 April 1919, and after that date the RCMP could no longer prosecute anyone for possession of IWW literature. Prosecution again became possible under amendments to the Criminal Code passed 6 June 1919, permitting not only prosecution, imprisonment, and deportation for possession of literature, but repealing the right of free speech and making membership in a "subversive" group a crime. The penalty for this crime of mere membership could be deportation or up to twenty years' imprisonment for "sedition".[22]

It is important to note that the perceived necessity for such measures was justified by such dubious evidence as RCMP spy reports on legitimate dissenting groups. The RCMP had long been using secret agents to spy on labour unions and various other organizations whose existence and activities were not illegal. Commanding officers instructed their subordinates in the intricacies of selecting and operating such agents. Spies were told to send photographs of their suspects if possible. It sometimes was not. Secret Agent 32 complained that his unionists were "suspicious" and "too wise" to be photographed. Since the spring of 1917 the Mounties had had spies in nearly all the trade unions and left groups. These agents sent in reports underlining the idea that socialists, radicals, Bolsheviks, and foreigners were interchangeable terms.[23]

These generally held views of the police, RCMP, and government officials (and probably a great number of Canadians) found expression in the drastic amendments to the Criminal Code and the Immigration Act passed by Parliament in June 1919. It is undeniable that these amendments were aimed at the suppression of the Winnipeg General Strike. But they were not an anomaly caused by wartime hysteria. The political deportations of the Department of Immigration were well within the mainstream of official persecution of dissent. And if the Department behaved illegally from time to time, the private view of government officials, as well as of employers representing business interests, would probably have been that the laws were too lax.

In this increasing persecution of radicals and "subversive" elements, Canada was following a path well tread by the United States. This was not the result of coincidence, or even of the two countries choosing comparable responses to similar problems; rather, it was a co-ordinated effort. Canadian officials were in touch with their American counterparts and each warned the other of radical incursions, real or imagined. The legislation of each country had similar provisions: a Section of the U.S. 1917 Immigration Act plus a special Immigration Act of 16 October 1918, were "very much along the line of Section 41 of our own Act." The U.S. and Canadian Acts had much the same "flaws", from the point of view of deporting subversives, and so in the United States, "a considerable number of alleged anarchists were arrested and deported during the year on grounds other than the charge of anarchy,'' just as radicals were deported on grounds other than radicalism in Canada. Gradually more formal lines of communication were developed, and by the end of 1919, the United States officially notified Canada of impending agitator entry attempts and vice versa: the initiator in this formal arrangement was Canada.[24]

Some Canadian officials of particularly severe persuasion felt that existing suppression was inadequate. As David Bercuson points out, many military and law enforcement authorities "advocated internment to deal with alien labour unrest." Any labour disruption came to be seen as "treasonous". Reactionaries found it easy to treat aliens as scapegoats; surely no real Canadians would be receptive to Bolshevist ideas, and surely no one unreceptive to such ideas would willingly go out on strike. Never a patient man, Cahan had resigned, claiming that he had no support from the government, which was not adequately enforcing the laws against radical propaganda.[25]

On the whole, Canadian officials of the Department of Immigration seem to have been satisfied with their own efforts in comparison to those of the U.S. One commented:

> I think we have been more successful than the United States in handling the Bolshevik element so far: at least we have not yet had such an exhibition as is now going on at Ellis Island where a considerable number of the anarchist class are under arrest for examination and they refuse to be examined or to give any information about themselves.[26]

The fiasco at Ellis Island was the result of the U.S. Immigration Service's policy of mass raids and lockups of radicals. The radicals, after coaching by competent lawyers, had refused to give any information or to respond to questions. The authorities could not deport them for lack of evidence. The American officials had become a laughingstock. They responded by changing the regulations to remove the right to counsel before questioning. The credibility and integrity of the U.S. Immigration Department had been damaged.[27]

The occasional American farce did not prevent Canadian officials from following with interest American tactics and attempting to winnow useful techniques from U.S. successes. One such attempt concerned the sailing of 248 deports from New York in December 1919. Secretary Blair wrote to the American Commissioner of Immigration, referring to the press reports of these deportation of "anarchists, communists, extremists . . .

on account of their opposition to law and order,'' wanting to know how the U.S. had carried it off, and particularly how they had gotten rid of the Russians.

> We have not so far been able to get rid of our undesirables of this class, particularly those of Russian nationality, while we have not got anything like the number . . . we would like to get rid of those we have.[28]

In fact, under the conditions of war, there were several alternative methods of procedure open to the Department. If the prospective deport were of enemy alien origin, an easy solution was to have the person interned, however briefly. In this case the deportation could be carried out ''as a matter of course and without any further examination or difficulty.'' There was no appeal, no hearing; deportation was automatic. Or, if an alien were caught with any type of arms, he or she could be convicted of violation of the regulation governing the behaviour of aliens, and thus deported automatically under Section 40 (criminality) if the person did not have domicile. It was possible to arrest someone on the grounds of some kind of political ''crime'' under Section 41, but it was a risky method. If the person turned out to be a member not of a proscribed organization but rather of a borderline one, or if they attempted to defend themselves, the Department of Immigration might find itself in the embarrassing position of ''having to put a man on the witness stand without first being able to establish that we have a case against him.'' Still, in the case of someone of enemy alien origin, ''if it is desired to get rid of him'' no matter what the reason, there was one guaranteed method: ''the best plan is to have him interned, and then his deportation is very simple.'' Deportations which were illegal under the Immigration Act were carried out by this simple expedient.[29]

After June 1919, the possibilities were widened by the infamous amendment to Section 41 of the Immigration Act, which defined a prohibited immigrant who could not be legally landed in Canada as anyone interested in overthrowing organized government either in the Empire (at the provincial level in Canada too) or in general, or in destroying property, or promoting riot or public disorder, or belonging to a secret organization trying to control people by threat or blackmail. If someone fell under this Section at any time after 4 May 1919 or even retroactively, ''this constitutes evidence that he is still a member of the prohibited classes,'' even if this person were not at that time doing anything prohibited.[30] The sole exception was someone who was a Canadian citizen by birth or naturalization. British immigrants could not be naturalized (their Canadian citizenship was automatic after the required period here); thus they were subject to this amendment, which caused much outrage.

The Department had a curious blind spot about British-born radicals. Its officials made statements such as ''so far as my experience goes, British-born subjects do not generally side with the classes opposed to continuing authority.'' Yet the June 1919 changes were aimed at removing British agitators, particularly those leading the Winnipeg General Strike. The amendments were not successfully used against the British-born in the Winnipeg cases nor, if the Department were to be believed (and it should not be on this point), in other instances. Moreover, provisions added at about the same time to the Citizenship Act provided for ''denaturalization'' so that naturalized citizens could be stripped of citizenship and then deported. Although denaturalization was possible, it was easier to avoid giving citizenship to radicals in the first place. The Department urged caution in this matter, ''with the number of Reds floating about this country, many of whom should be picked up and deported . . . .''[31]

Into 1920, the Department continued to respond to the alarms of the police, the RCMP, employers, and American officials about expected incursions of ''Reds'' into Canada. It reinforced border patrols, intensified inspections, and sent investigators from the Department into reputed trouble spots to search for deportables. In short, it was repression as usual. Yet by this time there was a difference. The beginnings of protest against continuing wartime measures to suppress dissent had appeared in the press and elsewhere. The response of the Department to this challenge was not sympathetic. The Winnipeg *Free Press* ran an editorial on 6 January 1920 opposing these measures as an arbitrary violation of the right to read and think as one pleased, and so on. Western Commissioner of Immigration Thomas Gelley sent the clipping on to Ottawa with the comment that ''It contains some very hot stuff.'' Secretary Blair commented rather resignedly, ''I am afraid there is a somewhat widespread disposition on the part of the public to discount the need of any further steps to control the element which has revolutionary tendencies.'' It was not just the press who were becoming skeptical. A widespread campaign by organized labour bore fruit at this time as well. The Department received dozens of cards urging the repeal of the 1919 Amendments which were a "menace to the freedom of workers" in Canada. The cards gave the numbers of union locals, and were usually signed by members of the executive, most often the President and the Secretary.[32]

The liberal ideas of some members of the public had little influence on the activities of the Department. The Red purge was at its height in the United States, Canadian officials still believed there was a menace, and the Department of Immigration continued to behave as if its duty lay in ridding the country of foreign agitators. It is quite clear that the U.S. situation continued to influence the Canadian scene. For example, Canadian Travelling Immigration Inspectors were given copies of a list of questions used by the U.S. Department of Justice to interrogate their "Red raid" prisoners, and were told to use this list as a guide to interrogate suspected "Reds" in Canada. The questions examined not only place of birth, name, employment, citizenship, date and mode of arrival, but also possible affiliation with the Communist Party, names of others likewise affiliated, knowledge of the bylaws, affiliation with other allegedly communist organizations, associates, and bylaws, and a series of questions to establish deportability on other political grounds. Did the prisoner believe in the overthrow "of any [sic] government" by force or violence? in killing public officials? in revolution? anarchy? and so on.[33]

A casually selected sample of cases from the Department's "agitator" file gives a sense of their actions at this time. There was, for instance, Anna Kanasto, who entered by misrepresentation, did not report for inspection when she became an immigrant, and spoke as an organizer for the Finnish Social Democratic Party, thus coming under Section 41 of the Immigration Act and deportable as a radical. The bureaucratic case report masks the real-life events, but some educated guesses are possible. Kanasto may have said she was entering as a visitor, concealing her intended political activities or deciding to become involved only after her arrival. Her change in immigration status may have involved intent, activities, length of stay, or violation of the wartime regulations. She may not have been aware of the legal niceties of her situation. The more arcane points of Immigration regulations were surely not common knowledge among the general public or even among immigrants. The important point in the Kanasto file is the Section 41 liability; the other charges are either preliminary or supportive. The second example is Elle Saborceki, a German national who had arrived in Canada 1 June 1914, and during the war had been associated with enemy subjects. She was allegedly a Communist Party member, a "revolutionist of a pronounced type." Her deportation had been ordered but could not be carried out during the war, so she had been interned and "repatriated" as a "prisoner of war", 27 February 1920. Saborceki's "association" could have meant with family members, friends, colleagues; it could have been personal, private, public, political, or all four. Given her nationality and alleged political leanings, it probably was all four. Almost any combination would do to create "crimes" with which she could be charged. Note also that "repatriations" did not appear in the deportation statistics, nor were they governed by the Immigration Act. Once an immigrant was ordered interned, whatever the ostensible cause, she had virtually no recourse and certainly had no appeal rights under the Immigration Act.

A third example, David Hirschfield, was a Russian, described as a "tool of others"; after two months in jail for an unspecified but clearly political offence, he had been "brought to his senses." He had been ordered deported on unspecified grounds, but the deportation was delayed because of problems obtaining his passport. He had been released on $1,000 bond until the paperwork could be completed for his deportation. The fourth example, L. B. Thorp, was an American from Detroit, and allegedly a member of the IWW and the Communist Party Secretary in the Detroit area. His case was in progress at the time of the Department record. Finally, there was Sava Elua, a Russian, arrested under Section 41 and sentenced to two months in jail for possession of forbidden literature. He had been examined for deportation by an Immigration officer acting as a one-man Board of Inquiry, during the time he was in jail. This case too was in progress.[34]

There is a wealth of evidence that the systematic persecution of aliens for their political beliefs and activities was part of the work of the Department during the period. Yet this was denied, as, for example, in 1920 in reponse to a question from the British Secretary of State for the Colonies sent to the Governor General of Canada, concerning the alleged "persecution of Russians, in . . . British Dominions, on account of their political views." The Department denied that such persecution existed in Canada.

> So far as I am aware there has been no persecution of Russian citizens in Canada. A number of Russians have been prosecuted for offences under the Immigration Act. Deportation has been ordered in a number of cases. We have 14 of these men detained at New Westminster,

British Columbia, pending arrangements for their deportation to Russia.[35]

Although the Department admitted to holding some Russians in this instance, at other times it had denied such detentions. In September 1919, the Port Arthur, Ontario Trades and Labour Council had protested the deportation of Russian radicals and had asked that these people be allowed to choose the Russian city to which they would be sent. The Director of Internment Operations responded to this request by writing to the Department of Justice that since there were no more Russians interned in Canada, no response was needed. Yet other correspondence revealed that the Department of Immigration had a number of "undesirables and agitators", the majority of whom were described as Russians, held under Section 41 for political "crimes", and awaiting deportation. Because the paperwork for Russian deportations was difficult to complete, some had been released on bail, others were being held in hospitals or asylums, and still others were imprisoned at Immigration Department Detention Hospitals (which despite their names were used as prisons) at Vancouver, Winnipeg, and especially at Montreal where the central Detention Hospital was located. The Department did not want these "agitators" to mix with other deports, and the segregated care of these political prisoners was a strain on Departmental resources. The Department had requested the use of an internment camp, and had been told by the Internment Operations Office that a camp was available. The Department's strategy was to designate such an internment camp as an "immigration station" within the meaning of the Immigration Act, thus making legal the use of an internment camp as a deportation detention centre in which "agitator" deports could be segregated from other prisoners. After the Department of Immigration had the Department of Justice verify the legality of this scheme, it was carried out. The internment camp was designated an "immigration station", and the Russian and other "agitators" became, legally and statistically, mere detainees for deportation for unspecified offences under the Immigration Act, rather than internees or prisoners.[36]

The Department could then deny any political persecution of Russians or other immigrants. Technically, their denial was true. Radicals were prosecuted for violations of the Immigration Act. The fact that certain political associations, beliefs or activities were in contravention of the Act was not mentioned in the answer given to the British Secretary of State in 1920 or on other occasions. Although the Department's answer was true, it was grossly misleading. As long as the Department proscribed certain ideas, then political deportations could be carried out perfectly openly, yet concealed by their very legality.

And so they were, during the war and into the early 1920s. Indeed there were indications that there may have been a movement within the Department to intensify the work of political deportation by increasing its effectiveness. The Winnipeg agent suggested that the RCMP, who were currently being used to help the Department trace and arrest violators, actually be made Immigration agents so that they could prosecute as well as arrest their victims. The legal position of the Department became more difficult after the War Measures Act lapsed, because political deportations had been much easier under wartime emergency legislation. Moreover, in December 1922 the Department of Justice ruled that the IWW was not an illegal organization, because its constitution did not contravene the relevant section of the Immigration Act. Yet undercover surveillance continued. Despite the fact that the Wobblies were neither legally excludable nor deportable as members of the IWW, the Department continued to reject known Wobblies at the border. That this was deliberate is clear from the files of the Department. As the agent at Winnipeg explained to a subordinate,

> Of course, if a man is known as an IWW agitator or organizer, our officers at the boundary would hesitate to admit him, and if such a man is found in Canada, and comes before your notice, he could be treated under 33-7.[37]

And even though the Department could no longer legally deal with the IWW as an organization,

> with individual immigrants we can deal, however, under the Immigration Act, and in the present circumstances . . . persons . . . entering should be held on reasonable suspicion of entering Canada by misrepresentation. No Boundary Inspector in my district would ever dream of admitting any IWW agitators or IWW organizer.[38]

There was also a suggestion that the Department would have liked to have gone even further. In one instance, a Travelling Investigating Officer refrained from taking action against two Wobblies out of fear of hostility from the men's local supporters, rather than out of any legal fastidiousness. The two men were both Canadian, one by birth, the other by long residence. The former did not come under Department of

Immigration jurisdiction under any circumstances; the latter could have been deportable under Section 41 if there had been grounds. The RCMP were very eager to deport the two men but could not prosecute them because they had not broken any laws. The Mounties relied on Immigration to deal with the matter, but the Department could not in any case act against them solely on account of their IWW membership since the Justice ruling. The Travelling Investigating Officer concerned feared that if he had taken any "high handed action", a situation "uncomfortable" for the Department would have been created. He still hoped that the Department could do something, but cautioned that these cases must be handled in a "very politic way" and the Department must be sure to have "very secure grounds before proceeding." Eventually the situation proved to be too difficult to pursue and the idea of prosecution was abandoned because there was no legal ground for it and none could be created.[39]

Continued IWW activity in the West resulted in continued requests from employers for the government to do something to remove the radicals. The Department of Immigration was responsive to such requests. In January 1924, for example, the Annual Meeting of the Mountain Lumber Manufacturers' Association called on the government to "rid the country of agitators." The Minister of Labour subsequently notified Immigration to keep all agitators out of the country. Immigration asked the Association for further information about aliens "advocating or participating in strike agitation among the lumber camps." The Vancouver Board of Trade asked the Prime Minister to declare the IWW an illegal organization, and wanted all IWW organizers deported and excluded from the country in the future.[40]

Eventually, protest emerged within the Department about the illegality of the methods used by the Department to deal with the IWW. Officer Reid, a stickler for detail, discussed the problem with the British Columbia Immigration Commissioner Jolliffe:

> As you are aware, we cannot exclude from Canada a member of the IWW solely because he is a member of that organization, and unless he is an idiot, insane person, criminal or diseased, we can only exclude him if, in the opinion of our officer, he is liable to become a public charge . . . . This has been done . . . but it is putting somewhat of a strain on the conscience of our officers.

One problem was that "in no case is there any danger of an IWW of any standing admitted to Canada for propaganda purposes liable to become a public charge'' because such a person would have money from the organization, and ''he usually has brains enough to keep him from breaking any laws'' while in Canada. This left officers in an awkward situation. ''Judging from the telegrams'' and letters from the Department asking British Columbia inspectors to keep out agitators, Reid believed ''the situation is not clearly understood'' in Ottawa. If it was intended to prevent members of the IWW from entering Canada, then the law should be amended to exclude them on the basis of membership. Reid was not refusing to exclude Wobblies. On the contrary, he explained, ''we are always willing to try to stop them from coming.'' Yet he feared that present practices connected with deportations could not continue. ''To pick them up and arrest and examine them'' after they had been legally admitted would ''only result in unfavourable criticism . . . and unless you instruct to the contrary, we will not do so.''[41]

This may have slowed down activity against the IWW but it did not stop it. Immigration was conciliatory but did not back down. Reid's superior justified the Department's position:

> There has been . . . a considerable amount of industrial unrest . . . either started or kept alive by agitators allegedly operating as IWW officers or delegates . . . . It is the desire of the Department that men of this type be carefully examined and the Act be strictly applied.

Clearly what was meant here by ''strictly applied'' was using any technicality in the Act to keep the Wobblies out. This was shown by the detailed instructions issued, including the admonition to use the ''liable to become a public charge'' category even if it were not likely to be caused by unemployment, but perhaps ''as a result of agitating and fomenting trouble in disturbed industrial areas.'' In other words, if these men were fired or jailed because of their organizing activities, they might then become a public charge (any resident of a jail was technically a public charge even if they were later found innocent, and even if they had the money to pay for their keep, because such bills were never tendered). Officers did not need to trouble their conscience, because

> it is not intended that our officers should be instructed to exclude members of the IWW (as such) . . . but it is of course intended that our officers shall intelligently apply the Act.[42]

Officer Reid of British Columbia continued to seek legal ways to deal with the IWW, writing weeks later that several IWWs had entered as tourists, and that if they took even a temporary job, he would "have some ground on which to take proceedings against them." He asked the Department if their investigations had found cases such as this. Except for catching the men in some violation of the Act, Reid said, "under the regulations as they exist at present, I have no means by which I can effect the return of these men to the U.S."[43]

The high point – or perhaps low point is more à propos – of the Department's persecution of the Wobblies was the badly fumbled attempt to deport Sam Scarlett in 1924. The Department must share the credit for this bumbling with the Department of Justice, for the case rested on a tiny technical point of law, and Justice gave Immigration some bad legal advice. The Vancouver office had been concerned about Scarlett but was hesitant to act against him without good grounds. The Department of Immigration wrote to the Department of Justice to ask if Scarlett were deportable under various sections of the Immigration Act. Justice said yes, and a warrant was sent to Vancouver for Scarlett's arrest and examination. Scarlett was a forty-three-year-old Scot who had first come to Canada in 1903, and then had entered the United States in 1904. In 1911 he became a member of the IWW. He was convicted of seditious conspiracy in a trial of dubious legality, in Chicago in August 1918 as a result of the Red raids and sentenced to twenty years' imprisonment.[44] The sentence was later commuted on the condition that he be deported, in January 1923. Deportation was carried out from New York that April.

In August 1923 Sam Scarlett legally entered Canada. He had come as a harvester, but took work as a machinist, claiming that he had arrived in the Prairies between harvests and the other job had come along while he was waiting for the next harvest. Later he worked as a labour organizer in Vancouver where he was arrested. After a hearing in which the Department tried unsuccessfully to show that Scarlett advocated violence and the destruction of property and did not believe in organized government (which would have brought him under Section 41), he was ordered deported under Section 3, subsections (o), (r), and (s) of the Immigration Act. The case rested on the Department of Justice ruling that the latter two subsections applied to Scarlett because he had been found guilty of conspiring against an allied government during the war, and had been deported from an allied country for this conspiracy. Therefore he was a prohibited immigrant who could not have been landed legally when he entered in 1923. It is unclear why subsection (o) was included in the order, since Justice had ruled nearly two years earlier that the IWW did not come under this subsection. The key points in his conviction, however, were the other two subsections; otherwise he was not deportable. Scarlett appealed his conviction, and his attorneys filed a brief arguing that neither the IWW nor Scarlett advocated anything illegal under the Act. The brief did not touch upon what was to be revealed as the real flaw in the case. The problem, as the Department discovered when it asked Justice for advice about the appeal, was that the United States had not been an ally of Canada during the war, but rather an "associated power". The case of the Department collapsed, and Secretary Blair noted, "In view of this we must sustain the appeal."[45]

Blair may have been relieved. He had expressed qualms about the case: "I think it would have been better if we had not started this at all," he had said, "because these upheavals usually do more to spread fire than to quench it." The upheavals to which he referred were a series of protests and demonstrations, well observed by the RCMP. They reported that the IWW did not expect to halt the deportation, but was determined to use it to promote the movement. The Department had received telegrams from a wide variety of British Columbia unions and other labour organizations, as well as from an MLA from that province. As well, in September it received dozens of letters from concerned individuals and organizations.[46] The long (and sometimes successful) campaign by the Department to suppress agitators in response to the demands of employers had received a serious blow. The campaign did not stop, but it fizzled. The Department did not lose its interest in eliminating agitators, but it became very cautious.

Sam Scarlett remained active. A letter from the Immigration Commissioner at Winnipeg in the summer of 1925 indicated that he remained a thorn in the side of the Department. It was a thorn with which the Department was prepared to live, however. The Winnipeg officer's superior wrote:

> While the Department fully appreciates the undesirable activities of Sam Scarlett, yet it is quite evident that no action at the present time can be taken under the provisions of the Immigration Act, the Justice Department having ruled that the case does not come within the provisions of subsections (o), (r), (s) of Section 3 of the Act . . . . If the activities of Sam Scarlett are not such that he can be arrested and convicted on any charge . . . it is hardly probable that the Department could successfully take any action against him in the matter of deportation, particularly when there are no grounds other than those upon

which he has already been examined. Therefore the Department is not prepared to sanction any action to arrest and examine Sam Scarlett unless he has been convicted of some offence and sentenced to a term of imprisonment in Canada.[47]

The return to the pre-war status quo took some time. There were numerous attempts to take Section 41 back to its original form as it had been before the June 1919 amendment. In each case, the Senate rejected the attempt, leading Blair to speculate to the Deputy Minister that this would probably not happen until the government had a majority in the Senate. In fact, Section 41 was not returned to its original wording until 1928. Section 98 of the Criminal Code was not repealed until 1937.[48]

The Department liked to claim that ''no person . . . so far as I am aware has ever been deported from Canada under the extended authority'' of Section 41.[49] If this were true – and it is not – it would not have been from lack of trying. Scott had written to the Department of Justice about legal technicalities of a series of Section 41 deportations that he wished to undertake, just before the Section was amended in June 1919. Scott had reported large numbers of cases coming within Section 41, including

> those who have been convicted for being in possession of revolutionary or other prohibited literature of an undesirable nature, and of similarly illegal and disloyal acts, and who are shown to or are known to profess disloyal or revolutionary tendencies.

Scott asked if these could be deported, even though they had acquired domicile, and even though under the Act at that time they were not classified as prohibited immigrants (which would have annulled their domicile). Scott also wanted Justice to confirm that such persons could indeed be deported under Section 41. On 21 July 1919 Scott wrote again to Justice, saying that no reply to his first letter was now necessary, as ''the amendments to the Immigration Act have provided the answer to our letter.''[50] The answer was ''yes''.

The files of the Department abound with examples of the use of Section 41. Successful deportations under this Section include those of Charles David Rose, Bernard Reed Thompson, and David G. Miller, David Porter Moon, and Fred Schultz, all of whom had entered from the United States in the fall of 1917. They were all card-carrying IWW members, and had ''stirred up trouble'' by encouraging their fellow workers to strike for higher wages. They were prosecuted under Section 41 for ''attempting by word or act to create riot or public disorder.''[51] There were also charged under Section 33: entry without proper inspection. A somewhat later example of deportations under Section 41 (as amended in June 1919) was that of two women, one a Finnish Social Democratic Party member and organizer, the other a German Communist Party member.[52]

A particularly blatant example of attempted Section 41 deportations was the case of the "Winnipeg Five", who had been rounded up in the Winnipeg General Strike raids. It was in order to legalize such proposed raids that Section 41 had been amended in June 1919.

Three of the five "foreigners" rounded up were Jews. The men were charged with seditious conspiracy, told that they would be deported, and taken to Stoney Mountain Prison. Several weeks later they were moved to the Immigration Hall in Winnipeg. Moses Almazov (né Samuel Pearl), Sam Blumenberg and Michael Charitonoff had all been classified as dangerous enemy aliens and for weeks before the raid had been under surveillance by the RCMP. Almazov, a University of Manitoba student in economics and philosophy, had come from Russia in 1913. He was editor of *Die Volke Stimme*, and a member of the Social Democratic Party and a communist. The RCMP said he was an "active revolutionary plotter." He was eventually acquitted by a Board of Inquiry and released after a scolding by Magistrate Noble (illegally appointed to the Board by Immigration authorities).[53]

Michael Charitonoff had been charged with attempting to create riot and disorder. The evidence against him was based on his presence at a public meeting in Winnipeg. He had sat on the platform but had not spoken. He had voted in favour of several resolutions which the Mounties said were not in themselves seditious, but had been supported by rather "hot" speeches. His deportation case was based on this flimsy evidence. Charitonoff was ordered deported by the Board of Inquiry. He successfully appealed the decision. The Department of Justice had ruled that although Charitonoff was "well within the meaning of undesirable," simply voting for these resolutions was not sufficient evidence for Section 41 charges. He would have been acquitted in a court of law.[54]

Although the Charitonoff case ultimately had turned on legal points of evidence, another factor was the public outcry following the Winnipeg General Strike raids. The government had been too alarmed at the fuss to make the use it had intended of the amended Section 41. The government was forced to resort to other tactics, including the use of other sections of the Immigration Act, to rid themselves of "troublemakers". The other four of the Winnipeg Five fared well under Section 41. Only one,

Schoppelrei, was deported, and that was for illegal entry. Their Board of Inquiry hearings were important in determining the failure of Section 41 as an instrument for automatically deporting political dissidents, as Donald Avery has pointed out. A group arrested in a second raid four days later did not have hearings before a Board of Inquiry, as provided by the Immigration Act. Instead, they were sent to an internment camp on the order of Judge MacDonald, and "secretly deported" at a later date.[55] This was, of course, exceeding the letter as well as the spirit of the law. It was not an uncommon excess.

What the government was trying to do in the war period was "to arrest a movement: it was trying to deport a philosophy."[56] Extra-legal methods were appropriate to problems that did not admit of legal solutions. These methods, like so much that had taken place under the auspices of the Department before this time, were indeed, as David Bercuson has pointed out, in "violation of the spirit of common justice."[57]

The political deportations of the war period displayed the sophisticated and systematic bureaucratic techniques of the Department. During this period, the Department managed to remove a whole category of people by applying to them purely administrative proceedings. Deportation's function as an extension of exclusion was made clear, and so were some lessons on how to manoeuvre around legal limits. For example, they could find other nominal reasons to exclude or deport; use the double bind tactic of excluding those who admitted their affiliations, and deporting for entry by misrepresentation those who concealed them. There was also the post facto technique: once the political undesirable had been identified, it was a matter of finding the legal grounds to fit the case. Before the war, this had been done on an individual, intermittent, and ad hoc basis. Now it was systematic and deliberate.

Four conclusions may be drawn from the political deportations of the war period. First, that systematic political deportation existed, overtly within the Department, but to a certain extent concealed from liberals and critics and the public in general. The main technique for concealment was the absence of a category called "political deportation" in the statistics on the causes of deportation that appeared in the annual reports of the Department. Second, from the evidence it is clear that the published statistics concealed the real reasons for deportation behind a screen of bureaucratic categories. Nominal categories could be used to remove a person deemed undesirable on other grounds. For instance, a person deported for having tuberculosis most certainly had the disease; but was that the real or only reason for deportation? The question for the Department was not so much "why is this person undesirable," but rather "for what legal cause can we deport this undesirable person." The evidence indicates that this method was commonly used for political deportations. Third, the Department deliberately and systematically extended its policy and role of actively searching out deports, by fitting political deportations into existing categories. Sometimes the fit was crude and obvious, other times easy and unquestioned because of wartime hysteria and the new "undesirability" criteria. But once the deportation of political misfits had begun on a large scale, it continued after the wartime reasons and the legal supports for it had disappeared, and indeed until the target group had itself faded away. Bureaucratic categories, practices and excuses had become self-sustaining. Finally, the question of whether the Department threw out a group depended not on the legal status of the group, but on its political status. If legal deportability confirmed the political deportability, as it did for interned enemy aliens, so much the better, but the a priori reason for deporting enemy aliens was political. In the case of the IWW, the Department continued to act against them whether or not the IWW was at a given moment a legal or an illegal organization: the techniques, not the activities, of the Department changed. The law was not a problem for the Department for much of this period, as the law was changed to suit the political needs of the government; not coincidentally, it also suited the administrative needs of the Department in its own war against radicals and agitators.

6

The Bureaucracy Matures, 1920s-1935

Throughout the 1920s deportation case-building and record-keeping increased in importance. Before the 1920s, the Department's emphasis on constructing solid cases was usually based on its desire to make the transportation companies pay the cost of deportation, and to avoid grave criticism or public uproar for shipping out paupers or the helpless. By the 1920s, it had begun to build legal cases that would demonstrate the fairness and completeness of its work.

To perfect deportation as an administrative proceeding, the Department had to show that deportations were legally carried out, for consistent reasons, by proper methods, in accord with the provisions of the Immigration Act. The evidence that was assembled and the cases that were created protected the Department rather than the immigrant. This is not to suggest that the Department intended to cover up gross violations of the rights of deports, or gross illegalities in its actions. The Department did not as a rule commit such offences, nor did it need to. Its violations of the Act were often technical and could be seen as petty and unimportant, were it not for the consequences for the people involved.

The 1920s were a period of intensified activity for the Department, not searching out deports – that system had been effectively set in motion in the preceding decades – but in creating an unassailable legal rationale for its practices, policies, and actions. The rationale was unassailable because it was based on prevailing social and sexual mores and discrimination, and because it was concealed from the public and, for that matter, from Parliament. If awkward questions were to be raised, the records created by the Department would show the occasional instance of regrettable necessity of a mixed and shifting type. It remained almost impossible for outsiders to discover how the actions of individual immigrants were related to the statistics on the causes of deportation published in the annual reports.

During the decade the Department had to develop techniques to cope with legal and procedural issues such as the extralegal detainment of immigrants who had not been convicted of crimes. The Department had been placing them in jails in lieu of designated immigration detention facilities. Its authority to detain immigrants for examination or deportation was limited by the Act to holding them in an "immigrant station". A jail was not an "immigrant station" within the meaning of the Act. Sometimes the Department could arrange to have a jail so designated, such as the penitentiary in New Westminster where fourteen Russian "agitators" were being held. The Minister simply sent a letter "recognizing" the Warden and his staff as "officers" under the Immigration Act, and the jail as an "immigrant station" in order to "clear up the question of legality of detention in a penitentiary." After the Department of Justice criticized several related practices as being illegal, the Department decided to follow more closely the procedures laid down in the Act, to use the proper paperwork, and to produce documentary evidence that its actions were legal.[1]

Certain illegal practices continued, however. For instance, under some sections of the Act, an immigrant could be arrested without a warrant, but not detained in jail. Nonetheless, the Department decided to continue to do this "at present until we can get the Act amended in such a way to make entirely legal such detention." The Department hoped that if problems arose it could prosecute the detained immigrant for being in Canada in contravention of the Act or entry by stealth or misrepresentation. It might gain a fine or even a conviction. "The moment a conviction is secured, the question of legality of detention awaiting the outcome of deportation proceedings, is no longer a question for us."[2]

The Department also used extralegal procedures with deports who were quite legally held in jail following criminal convictions. Contrary to the provisions of the Act, it was their "custom to deal with inmates of prisons, penitentiaries, and asylums without the formality of an examination by a Board of Inquiry." After 1920, the Department tended to hold Boards of Inquiry, although its methods remained questionable. One short cut was to keep a supply of blank orders signed by the Minister, so that they could be sent off at very short notice in response to a telegram from an agent.[3]

The situation in British Columbia illustrates the way the Department complied almost meticulously with certain legalities while at the same time violated the Act. By 1921, applications for writs of habeas corpus by defendents in Departmental deportation cases were "almost weekly occurences." British Columbia judges had repeatedly ruled that the courts could investigate to be sure that the Department had followed proper procedures laid out by the Act. As a consequence, Vancouver agents paid much greater attention to detail to be sure that their cases would stand up in court. It was to provide British Columbia agents with evidence that they acted legally that the practice of having the Minister sign blank orders for examination became standardized. By 1922, the Minister was signing blanks in batches of fifty.[4]

As the Department increased its attention to case-building, it gave outside officials detailed instructions about preparing deportation cases. To the head of the Canadian Pacific Railway Colonization Department, Secretary Blair explained how to deport some Yugoslavs who had refused to do farm work. It was first necessary to prove that they had entered as agricultural workers but had subsequently refused farm jobs. They could then be arrested without a warrant and deported under Section 33 for entering by misrepresentation. The CPR man was told to submit several cases to the Department, when he had prepared them along these lines, in order to have the deportation proceedings started.[5]

The Department increased its attention to record-keeping, as well. Agents were told to be sure to obtain a signed statement from immigrants who withdrew their appeals against deportation. Perhaps the most significant decision (at least from the point of view of later analysis of the practices of the Department) was to "save the deportation cases." This practice was initiated after the Department found that it could not proceed with a deportation ordered on the grounds that the immigrant had been previously deported, because the person's file had been destroyed. "It seems to me that in deportation cases it might be advisable to retain our files almost indefinitely, because such cases are liable to crop up over and over again and once a record is destroyed it is difficult to effect the second deportation without a good deal of trouble."[6] The general principle of saving the deportation records was consistent with the increased attention by the Department to creating and maintaining records, and building good legal cases for its deportation activities.

Developing precise definitions of deportable conditions or offences was an important factor in assembling solid deportation cases. The Department tried to define more precisely what constituted becoming a public charge. The answers to that question were sometimes inconsistent. For instance, the Deputy Attorney General of British Columbia said that a woman who received Mother's Pension (that is, welfare for the support of dependent children, usually paid to poor widows and other women in desperate circumstances) was not "a charge on the public authorities." Yet these "pensions" were paid from public funds. Women who lived in Salvation Army or YWCA or WCTU hostels were not public charges either, according to the Department of Justice.[7] First World War veterans receiving treatment for war-related problems at veterans' hospitals, however, were considered to be public charges, and could be deported as such.

The deportation of veterans had political implications, and raised complex questions. The issue centred on the question of whether or not a hospital maintained by the Red Cross, or a public institution to help veterans set up and run by the government, were "public charitable institutions" within the meaning of the Immigration Act. Members of Boards of Inquiry had not always agreed, and this had led to difficulties in reaching consistent decisions on deportation cases. In the opinion of the Immigration officials in Ottawa, Red Cross hospitals were public institutions, since funds had been subscribed in Canada by municipal, provincial and federal governments as well as by the general public. If the Red Cross gave help to people, particularly those not citizens or not members of the Canadian Expeditionary Force (CEF), they became public charges within the meaning of the Act. Further, government veterans' hospitals were maintained by public funds. Whether or not veterans using these hospitals became public charges depended on individual circumstances, particularly upon allowances deriving from former military service. According to the Department of Soldiers' Civil Reestablishment (DSCR), even when veterans' allowances entitled them to treatments paid for by the government, the payments did not cover the actual costs. Thus, "no matter to what treatment they are entitled," patients who had not been in the CEF, who became inmates of veterans' hospitals run by the DSCR, "become to a certain extent a charge upon the public funds and a public charge in Canada."[8]

Thus, veterans were deportable if they sought hospital treatment as veterans:

> If an ex-Imperial soldier is not receiving a pension and he receives treatment under the jurisdiction of the Department of Soldiers' Civil Reestablishment in Canada, he is regarded by that Department as becoming a public charge, unless they are reimbursed by the Imperial authorities for the cost of such treatment.

Such reimbursement was reported to be rare. Moreover, even if the veterans were getting a pension and the Imperial authorities paid all the costs of treatment, the DSCR stated that such payment ''does not cover the costs to their Department of the maintenance of such persons in Canada.'' Therefore, even a veteran with veterans' medical treatment benefits became a public charge if he sought treatment at a veterans' hospital in Canada.[9]

The Department of Soldiers' Civil Reestablishment did not stand by the veterans on this issue, but rather co-operated with the Department in deporting vets. The collaboration of the DSCR helped the Department to establish standardized procedures for veterans' deportations. The local offices of the DSCR sent lists of prospective deports to their central office in Ottawa, which in turn forwarded the information to the Department. At the same time, local DSCR offices sent carbon copies of the deport lists to the local Immigration Agents, to help start the investigations. By the end of 1922, the DSCR was requesting deportations in much the same way as the municipalities. The choice of who was deported was largely a question of class, however: as Immigration Secretary Blair remarked, lists of deportable vets seldom included officers.[10]

Even when deportation seemed inevitable under the Act, it was necessary to create detailed evidence in accord with legal procedures. This became increasingly evident in medical deportation cases where the deport had been in Canada long enough to acquire domicile. It was necessary to show that the immigrant could not acquire domicile because he or she belonged to the prohibited classes. In medical cases it was politic for the Department of Immigration to consult with the medical officers at the Department of Health (where the immigration doctors had been transferred in 1919), in much the same way as the Department consulted with lawyers at the Department of Justice about interpretations of the Immigration Act. In 1921, Secretary Blair wrote to the Deputy Minister of Health about a woman certified as mentally defective by Dr. Eric Clarke of the Canadian Committee for Mental Hygiene at Toronto. Clarke attested that the woman, now aged twenty-one, had been feebleminded when she had entered Canada as a Salvation Army immigrant at the age of fourteen. She had borne an illegitimate child, and was currently receiving treatment for venereal disease. Secretary Blair wanted confirmation from the Department of Health that this young woman was indeed a prohibited immigrant under the Act. "Feeblemindedness is an arrest of development of intelligence and is like an indelible scar on the brain cells," replied the Deputy Minister of Health. By definition, she had been so afflicted at entry, and thus was a prohibited immigrant, could never have legally entered, and thus could not have fulfilled the requirements for domicile.[11]

Sending records of all medical-related cases to the Department of Health did not necessarily mean that these deportations were actually carried out on medical grounds:

> Unless evidence is available that a person was prohibited at the time of entry, no action can be taken in the deportation cases of persons who are insane or mentally defective in any way or are suffering from venereal disease or tuberculosis or are physically defective to such an extent that they cannot work or earn a living, *unless* such persons have become inmates of asylums or hospitals for the insane, or the mentally deficient, or public charitable institutions or have become public charges.

Lacking the evidence that the condition or problem had existed at the time of entry, deportation was usually effected on the grounds that the immigrant had become a public charge.[12]

The Department of Immigration did not refer all deportations on medical grounds to the Department of Health, nor did it refer all public charge deportations:

> The term "for medical reasons" is rather elastic, and we must decide generally the limit within which we will report to the Health Department. If the *real* grounds for deportation are physical or mental, I think we should advise Health. But if otherwise, I would not report unless the record shows that a person had become a public charge etc., because of physical or mental conditions possibly present when entering Canada.[13]

For the most part the relationship between the two departments was smooth and they collaborated effectively on deportation problems. Yet sometimes there were hints of disagreement. In 1927, the Department of Health expressed concern that "too many cases were being deported on the ground of medical reasons." Immigration countered that although the Department of Health was given copies of all medical cases, this did not mean that such deportations were "effected on medical grounds." They explained, "the condition of health of the person under investigation . . . is frequently a determining factor in the decision finally arrived at, but this does not, of course, mean that the deportation is effected on the grounds of medical causes."

In the case of one man who was also a prohibited immigrant because he had tuberculosis, the deportation had been

> ordered solely on the grounds that the alien had become a public charge in Canada and was not in possession of Canadian domicile. The Examining Officer came to the conclusion that the alien was not disposed to work and that he appeared to be strong and healthy.[14]

Thus, the fact that the person had tuberculosis and was therefore a member of the prohibited classes was used only to disqualify him from domicile. The actual ground for deportation was that he was a public charge.

High numbers of deportations on medical grounds reflected badly on the Department of Health; since the transfer of the immigration doctors in 1919, incoming immigrants were inspected by medical officers under the auspices of the Department of Health. Although by the 1920s the medical officers no longer had the power to exclude or deport immigrants, they were still required to certify in writing the existence of any medical problems which might make each immigrant a member of the prohibited classes specified in the Act. Subsequent admission, rejection or, ultimately, deportation, was out of their hands. Yet outcry for stricter inspection focused on the inadequacy of medical inspections. High rates of medical deportation fueled such outcries.

Even though the medical inspectors had little real authority by the 1920s, it was essential that they note any defects that might have bearing on later deportation cases. Without such evidence, the Department of Immigration might find it impossible to deport someone. For example, in 1928, Jane Smith, aged seventy-four, suffering from senile dementia and varicose veins, was ordered deported. She had entered Canada in August 1919, destined for Fort William, Ontario, where her married daughter lived. She had been admitted to the Ontario Hospital for the Insane in April 1928, nearly nine years later. The Department of Health agreed that she had been certifiable at the time of entry under the medical prohibitions of the Act, because of ulcerating varicose veins. Her deportation order was based on Section 3, "prohibited immigrant", Section 40, "having become an inmate of a hospital for the insane," and "having become a public charge."[15]

The case rested upon her inclusion in the prohibited classes because of her varicose veins at the time of entry. She had admitted that she had suffered from varicose veins before entering Canada. Upon arrival at the hospital, she had been medically certified as physically unable to work because of old age and varicose veins. Moreover, there was also a letter from the Medical Superintendent of the hospital attesting that she was lame because of her veins, and thus had never been able to earn her living in Canada. Therefore, she had been certifiable under Section 3 at the time of entry. Nonetheless, the Department finally had to reverse her deportation order, because she had not been so certified when she entered Canada. Thus, there was no adequate evidence to show that she did not have domicile, and so she was not deportable under Section 40.[16]

The issue in deportation cases was not so much the real situation but rather what could legally be shown to be the situation. While medical factors gave the opportunity to build good cases for the deportation of some immigrants even after long residence, these medical factors were useful only if carefully constructed into evidence to support the case.

The Department acquired a new technique to use against domiciled aliens, with the amendment of the Opium and Narcotic Drug Act (O.N.D.A.) on 28 June 1922. Before, only undomiciled aliens could legally be deported after criminal convictions for drug-related offences such as possession of, addiction to, or trafficking in, illegal drugs. After the 1922 amendment, according to a Department of Justice ruling, "an alien coming under the provisions of the O.N.D.A. is deportable, notwithstanding the fact that he may have acquired Canadian domicile under the provisions of the Immigration Act."[17]

Such deportations did not go unchallenged: in fiscal 1922-23, fourteen cases from the Pacific Division (British Columbia) went to the courts. Five of these court cases were won by the Department and the persons were deported after their jail sentences. The other nine persons won and the Department had to release twenty-three O.N.D.A. deports who had served their jail sentences, and whose deportations would not have been sustained by the courts if challenged by writs of habeas corpus. Another important British Columbia Court of Appeals decision made O.N.D.A. deportations more difficult. The Court decided that deportation under certain Sections of the O.N.D.A. was a criminal proceeding. This increased the already high number of deportation cases being appealed in the British Columbia courts.[18] The Department fared better in closed administrative proceedings. Nonetheless, the use of the amended O.N.D.A. was subject to fewer constraints in other provinces, and its provisions did bring hundreds more each year into the ranks of the deportable.

The tactics used by the Department were flexible and varied according to the target. The O.N.D.A. deportation provisions applied only to "aliens". British subjects could not be examined for deportation for drug offences under the O.N.D.A., but if undomiciled they could be examined under Sections 40 and 42 of the Immigration Act for deportation as convicted criminals. Sometimes the Department's choice of legal tactics was affected by economic considerations. Some O.N.D.A. offences could lead to deportations of undomiciled immigrants under the Immigration Act. In these cases, the transportation companies were usually liable for costs. Drug cases "beyond" the Immigration Act, when aliens had Canadian domicile, had to be carried out under the O.N.D.A. In these instances, the Department paid the costs of deportation.[19]

The Pacific Division office in Vancouver, where most of the O.N.D.A. deportations were carried out, and where the Department had faced the most severe court challenges, helped other offices prepare O.N.D.A. cases that would survive appeals or habeas corpus writs. Agent Malcolm Reid, Assistant Chief Controller of Chinese Immigration at Vancouver, explained to Agent Regimbal, Montreal Controller of Chinese Immigration, that in British Columbia they had "successfully defended some Habeas Corpus cases . . . but have lost one or two as well." The most important points for the Board of Inquiry to bring out in such cases were that the accused was an alien, and that he or she had been sentenced under the relevant sections of the O.N.D.A. "The courts have told us that in all cases, the Warrant of the Minister of Justice . . . must be issued," as well as the warrant from Immigration. Further, the person would have to have been formally ordered deported by a Board of Inquiry. If these steps were properly taken, Reid advised, the Department "will not have much trouble with these cases."[20]

The statistics of the Pacific Division showed the usefulness of the new Act. In fiscal 1923-24, 38 per cent (116 : 307) of its deportations were under these provisions; in 1924-25, 22 per cent (77 : 374); and in 1926-27, 16 per cent (52 : 328). Moreover, within the statistics of "criminal" deportations, there were other instances of those not yet domiciled, and thus liable to be deported for criminal convictions (violations of the O.N.D.A.), under the provisions of the general Immigration Act.[21]

The O.N.D.A. was aimed at the drug trade in Canada, particularly at the Chinese, who were thought to be disproportionately involved in it. Indeed, most of the deportations under the O.N.D.A. were of persons of Chinese descent. Chinese immigration had been restricted since 1885 by the imposition of a $50 head tax, increased to $100 in 1901, and $500 in 1904. In 1923, the Canadian government's Chinese Immigration Act cut off Chinese immigration by restricting entry to Canada to: diplomatic personnel and their families; returning Canadian-born Chinese who had been away for educational or other purposes and who could prove they were Canadian-born; returning long-time Canadian residents who could prove their status; students; certain classes of merchants; visitors; and persons in transit to other countries. Persons of Chinese descent presently in Canada had already been required to register with the immigration authorities. Their subsequent exit and re-entry was controlled by a system of certificates valid only for a certain length of time.[22]

This anti-Chinese prejudice expressed in policy in the 1923 Act was also expressed in Departmental practice. The Winnipeg Commissioner wrote to the Ottawa office in 1923 to complain that he had not been consistently notified of the impending arrival of Chinese deports coming from the East to be deported from a Pacific port. Winnipeg officers met the train, and took over escorting the Chinese deports to Vancouver. Winnipeg officers needed adequate notice to arrange a transfer of custody at the station, ''so that these Chinese will not be kept over in the Immigration Hall here.''[23]

It was not just the Department who objected to close contact with Chinese deports. In 1929, Charlotte Whitton of the Canadian Council on Child Welfare complained to the Department about a series of child deportations. A fifteen-year-old girl and a fourteen-year-old boy, escorted by a Department Matron on the Vancouver eastbound train, had found no sleeping accommodations. Their car had been filled with Chinese men. At first the Department presumed that it was the colonist car accommodations rather than the Chinese passengers to which Whitton objected, and responded that the colonist car was no worse than that in which the children had immigrated to Vancouver. Moreover it would be exceedingly rare for [white] child deports to travel in a colonist car, or to be sent in a car full of Chinese. As a result of this case (and others before), the Vancouver Children's Aid Society asked that all child deports be given better accommodation. As the Society argued, when the children had travelled to Vancouver with their parents, it is unlikely that they had been the only non-Chinese occupants of a car. The Society wanted assurances that child deports travelling without their parents would be placed in a car "where the other passengers are not Orientals and the girl deportees should not be made to travel in a car entirely filled with men." Someone from the Department noted in the margin beside these two requests, "quite right," and suggested using tourist rather than colonist cars.[24]

The O.N.D.A. amendments added another weapon to the arsenal of the Department, but the instructions had to be carefully followed to avoid backfiring. The provisions of the Immigration Act did not so much limit the power of the Department to carry out deportations, as did they specify the methods and procedures through which the Department was to exercise that power. As long as the Department was meticulous in paperwork, used the correct forms, and adduced evidence in its Board of Inquiry hearings to prove the immigrant's membership in a particular group specified in the Section of the Act under which the deportation was to take place, its authority would be virtually unchallenged.

Immigrants in Canada more than five years could be deported in the 1920s only under certain conditions: discovery of political offences, bringing them under Section 41; discovery that they had not entered legally and could not have fulfilled the requirement for five years' residence after legal entry; or discovery that some medical problem or condition brought them under the prohibited classes, which meant that they could never acquire domicile. Otherwise, domiciled immigrants were usually safe from deportation. The amended O.N.D.A. added another category to the list of exceptions, and it focused on groups who were widely seen as undesirable: drug addicts or traffickers, criminals and, often, the Chinese. Deportation of these groups was politically safe, morally attractive, and in accord with the popular prejudices of the general public and of the "progressive" elements such as doctors and moral reformers of the period.[25]

Morality was a particularly important consideration in the deportations of women. The attitude of the Department was ambiguous. On one hand, the Department routinely deported women because of little more than sexual transgressions at which they had been caught (for instance by pregnancy or venereal disease). On the other hand, the Department cautioned its various agents to be sure that women reported for deportation for sexual immorality were not merely victims of someone's desire to get them out of the way. During the war, Superintendent Scott had issued a notice to all agents and officers in the West concerning such cases. The Department was sometimes criticized, Scott said, for deporting young women, especially single women. It was claimed that "interested persons" were bringing about such deportations to "avoid local trouble" and the women were "unable to defend themselves and more to be pitied than blamed." The Department had no desire to find itself blamed, however. Scott instructed, "With the object of further safeguarding our interests . . . where the deportation of a young woman is under consideration, the greatest care should be taken to see her side of the story is considered and, if necessary, investigated."[26]

Bruce Walker, then in charge of the Winnipeg office of the Department, responded that he had "for several years . . . made it my personal business not to pass a woman for deportation, old or young, married or unmarried, without a thorough investigation. . . . Interested parties do not hesitate to bring unsupported charges to compel political or other influence towards the removal of a woman whose presence is considered dangerous or inconvenient to them. I have a case in Ft. Frances this morning, where local influence is being used against a young woman . . . by local interests, in which one of the parties concerned is guilty of a serious crime against the girl and seeks to protect himself from further exposure. . . ."[27]

The Department was paternalistic towards female immigrants, especially the respectable and the "fallen". This can be explained in part by connections between the Department and the women's reform movement in Canada, especially that part of the movement involved in female immigration promotion and management. Bruce Walker was sympathetic to maternalist feminist circles such as the Young Women's Christian Association. Walker addressed meetings sponsored by the YWCA, wrote on female immigration in their magazine, and approved of YWCA efforts to control and protect female immigrants in the West. The YWCA had been a leader in the efforts by women's organizations in Canada to protect young women immigrants. In 1909, a Canadian representative to an international conference of women reformers had suggested that young women coming to Canada be made wards of the state, to keep them on the straight and narrow; unsupervised young women would be "ruined".[28]

By 1914 the YWCA had helped to set up an elaborate system of reception and supervision of female immigrants arriving in Canada. The YWCA's part in this network was mostly Travellers' Aid work. "TA" workers wearing badges met incoming women at stations all over the country, and through local committees of women's church missionary societies, associations of girls' school graduates, home economics societies, women's institutes, other women's organizations, and through local clergymen, tried to supervise and assist newcomers. The YWCA had received permission from the railroads to put up placards in stations, and had obtained promises of further co-operation. The Canadian delegates at an international YWCA conference in Stockholm had suggested that a system of compulsory reception and registration centres be set up in each Canadian city station, where female immigrants would check in so that they might each "be located and guarded."[29]

Bruce Walker echoed many of these same concerns in his 1914 article in the YWCA periodical *The Young Women of Canada*. He described the moral dangers of unescorted and unprotected travel, and advocated the investigation of prospective employers to protect women against moral dangers. He explained the importance of supervising female immigrant newcomers so that they would become the kind of wives and mothers upon whom the building of Canada and the moulding of "the destinies of future Canadians" could safely depend. He urged that there be a female immigrant receiving home managed by women (especially YWCA women) in every province, and that the presence of female supervisory escorts be made compulsory on all ships and trains carrying female immigrants. He urged his readers to pressure the government to bring about these reforms.[30] (They took his advice.)

This was the context within which Department agents approached concerns related to female immigrants. The YWCA and other women's groups working with these immigrants continued during the 1920s to press for more systematic and thorough contact with immigrants after they had been settled in new jobs and homes. With the creation of a Women's Division in the Department of Immigration after the war, the ties between the women reformers and the Department were formalized and legitimized. Jean Burnham, head of the Division, instituted many of the procedures which women's groups had developed and lobbied the government to support since the 1880s. Burnham advocated "follow-up work", as this supervision and contact was called. She told the YWCA Immigration Committee in 1925 that she believed it should be "not just protective," but also embodied in "club opportunities for making friends and keeping straight." The social activities of women immigrants should be a part of this follow-up system. Burnham was sometimes more thorough than the YWCA on this question, for she had suggested, as well, a letter and "follow-up visit" to every employer ("mistress") of immigrant domestic servants to assure that effective supervision and protection could be maintained.[31]

On other occasions, Burnham used the YWCA and other follow-up workers "to locate missing girls," that is, women who had dropped out of the records of the Department. Women reformers had focused mainly on British female immigrants; Burnham extended the system to non-British women. Agreeing that female escorts were needed for women travelling to their new homes, Burnham expressed concern that "conductresses" were "rarely sent out on an immigrant train that is wholly foreign," so that "foreign" women did not receive the same "protection" as British women. She was able to report a few months later that the situation had improved, and that fewer "foreign" trains were sent out without a "conductress". Some aspects of this close relationship between the women reformers of the YWCA and the government, however, had deteriorated by the last half of the 1920s.

In 1926, Burnham notified the YWCA that she would no longer send them corrected and updated addresses for all single female immigrants in Canada. "The government safeguarded the interests of the new arrivals and . . . our general follow-up work was therefore not needed," reported an upset YWCA worker to her headquarters. In 1927, Burnham discontinued the practice of notifying the YWCA of the arrival of married women; only single immigrants were to be named henceforth in the Department lists given to the YWCA.[32]

Three factors were significant in these decisions. First, the Department had become more deeply involved in the work of female immigration management; women immigration officers and other workers were employed by the government, and systems for the "care" of female immigrants were well established, particularly with the advent of the Empire Settlement Act and the Aftercare Agreement for the supervised immigration of British domestic servants. The Aftercare Agreement promised that the women would be personally conducted to their ships, supervised on the voyage, met at the Canadian port by women officers of the Department of Immigration, and kept under government supervision until they were placed in suitable positions. After placement, the government would maintain contact with the immigrants for several years. The government no longer needed to supply information to the YWCA in order to have follow-up done. Secondly, the pressure of work increased as paperwork became more voluminous, more specific, and more important.

The special responsibilities of the Women's Division meant that Burnham and her staff were under constant pressure to generate a staggering array of statistics and reports on women immigrants. Moreover, it was their duty to keep track of every single female immigrant who entered the country. The Division could no longer afford extra time and money to send this information to the YWCA. Finally, by the 1920s, Jean Burnham may well have been exasperated by the difficulty of bringing together women reformers to work with her under new and more professional terms and conditions.

In 1919, when the Women's Division had been formed, a publicly funded advisory and coordinating committee of representatives from provincial and federal governments and women's reform groups working in female immigration had also been established. The Canadian Council of Immigration of Women functioned for several years and then gradually faded from the scene, perhaps because its role was token. Ever more of the responsibilities of the Council were taken over by government representatives and professional social workers, while the volunteer reformers became ever less necessary and available. Dr. Helen Reid, a Montreal feminist and physician who was very active in immigration and public health matters, in 1927 suggested calling up the Council again, to strengthen the Women's Division, to lessen the overlapping of organizations doing immigration work, and to develop information on the actual work done by organizations. Reid stressed the importance of co-operation between governments and women's groups in this work. Burnham had been working without much success since 1926 to organize a conference to revive the Council, and had written to Minister of Immigration Robert Forke to gain support for the idea. She hoped that women's organizations could use the Council to ''help mould government policy.'' The meeting was eventually held in 1928 but the role of voluntary organizations in female immigration work was never to regain the importance of previous decades. Although the work of the Women's Division continued to show maternal feminist features of the earlier period, its outlook had become professionalized. The women's immigration reform movement that had helped to shape the Division had also changed, with some of its activists becoming professionals themselves, and some turning to other tasks.[33]

The establishment of a Women's Division can be seen as one response of the Department to decades of working more or less in co-operation with women (and to a lesser extent, men) reformers in the area of female immigration. There is little evidence of conflict between Jean Burnham and other Department officials. Since most of the work relating to women took place under the ostensible supervision of the Women's Division, there may well have been relatively few occasions for clashes. It was the practice in the 1920s to use female officers to carry out escort and other deportation-connected duties. Despite the Department's sometimes harsh deportation practices, it did display a paternalistic (or maternalistic) "protective" attitude towards women immigrants.

The Department routinely deported women who strayed from well regulated and respectable behaviour. The Department in some instances deported women solely because they had illegitimate children. In one case in 1922 the child had died, so "the care and maintenance of the child was not a matter to be taken into consideration"; still, the mother was deported. "Fallen girls" were deported, often at the behest of municipal officials. In one such case, the Department's Assistant Accountant explained to the Secretary of Immigration that Calgary authorities were doing their best to "get rid of" one woman, whether she was "legally deportable or not. I think experience has shown the Department that this is pretty much the attitude of at least all the Western Municipalities . . . ."[34]

When a woman in such a situation wanted to go back to the British Isles (most single women immigrants in the 1920s were British) the Department "might have helped her home without bothering about whether or not she was deportable." But if she were not willing to go, and not legally deportable, she could not be shipped out so easily. In the case of Nellie Fry, for instance, the Department was stymied. She had entered before the 1919 Act had come into effect, so could not be found in the prohibited classes, said Blair. She had been examined to see if her "mental state" would bring her under the prohibited classes under the provisions of the 1914 law. It did not. Noted the Department, "when the girl herself stated that she did not want to go back, that her misfortune and her offence had taken place in Canada and that she had paid here for her error, it became necessary to deal with her case in an absolutely legal manner."[35]

Whether or not women were deported for causes related to sexual "immorality" seems to have been determined also by such factors as with whom they were "immoral". Grace Evelyn Baker had come to Canada as a domestic in November 1926, left her job after a month, and then was apparently courted at the same time by Padgen, a naturalized

Canadian of Austrian origin, and Hoy, a Chinese cafe cashier. The Department had implied that she had been sexually intimate with both before she had married the former. In July 1927, she obtained a legal separation. In September of that year she gave birth to a child who was registered as Hoy's son. Hoy had been "looking after" her since that time. Moreover, upon examination she had "admitted to having been intimate with a young man in England prior to emigration to Canada, and from the evidence it is quite conclusive that she is an undesirable."

She was charged as a prostitute under Section 40 of the Act and ordered deported, because she had admitted having a room at the same hotel as Hoy, and also admitted that she had "frequented the room of this Chinese and had intimate relationships with him, who gave her money as well as presents." Her appeal against deportation was sustained only because she was legally the wife of a Canadian citizen. It is also clear from the records of the Department that it was on account of her sexual relationships outside of marriage (albeit one of the three had been long before) that she was deportable. While the Department professed sympathy for respectable women who had "fallen" victims to sexual predators, and sometimes did help them, it reacted to those who willingly and knowingly transgressed, with little but the desire to remove such a menace to public morals.[36]

The Department was concerned to show that deportations were not arbitrary, but just and legal. The Act offered a variety of statutory causes for deportation. The Department had to build evidence to show that particular cases came under the general categories of the Act. The evidence was the link between the actions of the immigrant and the ability of the Department to deport him or her as a consequence of those actions. There may well have been a direct cause-and-effect link between action and deportation, but the records created and displayed by the Department in its annual reports did not necessarily reveal this causal connection. Rather, nominal or legal causes given to explain deportation tended to obscure the "real" reasons.

The extent to which nominal causes for deportation concealed the real or a priori reasons can be seen in the deportations of British women who had come to Canada as domestic servants during the 1920s. Between 1923-31, a total of 23,804 women had come out as household workers under the Empire Settlement Act. Of these, 18,790 came after January 1926 under the Aftercare Agreement. This agreement brought over women in five different categories under various schemes set up between the

Imperial authorities, the federal government, and such bodies as the Province of Ontario or the Salvation Army. The Aftercare Agreement offered household workers guaranteed work at standard wages. Between 1923 and 1925, women could obtain passage loans. In 1926 a cheap fare of three pounds (reduced to two pounds in 1927) was made available for the ocean passage, and rail fares in Canada were also greatly reduced. The post-1926 immigrants had to pay their own ocean passage, but could get loans for their rail fares. (By 1937, eighty-nine per cent of the loans had been repaid.)[37]

The Aftercare Agreement did not entirely succeed in eliminating the problems traditionally associated with female immigration. The Department classified difficulties experienced by these immigrants as "minor" and "major" problems. Minor problems listed for fiscal 1931-32 included ill health, job changing by unskilled houseworkers, immigrants being "unsettled owing to poor character", houseworkers taking other kinds of work, address unknown, and unemployment. Minor problems in themselves seldom led to deportation. Yet minor problems might become "major", and major problems often led to deportation. Despite the supervision ("protection") promised by the Agreement, numbers of domestics became pregnant and bore children out of marriage.[38]

The Department of Immigration claimed that it did not deport these women simply because they had illegitimate children. This claim was regarded with some skepticism. The Overseas Settlement Office in England, a British government agency, had complained as early as June 1926 that Canada was too eager to deport Empire Settlement women. In 1928, Terence Macnaghten, Vice Chairman of the Overseas Settlement Committee, wrote on behalf of the Overseas Settlement Office protesting the deportation of unwed mothers. "We take the view that when an unmarried woman from this country becomes a mother after she has resided in Canada for a year or more, i.e., when the presumption is that she was led astray after she had arrived in Canada . . . the mother and child should remain in Canada and be dealt with like any other unmarried mother and child in Canada."[39] He urged the Department to seek permission from the Overseas Settlement Office to deport such cases.

The Department was indignant at the suggestion that it should consult British authorities in deportation cases. In an internal memo the Commissioner of Immigration hotly denied that the Department had a programme of wholesale deportations of unwed mothers. "We are continually in hot water owing to our refusal to deport" many such cases, he claimed. As for Macnaghten's idea that these women had been "led astray" in Canada, "no doubt some of them are, but . . . from a perusal of most of these cases, I would judge that there has not been much leading astray . . . the examination frequently indicates the girls were immoral before ever they came to Canada."[40]

Deputy Minister of Immigration William Egan replied to Macnaghten, "we never deport an unmarried mother nor do we deport any British subject if it is at all possible to establish them in this country but we subsequently discover migrants who belonged to the prohibited classes at the time of their entry, and we have . . . no authority under the law to permit such persons to remain in this country." The Canadian law was "designed to protect a municipality" from immigrants who had become public charges, and unwed mothers fell under this law. Shortly thereafter Blair forwarded Macnaghten a copy of a report from an urban charitable organization which complained strenuously about a very low rate of deportation for illegitimacy, arguing that these mothers had become public charges, and that "socially unadjusted cases of this type" should be deported. The organization had decided to refuse to grant relief to such cases, and warned that it would not accept responsibility for the "serious and permanent social problems due to the Department not taking action." Blair cited this report as an example of the problems faced by the Department in dealing with these cases, and as evidence that the Department did not automatically deport unwed mothers.[41]

Macnaghten was persuaded that such cases were dealt with "sympathetically and justly." He accepted the claim that these immigrants were not deported "unless there is evidence of constant immorality and disease." Further, he believed that only a small percentage of deportations ordered had actually been carried out.[42]

Departmental files challenge these claims. The rate of deportation for British female domestics brought to Canada, under the Aftercare Agreement (with its supposedly stringent procedures of selection, supervision and assistance), between 1 January 1926 and 31 March 1931, was 4.6 per cent. This is considerably more than the average of one per cent cited by the Department in its published annual reports. A report by the Department on 670 "unwed mother" cases between 1926 and 1933 revealed that 27.5 per cent of these unmarried mothers were deported, and a further 5.4 per cent were ordered deported, but the deportations stayed. Ten per cent "returned to the Old Country"; it is unclear how many of these returns were in fact informal deportations. These figures do not reveal the extent of illegitimacy deportations, because of the high percentage of cases not yet settled at the time of the study: 36 per cent. Department memos and internally circulated reports indicate that there was not necessarily a direct connection between the "problem", and the stated cause given by the Department for deportation. An analysis of the causes for the deportations of 689 Empire Settlement Aftercare domestics between 1 January 1926 and 31 March 1931[43] showed that the same "problem" – immorality – was listed as a "contributing factor which necessitated deportation" in four of the five statutory causes for these deportations.

The Department gave seven reasons for these 689 deportations: "illegitimacy" (169), "immorality" (64), "criminal convictions" (68), "bad conduct" (64), "medical" (233), "marriage" (deported with husband, 83), and "becoming a public charge" (8). These reasons were not necessarily legal causes for deportation, nor did they correlate directly to the legal causes. The statutory (legal) causes for these 689 deportations were: "public charge" (528), "insane" (24), "prohibited immigrant" (66), "inmate of gaol" (56), "misrepresentation" (15). The same reasons appeared under more than one statutory heading. "Immorality" was in four; "mentally deficient" and "medical" appeared in three ("public charge", "prohibited immigrant", and "misrepresentation"). "Venereal disease" appeared as a subcategory of "medical reasons" under the statutory cause of "public charge", and again as a category itself under the statutory cause of "prohibited immigrant." "Inmates of gaol" deportees (56) had been jailed for "immorality" (80), "vagrancy" (21), "theft" (16), "forgery" (1), "breach of the liquor act" (1), "child desertion" (1), "bigamy" (1), and "contributing to delinquency" (7). Those deported as prohibited immigrants under the Immigration Act (66) were "mentally deficient" (37), "immoral" (8), "previously deported" (2), "convicted prior to arrival" (2), or had "venereal disease" (6), "medical problems or conditions" (11). Of the fifteen women ordered deported for entry by misrepresentation, four were deported for "immorality", "mental deficiency", "medical reasons" or having been "previously deported", while eleven were ordered deported for having "misrepresented" their marital status, that is, for claiming to be single. Even so apparently straightforward and frequently used a statutory cause as "being a public charge" (528) included a variety of stated reasons: "illegitimacy" (142), "immorality" (33), "bad conduct" (69), "medical reasons" (159), "mental deficiency" (32), "vagrancy" (5), and "unemployment" (88).[44]

Illegitimacy figured prominently in the "Reports of Aftercare Agreement problem cases." The Department claimed that it did not deport an immigrant solely for having an illegitimate child; however, it did deport women for other, often related, reasons. Another Departmental study outlined the causes for deportation of a group of 574 Empire Settlement Aftercare Agreement immigrants who had borne illegitimate children by the end of March 1934. Of this group, 137 were deported for illegitimacy combined with other charges: "becoming a public charge", "immorality" (living with men to whom they were not married), "having a second illegitimate child", "theft", "feeblemindedness", "venereal disease", "being thoroughly undesirable". Of the deportations not tied to illegitimacy, fifty-four were deported for "immorality" (living with a man) in combination with "prostitution" or other offences. A total of sixty-one more were deported for "conviction of a criminal offence", such as "keeping a disorderly house", "theft", "forgery", "immorality", or "contributing to delinquency". Another fifty-three were deported for "bad conduct": "attempted suicide", "petty theft", "incorrigibility", "refusing to accept employment". Medical reasons accounted for 208 deportations: "feeblemindedness", "asthma", "epilepsy", "rheumatism", "tuberculosis", "arthritis", "venereal disease", "kleptomania", and "foot trouble". "Becoming a public charge" was the reason given for the deportation of sixty-one, of whom fifty-nine were sent along with their deported husbands, and two more with their husbands and children.[45]

The Department had not expected these problems with the supposedly carefully screened and supervised Aftercare Agreement immigrants. It attempted to compare them with other single British women immigrants who had arrived in Canada between 1926 and the end of March 1934.[46] This group produced 472 "problems" for the Department. Of these, 194 concerned "illegitimacy", 38 "immorality", 18 "criminal convictions", 32 "bad conduct", 124 "medical conditions or problems", 18 had unemployed husbands (and thus were deported with them), and 48 were themselves unemployed. Of the total, 202 were deported and another 50 "returned" home by the Department. "Returned" home often was de facto if not de jure deportation, in cases where statutory causes might not exist, or where the person had been resident too long to be deportable, and he or she would consent to be sent back. Some returns were indeed voluntary, but it is clear that many, if not the majority, were voluntary only in the sense that consent had been given, sometimes under duress.

In the Empire Settlement comparison group, by December 1932, of a total of 18,528 Empire Settlement arrivals between 31 March 1926 and 31 March 1931, 377 had become problems. There were 120 cases of "illegitimacy" (19 deported, 7 "returned"). Two women had been pregnant on arrival in Canada. There were 52 cases of "immorality" (7 deported, 2 "returned"), and ten "criminal convictions" (5 deported). Sixty-one women had been noted guilty of "bad conduct" (11 deported, 2 "returned"). "Medical problems" numbered eighty (27 deported, 2 "returned"). A total of 45 were deported with their unemployed husbands. Seven themselves had become public charges, and two of these were deported. Of the total, 114 were deported and 22 "returned".[47]

A study of a slightly larger group of Empire Settlement arrivals produced 1,885 problem cases by the end of March 1933. There were 670 cases of "illegitimacy" (179 deported), 184 of "immorality" (67 deported), 95 "convictions" (69 deported), 313 cases of "bad conduct" (67 deported), 451 "medical problems" (248 deported), 108 deported with their unemployed husbands, and 64 "public charges" (10 deported). A total of 748 were deported, and a further 202 were "returned" home. Somewhat more than half of the immigrants identified by the Department as "problem cases" were deported in one way or another.[48] There was a considerable increase in the rate at which the Department labelled these immigrants as "problem cases" by 1933: over 1,400 new "problems" arose in one year. One must speculate about the reasons for this increase: did the economic and social pressures of the Depression produce more real difficulties for these women, or were their experiences typical of domestic servant immigrants? Were the new "problem case" immigrants on the verge of gaining domicile, after which they would be harder to deport? Whatever the case, the Department used deportation as a solution for problems experienced by female as well as male immigrants in Canada.

In 1936 the Department undertook a study to determine the success of the Aftercare Agreement programme. This report is useful as a summary of what did happen to those women who came over as domestics under Empire Settlement in the 1920s. By the end of March 1936, of the total of 18,970 arrivals, 2,189 had married, 402 had gone to the United States, 85 had died, 305 had become "re-established" and 1,356, or a total of twelve per cent of the 18,790 "girls" went back to the Old Country, by deportation and "voluntary " returns. Of the total Aftercare immigrants, 2,169 had constituted "major problems" for the Department. A total of 877 (forty per cent) had been legally deported. Another eighty deportations had been ordered but never executed.[49]

This breakdown of major problem cases reveals interesting data not only about the difficulties experienced by this group but also about the response of the Department to these difficulties. Of the 2,169 cases, 773 were deported for "illegitimacy", 201 for "immorality", 107 for "convictions", 339 for "bad conduct", 519 as "medical", 135 "deported with husband", and 95 as "public charges".[50] These cases show how the Department translated immigrants' "problems" into legal deportations.

TOTAL "Major Problems": 2,169			
	Numbers	% of 2,169	% of 18,790
Deported	877	40.4	4.6
Deportation stayed	80	3.6	.4
Returned to Old Country	257	11.8	1.4
Went to United States	27	1.2	.1
Died	38	1.7	.2
Married	388	17.9	2.1
Re-established	305	14.0	1.6
Cases under supervision	195	9.0	1.0

These legal deportations were carried out under five statutory causes: "public charge" (690), "prohibited immigrant" (82), "insane" (29), "inmate of gaol" (61), "misrepresentation" (15). The reasons listed under these causes are illuminating.

Although "public charge" was the most frequently used statutory cause for these deportations, identical offences were used to build up a case under several different statutory headings. Only 2.9 per cent of public charge deportations were because of the woman's own unemployment, 15.3 per cent were because of her husband's unemployment. Those defined as "immoral", bearing illegitimate children, deemed "mentally deficient", arrested for "vagrancy" (even if they did not all serve sentences), with "venereal disease" or "tuberculosis", or who lied about marital status, or were guilty of bad conduct (attempted suicide, petty theft, refusing to accept a job, being incorrigible), might be deported under any of the five legal headings.[51] For these particular immigrants, at least, and probably for female immigrants in general, moral considerations played a significant role in determining whether or not the Department would allow them to remain in the country.

TOTAL DEPORTATIONS: 877

79.9%	PUBLIC CHARGE		690	9.4	PROHIBITED IMMIGRANT	82
21.0	illegitimacy		182	5.0	mentally deficient	22
8.7	bad conduct		76	2.5	medical	
22.1	medical		194		(.8 VD 7)	
	(2.4	VD	21)		(.1 TB 1)	
	(3.1	TB	27)		(.3 Epilepsy 3)	
	(16.6	Other	126)		(1.3 Other 11)	
3.1	mentally deficient		27	.3	previously deported	3
1.0	vagrancy		9	.6	immorality	8
15.3	deported with husband		134	.9	conviction prior to arrival	5
4.1	immorality		41	3.3	INSANE	29
.1	theft		1			
2.9	unemployed		26	1.7	MISREPRESENTATION	15
	(married 19)			.1	medical	1
	(single 7)			.1	previously deported	1
				.9	married woman	8
6.9	INMATE OF GAOL		61	.2	mentally deficient	2
2.4	vagrancy		21	.1	immorality	1
2.2	theft		19	.2	illegitimacy	2
1.2	immorality		11			
.1	forgery		1			
.1	breach of liquor act		1			
.1	contributing to delinquency		7			
.1	bigamy		1			

Whatever the "real" reasons for these deportations, it is clear that this was a period of brilliant legalisms interspersed with petty illegalities. Factors secondary to the real reason for deportation were used to a hitherto unsurpassed extent to build a legal case for deportation for a statutory cause that might be quite peripheral to the real reason. The records of the deportation of the disabled, the ill or handicapped, the criminal, the immoral, and the unemployed or impoverished reveal indisputably that the Department manipulated the factors in a case to build up evidence to support deportations for legal causes that often had little to do with the reason the Department wanted to deport an immigrant. This was perfectly legal, and no more than good administrative sense, from the Department's perspective. Attempts by the courts to assure that the Department followed legal procedures helped to strengthen this tendency, but they did not create it. For the most part deportation took place out of public view, and almost entirely beyond the control of anyone but officials of the Department. The maturity of the Department as a bureaucracy had become increasingly visible in the 1920s. All of the skill that it had developed became necessary in the 1930s, when the activities of the Department became almost entirely centred around the deportation of the immigrants that it had brought into the country in previous years.

Troublemakers and Communists, 1930-1935

Deportation of radicals in the 1930s was made to order by political fiat. It was a logical extension of earlier deportations of similar troublemakers. The techniques used for the political deportations of the 1930s were similar to those developed during the period of the First World War. In both instances, political deportation was made easier by special legal powers to deport radicals overtly for political "crimes" as enemies of the state. Although the Department of Immigration openly deported radicals for political reasons, it also continued to throw up a documentary smokescreen to disguise this target group and its specific undesirability by deporting radicals under various nominal legal causes. There was no category in the Department's *Annual Report* for "political deportation". By using other legal categories, the Department could avoid unfavourable publicity, make legal appeals against their deportation more difficult and less effective, and make the administrative management of deportation smoother, more efficient, and easier.

The longstanding policy of the Department to deport radicals and troublemakers whenever possible found its logical extension in the communist cleanups of the 1930s. A good many of the deportations of radicals had previously taken place under normal headings: medical causes, entry without proper inspection, public charge, or criminal conviction. These tried and true measures lost none of their effectiveness during the first half of the 1930s. A new legal weapon against the Communist

Party of Canada gave the Department the powers it needed to deport communists simply and openly for being communists. The Communist Party was declared an illegal organization in Canada on 11 August 1931, under Section 98 of the Criminal Code.[1]

Since the 1920s, communists and other radicals had been involved in activities which deeply alarmed the government and the business community of Canada: organizing industrial unions, building leftwing groups within existing unions, organizing the unemployed, leading militant strikes, and conducting successful publicity campaigns, such as the one that collected 100,000 signatures on a petition for unemployment insurance, a five-day work week, and a $35 weekly minimum wage for both women and men workers.[2]

Anti-radical drives were flourishing in several Canadian cities by the end of the 1920s. Police and civic officials, as well as provincial politicians, were prominent in such campaigns. At conferences, in groups and individually, officially and privately, they warned that the "communist menace" was growing, and urged clampdowns and wholesale deportations. In Toronto, regulations were passed in 1929 against non-English language public meetings and disorderly or seditious utterances. Anyone renting a public facility to a group for such a meeting could lose their licence. Police Chief Denis Draper and Mayor Sam McBride promoted police harrassment and assault against radicals, for which the radicals frequently found themselves arrested. The "free speech" issue became a cause célèbre; Toronto remained a hotbed of radical action and repression by the authorities until the mid-1930s.[3]

It was not only Toronto; anti-radical sentiment was high in smaller centres. In Sudbury, the City Council passed a resolution that the government should deport "all undesirables and communists", and sent it round to all the members of the Union of Canadian Municipalities in April 1931; over seventy sent in the resolution to Ottawa. As well, provincial premiers and other officials wrote urging action.[4]

Winnipeg Mayor Ralph Webb, a staunch supporter of law and order, carried out a one-man campaign, writing regularly to R. B. Bennett demanding action against communists and agitators. In May 1931, Webb sent Bennett the names of fifteen Winnipeggers who had gone to Moscow to study revolutionary organizing, asking that Immigration be told to bar their re-entry. In July, Webb wired Gideon Robertson urging him to press for "deportation of all undesirables" including behind-the-scenes radical activists and administrators. A number of local veterans' and employers' and fraternal associations supported Webb's position; the Bennett papers contain many resolutions and demands for stiffer laws and intensified or automatic deportation of radicals. The local Immigration official, Western Commissioner of Immigration Thomas Gelley, shared the prevailing views: he wrote to Commissioner Jolliffe in June 1931, suggesting a revival of the draconian provisions of the June 1919 version of Section 41 of the Immigration Act, repealed only three years before. His explanation of the problem was at least original (although perhaps not his own): Gelley argued that to allow the "communistic element" to come into contact with young people was like a farmer allowing potato bugs to multiply until the whole potato patch was endangered. In his opinion the Department must take some "radical action . . . to stamp out this element from Canadian life."[5]

Such sentiments were not surprising from the influential classes of a city that had survived Canada's only attempted Bolshevik revolution (or so they thought) a scant dozen years before. As well, there was a fear in some quarters that such an event might again be in the making. RCMP and Provincial Police headquarters, especially, were prone to such alarms. Among their contributions to the suppression of the Red menace were warnings to the Premier that the local Communist Party was setting up a "fighting group . . . to obtain funds" by "rob[bing] banks and stores," and a report that the Communist Party had insinuated many of its important members into municipal and other government positions, which was supposed to offer them protection against the authorities.[6]

The federal authorities in Ottawa were receptive, indeed enthusiastic. Prime Minister Bennett revived Section 98 of the Criminal Code and the government used it to go after the Communist Party.

Police signalled this campaign by raiding the offices of the Party and the homes of three of its leaders, and the offices of the Workers Unity League and the official paper *The Worker*, on 11 and 12 August 1931. The raids had been planned by Ontario Attorney General William Price, and co-ordinated by Ontario Provincial Police (OPP) Commissioner Victor Willimas, who had arranged for a squad of federal, provincial, and city police to carry out simultaneous raids in Toronto. There was a slight hitch; Willimas had failed to keep the leaders under surveillance, so six of the eight leaders sought were not there when the police appeared. A second series of raids had to be carried out to finish the operation.[7]

Although the OPP initiated the crackdown, it was strongly supported by the federal authorities. The federal Justice Minister had been sending spy reports obtained from the RCMP and other material to the Ontario authorities and offering "the fullest co-operation" from Justice and the RCMP, in any actions taken. The actions resulted in the arrest of eight Party members and officials; all were charged with being members of an unlawful organization, and seditious conspiracy.[8]

The eight were: Tim Buck (aged forty, married, three children, British-born, here since 1912), chief official of the Communist Party in Canada; Sam Carr (aged thirty-one, of Ukrainian origin, immigrated in 1924), in charge of the Party's organizational work; Malcolm Bruce (aged fifty, born in Prince Edward Island), editor of *The Worker* and on the Party executive; Matthew Popovich (aged forty-one, Ukrainian-born, in Canada since 1911), was former editor of *Robochny Narod* and a leader in several organizations such as the Ukrainian Labor Farmer Temple Association; John Boychuck (aged thirty-nine, married with one child, Ukrainian origin, immigrated in 1913), was a long-time organizer and official Ukrainian representative on the Central Executive Committee; Tom Ewan (aged forty, widower with four children, in Canada since leaving Scotland in 1911), was National Secretary of the Workers Unity League; Amos Hill (aged thirty-three, married, one child, Finnish-born immigrant to Canada in 1912), was active in various Finnish organizations, and Tomo Cacic (aged thirty-five, Croation, in Canada since 1924), was active in various ethnic branches.[9]

The eight were tried in front of a Toronto jury. The Crown's chosen method of presenting evidence was to be a precedent for the numerous prosecutions that followed. Rather than arguing that these individuals advocated force or violence, it argued that as communists, they were under the direction of the Communist International which advocated revolutionary violence. The views or actions of the individual were not germane; all that was necessary was to show that a person was a member of the Communist Party, which was bound to follow Comintern policy. The Crown's case rested primarily on Comintern policy documents, publications, etc., and on the testimony of a Mountie spy who had been an undercover member of the Party for ten years. Sergeant Leopold's statements were used to establish the subordination of the Canadian Communist Party to discipline from abroad, and the seditious nature of the organization.[10]

All eight men were convicted. All save Tomo Cacic were sentenced to five years' imprisonment; he got two (because of his relative youth, according to Anthony Rasporich's account, but Sam Carr and Amos Hill were younger than Cacic). All were supposed to be deported, but in the end, only Cacic was. On appeal, the seditious conspiracy charges were dropped, but the Section 98 charges stood. Thus, after February 1932, the Communist Party's status as an illegal organization was confirmed; all of its members were chargeable under Section 98. Such an outcome had been the hope of the authorities.[11] It was particularly pleasing to Immigration officials. Now political deportation could proceed smoothly, either overtly under Section 41 of the Immigration Act, or under the criminality category; an immigrant convicted of a crime was automatically deportable upon completion of sentence.

Not that they had not been busy. By 1931, Immigration officials were routinely exploring various avenues to expedite the deportation of radicals. They received names from the RCMP and other sources, investigated the immigration status of the prospective deports, and set in motion the appropriate machinery. By the fall of 1931, intensified political deportation had become federal policy. In October, the Minister of Justice hosted a special meeting to discuss the need to increase deportation. It was attended by the Minister of National Defence, the Commissioner of Immigration, the Military Chief of General Staff, and the RCMP Commissioner. They decided to use the RCMP barracks in Halifax to house the expected deports.[12]

Naturalized citizenship was no sure defence against deportation. In June 1919 the citizenship laws had been amended to permit revocation of naturalization certificates, as a preliminary to deportation. In the 1930s, the Department of Immigration used this route to move radicals from an inviolable to a deportable category. Stripped of citizenship, an immigrant could revert to being a member of the prohibited classes, unable to gain domicile no matter how long in Canada, because persons of that class could never legally enter. In November 1931, for example, Jolliffe of the Department of Immigration sent Thomas Mulvey of Citizenship Branch of the Department of the Secretary of State a list of thirty-five names to be checked for citizenship, as part of deportation proceedings. Thirteen were naturalized; eighteen had no record of citizenship, two had been rejected, and one case was being held in abeyance. Mulvey's staff obligingly identified four likely candidates for deportation: one was Michael Novakowsky, an Alberta farmer in Canada since 1912, and a citizen since 1920. Some of the names were those of men sentenced in Montreal to one year for sedition by Mr. Justice Wilson in the Court of Queen's Bench, the past June.[13]

An Immigration memo on one case illustrates the process. The Immigration official had been reading the RCMP file on a political case, and was lamenting the poor quality of evidence. The case against the man was shaky. ''None of his speeches, nor the article in the *Montreal Star* and the one in the Worker . . . are of a seditious nature.'' The only evidence given at the trial had been that of ''two secret agents'' working for the RCMP, and it had been of ''very little value.'' But it had been good enough to have the man sent up for sedition. For Immigration to deal with him, however, a preliminary step was needed. Their strategy would be to have his naturalization ''revoked and then attack the case on the basis of the fact that the conviction on a charge of sedition brings him within the meaning of Section 41.'' The order went out: ''request Mulvey to cancel naturalization certificate – and Board him after – tell Mulvey he must act at once.''[14]

Although it is impossible to be sure of how many political deportations were carried out during the Depression, it is possible to verify that these were numerous. Usually they were carried out under public charge, criminality, or other legal categories, and they were not explicitly acknowledged as such in the public documents of the Department, such as the *Annual Report*. Internal documents are somewhat more revealing, but it is frustrating to try to pin down specific cases, not least because the problem is ultimately not quantifiable.

The sources of information are fragmentary. In one memo, a total of eighty-two names were listed by the Department as having been deported as communist agitators. Many of the names are not those of well-known communists, and few appear in the historical literature on the Party. Many, but not all, of the individuals listed had been convicted of a crime prior to their deportation, usually under Section 98. Charges cited in the file include: unlawful assembly, distributing communist literature, inciting riot, assault of police, concealing weapons, communist demonstration, unlawful association, and simply communist. By far the most common was membership in an unlawful association or member of an unlawful assembly – in other words simply being a communist or participating in a communist meeting or demonstration. Three of the eighty-two were also noted for other violations of the Immigration Act: Section 33, subsection 7 (prohibited classes) and communist; unlawful association and previously rejected; unlawful association and epilepsy. This notation suggests that in these three cases, the Department may have used other legal grounds for deportation than those in Section 41, or may have used provisions of Section 33 specifying membership in the prohibited classes on other than political grounds. Epilepsy was a medical condition interdicted in the regulations; epileptics could never legally immigrate to Canada. Medical prohibitions were not subject to appeal.[15]

A second source of information in the records of the Department is a list of thirty-five names compiled to have citizenship status checked and naturalization certificates revoked, in order to effect deportation. Among the thirty-five names are those that do not appear on the list of eighty-two communists deported as such. A third list of twenty-six names of alleged communists also contains several names not elsewhere listed.[16]

A fourth file concerned with political deportation also contains lists of names, for example of thirteen immigrants arrested in Rouyn in 1932 for participating in a May Day demonstration. A note by a Department official explained that all legally deportable immigrants were to be ordered deported by Boards of Inquiry, and in the case of those with domicile, the Boards were to be adjourned until the Department could decide how to proceed. Eight of the names on the list of eighty-two radicals deported also are on the Rouyn list. Five other immigrants appearing only on the Rouyn list include just one who might have been in Canada barely long enough to acquire domicile, and who consequently might have been somewhat more difficult to deport. Cross-checking reveals that domicile was no bar; for example, one of the men on both the Rouyn list and the list of eighty-two names, Wasyl Semergo, had been in Canada since July 1913. He was deported almost twenty years later in March 1933.[17]

Another reference to those arrested in the 1932 Rouyn May Day demonstration contains information about Polish nationals involved in deportation proceedings on account of their alleged communist activities. The names of two women and one man, not elsewhere mentioned, are given.[18]

Other Department files, memos, and correspondence contain names, or discussions of cases, of other radicals not appearing on the list of eighty-two names. Internal and external evidence indicates that these people were deported under the legal grounds of public charge and other categories, or that the Department tried but failed to obtain such deportations. Whatever the details of individual cases, it is clear that such practices were routine and widespread. For example, in the fall of 1931, a group of Polish nationals who had been detained at Winnipeg for deportation, refused to co-operate in the documentation process necessary to arrange their departure. The Winnipeg Immigration official sought and received advice from his superiors in Ottawa about how to proceed. Further substantiation is given by accounts in the local press about the detention and deportation of those twenty immigrants as public charges, over the protests of the Polish consul.[19]

Another source of information on individual cases is the *Canadian Labor Defender*, the organ of the Canadian Labor Defense League (CLDL), which cites numerous instances of deportations for political activities. Some of the names given here can be cross-checked against Department of Immigration and other sources, although many names cannot be verified. Although the CLDL had an axe to grind and would have found it advantageous to portray the situation in the blackest possible terms, it was also to the advantage of the League to trumpet its successes in averting deportation in individual cases. On balance, it seems reasonable to accept as valid their descriptions of deportations completed. As well, their sporadic forays into statistics may also be useful for cross-checking other sources. For example, the CLDL claimed that between January and June 1932, thirty-three workers had been deported for political offences. The files of the Department list only fifteen persons deported as communist agitators during that period, suggesting that eighteen were probably deported under other legal categories.[20]

Also informative are oral history interviews with people who participated in the events of the time. Satu Repo's interview of Einar Nordstrom, a Lakehead radical, provides details not only about Department practices, but about community responses. In Thunder Bay, an October 1932 protest drew 1,000 demonstrators demanding services from city officials. According to Nordstrom, at the time the city had no soup kitchens, and unemployed single men had been denied relief by the City Relief Officer. They marched, and were turned back, some beaten, by the RCMP, OPP, and city police. Many were arrested. Most were later released, but a few leaders were held and eventually deported.

One of these was Emil Sandberg, a twenty-one-year old Swede, in Canada three years, who was very outspoken and active in the local Scandinavian Workers and Farmers Club. He was charged with vagrancy and being instrumental in causing a public disturbance. Deportation had by that time become so common, according to Nordstrom, that ethnic associations had developed the custom of holding dances and other fundraisers to pay a tailor to make a suit of clothes for the person to wear on the trip home. The tailor who measured Sandberg was the only visitor he was allowed. Even when he developed appendicitis and had surgery, he was guarded so closely at the hospital that a Swedish hospital worker could not slip in for a word.

Somehow Sandberg smuggled out a piece of toilet paper giving the time of his departure on the train East to be deported. A large crowd went to the station to see him off. Sandberg was handcuffed to two OPPs and not allowed to speak to anyone.[21]

Emil Sandberg's case does not appear in any of the Department lists of radicals deported. No information is available on the legal category under which his deportation was carried out. The circumstances of the case suggest that criminality would have been likely (his prison sentence), or public charge (if he had succeeded in obtaining relief) – either of which could have been smoothly executed procedures.

Causes for deportation were reported under five headings. "Public charge" covered those who were non-paying inmates of any publicly funded institution (medical or charitable), or who received some form of welfare payment from the public purse. "Criminality" covered those who had served sentences in penal institutions. "Accompanying" referred to members of families who were themselves not necessarily deported or deportable (Canadian citizens by birth, for example), accompanying a deported family head or member. "Medical causes" included those who were ill, injured, or incapacitated in ways that contravened the Immigration Act. They were usually not self-supporting at the time when ordered deported, and might have been non-paying inmates of hospitals and so on. Some may have been self-supporting but had a contagious disease, or were afflicted in some way that might in the future affect their ability to be self-supporting. Causes ranged from industrial accidents, tuberculosis, epilepsy, heart disease, varicose veins, venereal disease, retardation, and psychological problems (from raving insanity to masturbation). "Other causes" referred to various violations of the Act, usually related to improper entry, or belonging to some prohibited category.[22]

"Other causes" covered a multitude of sins. A Board of Inquiry could use Section 33 for an immigrant whose entry had been improper (sneaking in, lying, failing to comply with regulations), or Section 3 for an immigrant belonging to the prohibited classes on account of medical conditions, political beliefs or activities or intentions, criminal records, or morals at the time of entry. Many cases falling under sections 3 or 33 could be deported regardless of the number of years of residence subsequent to entry.

The charge of "entry by misrepresentation" was a handy catch-all used by the Department to deport those who undertook activities at variance with those they stated as intended at the time of entry. For example, Mikolaj Dranuta was brought over under the auspices of the Ukrainian Colonization Board in 1926 to do farm work. Instead, according to an RCMP spy report, he took a job in an Edmonton meat packing plant, joined the Ukrainian Labor Temple and taught in a Ukrainian school, helped to organize cultural activities such as the visit of a dance troupe, and so on. The Mounties described him as a communist, and noted that while he had not made any public speeches ("yet"), he was open about his views. After reviewing the spy report, an Immigration official perused Dranuta's photograph (from his Canadian Pacific Railway Occupational Certificate) and decided on that basis that Dranuta was not the farming or peasant type. "Under the circumstances" wrote the official, the Department would take "action . . . with a view to deportation on the ground of entering Canada by misrepresentation."[23]

"Vagrancy" was a common criminal charge against radicals. John Ferris recalls that in Sault Ste. Marie, activists in unemployed workers' movements were picked up and charged with vagrancy because they were "without substantial means of support." Margaret Patterson was reportedly charged with vagrancy in Toronto when she was arrested after singing "The International" at a 1930 May Day rally.[24]

Although any activist could find him or herself in trouble with the law, immigrants – especially the non-British – were particularly at risk. Mauri Jalava's interviews with Sudbury Finns revealed that deportations were a strongly feared feature of Finnish life in Canada during the Depression. By the early 1930s, many Finns still did not have citizenship, and others were refused when they applied, so any contact with the authorities could prove dangerous. Political persecution could take place even if no laws were broken: translators for companies hiring Finns were often anti-radical informers.[25] Protesting poor working conditions or the lack of work could have grave consequences. The political climate in Finland was not friendly to radicals; there might be a danger to liberty or perhaps to life for those deported.

A further problem for immigrant radicals was that existing laws were unevenly enforced. As Leslie Morris of the CLDL pointed out, many thousands of unemployed transients rode the rails and were usually ignored by police (partly because there was no space in the jails for a fraction of them). But anyone identified as a radical was far more likely to be arrested. For an immigrant, that might mean a one way ticket out of the country, marked only by a number in the criminality deportations listed in the *Annual Report* of the Department of Immigration.[26]

Deportation for any cause except violating Section 41, that is, under any category not overtly political, was considered so problem-free, so automatic, by the Department, that it did not normally hire lawyers for the Boards of Inquiry. So long as the Department followed properly all the procedures outlined in the Immigration Act, there was little likelihood of any successful challenge, even by the courts. The Department processed many thousands of deportations without any interference whatsoever during the 1930s. Most were carried out under the heading of "public charge". Many were in fact political deportations. For example, the City of Winnipeg had requested the deportation of a group of Polish immigrants reputedly "members of organizations connected with the communist movement," some of whom hired lawyers to represent them at their Boards of Inquiry. But the Department made no attempt to hire its own lawyers, and any tactics of resistance on the part of the Poles were futile because, although their political affiliations were their real crimes, their deportations were "based on public charge grounds." It is clear from the records that the Department was nervous about public protests in these cases (civic elections were coming up in Winnipeg and the communists were active in politics), but the facts were irrefutable. The immigrants were public charges, and were legally deportable as such after hearings in conformity with the Immigration regulations. And as such, they were deported.[27]

The real causes for which radicals were deported were varied. Arvi Johannes Tielinen, Thomas Gidson Pollari, Viljo Adolf Piispa, and Jaako Emil Makynen were convicted (along with several others) for taking part in an unlawful assembly after they had marched in a parade at Timmins, and deported in 1932. Of thirty-four people convicted of unlawful assembly for a similar parade in May 1932, eight were deported. Those deported for organizing or participating in relief strikes or demonstrations included Matti Hautamaki of Port Arthur, Leontie Karpenkower of The Pas, and W. Jacobson of Vancouver. Askeli Panjata was arrested for marching in a Port Arthur parade of unemployed workers in November 1930. He was sentenced to three months, then hastily removed from the local jail to Halifax, "before any of his friends were aware of it." He was deported to Finland in March 1931, in spite of his protests that his life would be in danger.[28]

Hymie Sparaga was arrested in Toronto in January 1931, on the picket line of a garment worker strike, sentenced to two months in jail, then deported (and according to Annie Buller, he was later killed by the Nazis). Louis Revay and John Gryciuk were convicted, respectively, of unlawful assembly and rioting during the 1931 Estevan strike, and deported.[29]

Often little information has survived about events such as these. In other cases, more can be learned. The details are different but the patterns are predictable. Sophie Sheinen's experiences were in some ways typical.

Sophie Sheinen was a Russian Jew who had immigrated to Canada in May 1927. Little is known about her subsequent activities save that she was involved in protests. She was arrested in Calgary and convicted in July 1931 of unlawful assembly. The case went to appeal; she lost, and served a six-month sentence in the Fort Saskatchewan Gaol, at the end of which she was ordered deported to the U.S.S.R. Her sentence was completed 11 May 1932, but she was held until 31 May, partly to induce her to sign some of her deportation documents. Worried about her ill health, eventually the CLDL stepped in and signed on her behalf.

Apparently she was ill-treated in jail. It is unclear if such treatment was typical of prisons of the time, or if she was singled out. Her cell was allegedly overheated and unventilated, the water periodically turning black and undrinkable. She complained of being harassed by a night matron who refused to turn off the noisily running water in the toilet and who rattled the door. Sheinen said that she was kept in solitary confinement as punishment, and was refused medical treatment until she threatened to complain to the warden. The CLDL passed on to Immigration a letter in which she detailed her complaints, claiming that by the end of her sentence she was spitting blood and had lost nearly thirty-five pounds.[30]

By September 1932 protests against her deportation were gaining Bennett's attention. He sought advice from Immigration officials, who told him that Sheinen had been ''mutinous'' in jail and vociferous about ill-treatment. In the opinion of the Department, her claims of ill-health were simply a device to avoid deportation; they had her medically examined and pronounced ''fit to travel''.

The Department's advice to Bennett was typical and revealed a consistent policy in political deportation cases. They admitted receiving many protests, but the sources were suspect. All seemed to be from communist sources. The Department had thus ''decided to ignore such communications unless they were from responsible parties.'' Unless there were protests of a ''special nature'' or from a ''source which obviously should be recognized,'' they would continue to follow this policy. They advised Bennett to do likewise. (Bennett needed little encouragement; he was rabidly anti-communist.) Sophie Sheinen was picked up at her home and deported in November 1932.[31]

Not even that much is known about the experiences of some of her colleagues. Edward Reinkanen was arrested (and beaten) at a Toronto anti-deportation demonstration in June 1931; he served one month at the Jail Farm, then was held at the Don Jail until deported to Finland in November 1931. Sam Langley, an activist in Northern Ontario, was deported to England on the *Ascania*, 23 December 1931. He had been previously ordered deported after a 1929 jail sentence for a free speech demonstration, on charges of vagrancy (the disorderly conduct subsection) – part of a whole series of arrests by Toronto police beginning in February 1929 and continuing into the summer. An uproar organized by the CLDL was effective in stopping Langley's 1929 deportation, probably because of his nationality as much as the dubiousness of the vagrancy conviction as the ground for a criminality deportation. By 1931 the political climate had changed; he was picked up in Port Arthur at 5:00 p.m., and on the train to Halifax by 9:00 p.m. that same evening, to be deported under the reactivated 1929 order. Essentially the same thing happened to Joseph Farley who had been arrested and jailed with Langley and four others in 1929. The old order was activated and used to deport him after he completed a ten-month sentence in Lethbridge. He was sent back to England in December 1931. Peter Zepkar, a Croat long active in Yugoslav organizations in the Party, and in Canada since 1924, was sentenced to one year in jail for his part in a Fort Frances lumber strike (unlawful assembly), and deported in December 1934.[32]

John Ferris of Sault Ste. Marie, a young man during the Depression, recalled pressures against radicals. Women canvassing for the Canadian Labor Defence League were arrested, then released without charges being laid. These cases were merely adjourned and left hanging so that they could be picked up long after. He remembers numerous cases where radicals were picked up and deported – sometimes so fast that friends did not even know that they were gone. Most of these cases involved non-British immigrants. The Sault Ste. Marie City Council, like others, passed a resolution to ''deport all known Reds.'' ''Reds'' was synonymous with activists.

Although Ferris himself was subject to arrest, he could not be deported, as he was born in Canada. Partly for this reason, he was responsible for conveying the hidden mimeograph machine to meetings. Accompanied by a left-leaning Free Methodist preacher (later forced by his congregation to resign), Ferris concealed the press in the family baby buggy and took it for innocuous strolls. The police never caught on, and never managed to confiscate the press. But there were other repercussions. The superintendent of the local steel plant told Ferris that he would have to change his politics if he ever wanted a job. "Practically blacklisted", Ferris gave up and left for Cochrane, Ontario, to look for work in 1935. If he had been a recent immigrant, and unable to find work, he would have had to apply for relief eventually; deportation would have resulted, although the real issue would have been his politics.[33]

Departmental files on individual deportation cases reveal disquieting evidence about the grounds on which the officials were prepared to act. Cases were built on the personal impressions of officials about the attitudes of the accused; the immigrants were not privy to this material and even if they had been, such stuff is impossible to refute, slippery as it is. Worse, Red smearing based on such impressions could remain in someone's official records for years, decades, and later be used against them – all without any foundation in fact, or at least without substantiation. Innuendo was good enough. For example, Sam Kluchnik of Winnipeg was reported for deportation by J. D. Fraser, Superintendent of the City of Winnipeg Relief Department in June 1932. His experiences in Canada were typical of many relief cases. He had entered as a farmworker, in 1928, but quit in disgust at the wages (seventy-five cents a day). In the ensuing years he worked seasonally in railway construction. More often than not unemployed, he lived "on the charity of friends" through most of 1930 and 1931. By October 1931 he was sufficiently desperate to apply for relief, and when the deportation complaint was recorded he had received a total of $101.50 in beds, meals, and clothing, in exchange for which he had worked a number of weeks on the Grassmere Ditch.

At his deportation hearing he said quite clearly that he was prepared to accept any kind of work, including farm work; he hoped to be hired for the harvest. He was ordered deported as a public charge, an order which he appealed. The regional Immigration official prepared a memo concerning the appeal, to be used by Ottawa in the ruling. In the memo, another reason for the ruling appears. Kluchnik's appeal should be dismissed:

There is a memorandum in my file from the Chairman of the Board of Inquiry in this case, stating that at the time of the Board, the appellant was surly and gave the impression of one who belonged to one of the "Red" organizations of this country, although he denied this. The Chairman of the Board is of the opinion that Canada would be well rid of the appellant.

The next step in the proceeding was to have the steamship company pay the costs of the deportation. If an immigrant were proven defective, the transportation company which had brought the immigrant to Canada would also be responsible for removing him. In the case of Kluchnik, the Department letter to the company displayed careful use of the opinion of the Chairman of the Board of Inquiry, and was an excellent example of distorted and fabricated evidence. It was based on an internal memo to the Commissioner of Immigration and the Deputy Minister, claiming that Kluchnik had admitted that he

> had not fulfilled the conditions of entry to Canada and apparently has no intentions of doing so. While he claims to be anxious to remain in this country he does not desire to take farm work and in the opinion of the examining officer he is a surly individual and gave the impression of being a Red although he denies this.

To the steamship company, Commissioner Jolliffe wrote that Kluchnik "refuses to accept farm work". The transcript of the Board of Inquiry reveals that Kluchnik made no such statements nor could anything he said be so interpreted.

Sam Kluchnik's deportation was not effected; by the time that the order got back to Winnipeg, he had found farm work. He was lucky; there had been such an outcry against deporting the unemployed that the Department had begun suspending deportation orders against those who had been on the dole but had found work by the time that their orders were ready. Had they again gone on relief, the orders would have been activated and carried out; otherwise they remained suspended.[34]

Kluchnik was under suspended sentence of deportation for more than twenty years. In December 1949 he hired a Winnipeg law firm to try to obtain his passport. The Department of Immigration investigated the request. Their records show that since 1932 Kluchnik had worked in farming, construction, and finally had gone into mining. By 1949 he had a family, owned a home and other property, and had savings. The local Immigration official declared himself ready to quash the outstanding deportation order, but the RCMP demurred. In a confidential memo, Special Branch replied, "We have no alternative but to say that he is 'NOT CLEAR FOR SECURITY' on the grounds of 'A'." On this basis, the Department of Immigration decided to retain the deportation order, although Kluchnik had never done anything to warrant its use.[35]

The federal authorities had a heyday in 1932. The previous autumn they had undertaken preparations for another showcase raid of communist functionaries. Internal documents show names of prospective targets whose arrival dates were to be verified; lists of naturalized citizens, some of whom might have their certificates revoked; and a sampling of warrants issued for arrests. Immigration records are scattered and incomplete, but there is sufficient evidence from a number of sources to piece together an account of the events.[36]

In February 1932 the appeal court decision in the Buck et al. cases gave the green light. Now it was legally established that the only evidence needed for deportation on political grounds was to prove that the immigrant was a member of some communist organization. A conviction under Section 98 or any other section of the Criminal Code was handy but no longer necessary. Deportation had never depended solely on conviction in a court of law; now it was even simpler.

On May Day 1932 the authorities swooped down on eleven radicals in Montreal, Oshawa, Sudbury, Winnipeg, Edmonton, and Vancouver. Offices, homes, and persons were searched for evidence of communist affiliation.[37] All arrested were kept incommunicado and quickly sent to Halifax for deportation hearings. The swift removal to Halifax was intended to avoid public outcry, prevent any effective defence, and effect swift deportations. The tactic had been a clever choice.

As details of the proceedings became known, there were widespread protests. There was good reason. Questioning of the Immigration Minister in the House by Woodsworth and others revealed an arbitrariness and disregard for due process all too typical of deportation methods. Gordon evaded questions concerning the nature of the charges and the where-abouts, date, and nature of the hearings. Cornered, he excused the hurried removal of the men by saying that when Immigration officials were sure that an immigrant was illegally in the country, they frequently chose the "nearest most convenient port" for deportation as the site of the hearing.[38]

Feeble on the face of it, subsequent revelations suggested that Gordon was trying to cover up star chamber tactics. Three men had been arrested in Winnipeg: one, Orton Wade, had been taken to jail after speaking at a May Day rally. He was visited the next day by a CLDL lawyer who then demanded (and was promised) a look at the order for arrest. Instead, RCMP Inspector Mellow stood up the lawyer and put the handcuffed men on the train for Halifax. What made all this more than just awkward was that Wade was a Canadian citizen by birth, under no circumstances deportable, and not accountable to the Department of Immigration for any reason. The Department had not done its homework.

Wade was not released until after his hearing with the Board of Inquiry in Halifax. He sued the Deputy Minister and others for false arrest and imprisonment. His case was dismissed by Winnipeg's Court of Queen's Bench, but heard by the Manitoba Court of Appeal. Wade lost the case by a narrow three to two decision, one judge ruling against him solely on a technicality.

The hearing produced a number of scandalous revelations for which the Department was roundly criticized by the Bench and the public. For example, Deputy Minister Egan had signed the warrant for Wade's arrest five months before it was used, but had made no effort to verify that Wade was subject to Immigration's authority. Nor did he think it reasonable to do so. If the Department verified particulars before issuing warrants, it would never get its work done, he said. The court was willing to agree that although the Department had acted improperly in failing to verify Wade's status, it may have had some justification in arresting him because Wade had previously told a police official that he had been born in the United States. But Wade's treatment after arrest "amounted to a denial of justice . . . actuated by motives which are not permitted by the law," said Justice Dennistoun. Further, even if Wade had been deportable, there was no excuse for his removal from Winnipeg (close to the U.S. border, thus the nearest port for his deportation) to Halifax. Justice Trueman compared the Department's conduct to "parallel high handed proceedings" of 1667 when Clarendon shipped off various of his opponents to islands and other remote outposts so that they could not have the protection of the law.

Egan's response was as revealing as his apparent imperturbability. He defended the Department's actions on the grounds that these were perfectly routine and normal procedures used in a "great number" of instances. Thus, if there were anything wrong in the Wade case, by implication, it was wrong in most deportation cases. And indeed it was. A victory for Wade would have put a serious crimp in the Department's activities.

Orton Wade succeeded only because he was Canadian-born. The remaining ten prisoners taken in May 1932 had little chance to escape deportation. There were as yet few constraints on the Department. The ten were a diverse lot, fairly representative of men in the Party. Typical, too, was the handling of their cases by the Department. At their Boards of Inquiry, held within a few days of their arrival, all ten denied that they were currently Communist Party members (the Party no longer existed, they said) or that they advocated the use of force or violence to overthrow the government. The Department depended on Sergeant Leopold's testimony to dispute both claims. All were members of communist affiliated organizations; all were subject to Party discipline. If Party policy advocated force or overthrow by violence, their individual beliefs were unimportant.[39]

Whatever else might be said of these men, the outlines of their activities contained in Departmental records show them to have been phenomenally energetic. Each was involved in numerous organizations. The Department's distaste for them and their ilk was hardly concealed; the more active the man, the more the Department urged his deportation.

Conrad Cessinger was German, single, aged thirty-one, and in Canada since August 1927. He did farming and bush work, and was active in a plethora of ethnic and other Party organizations, and on the executive of several. He was deported 18 December 1932. Dan Chomicki, a Pole who used the name Holmes, was thirty-four, married, and the father of one child; he had come to Canada with his parents from Austria in June 1913. He was a printer, and had worked for eleven years for the publisher of *Ukrainian Labor News*, *Working Women*, *Farmers Life*, and *Militant Youth Magazine*. Although it was awkward to deport him when he had been here since childhood, and all his relations were in Canada (his wife and child were Canadian-born), nonetheless the Department saw him as a leader "of a particularly dangerous type . . . entitled to no consideration whatsoever." He received none and was deported 17 December 1932.[40]

From Edmonton, Iwan Sembaj (John Semboy) had been arrested. He was then forty, born in Poland and claimed U.S.S.R. citizenship, and had been in Canada since 1923. He was married with Canadian-born children. He had done farm work for a short time, joined the Ukrainian Labor Farmer Temple, and had become a member of the executive. He was also active in the CLDL and other organizations. A Mountie spy in the Ukrainian Labor Farmer Temple Association (ULFTA) had reported that Sembaj had made "radical utterances" at meetings, and had advocated the establishment by force and violence of a Soviet-type government in Canada. He was regarded as a "more cultured type than average" and more dangerous for it. He was deported 16 July 1933.[41]

John Farkas was thirty when he was arrested in Oshawa. Single, he had come from Hungary in 1926 as a farmworker. He tried farming for less than six months and then headed for the city. He went from Toronto to Oshawa, where he remained after February 1928. He was involved with the CLDL, the Unemployed Workers Association, and various ethnic groups. When raided he had in his possession literature of an "extremely radical nature, revolutionary in its teachings and distinctly Communistic in its expression." He had "caused considerable trouble in Oshawa due to his radical tendencies and his active participation in various demonstrations there," and the OPP were eager to remove him. So was the Immigration Department; they deported him in December 1932.[42]

Martin Parker (Pohjansalo) was only twenty-two, but a threat to the security of the state, nonetheless. He had come to Toronto with his parents in 1913. Since 1928 he had been involved with *Vapaus* in Sudbury, and when arrested, he was associate editor. He was also active in the Finnish Organization of Canada. At his Board of Inquiry, while he denied advocating violence, he admitted that he thought a revolution was inevitable, and that the masses might retaliate if the bourgeoisie used violence against them. Immigration was impressed with his intelligence (of a "higher standard than average") and was keenly committed to his deportation. He left with his colleagues on the 17th of December 1932.[43]

Hans Kist was also young. At twenty-seven, he was married (common-law) and had lived in Vancouver since deserting his ship in May 1930. He was charged with entry without inspection (Section 33, subsection 7) as well as under Section 41. He had been active in a strike at Fraser Mills and in several unemployed organizations. Immigration had a good deal to say about him: obviously he had stepped on some toes. He was "saturated with Communist beliefs and revolutionary ideas of a particularly virulent nature . . . a thoroughgoing troublemaker" with "no respect for the law": a "dangerous type." He was deported in December 1932 and died a few years later after being tortured in a Nazi concentration camp.[44]

Arvo Vaara was an old hand at this sort of thing. Aged forty-one, single, he had immigrated in 1909 and settled in Sudbury. He had previous brushes with the authorities: he had been rejected at the border in 1928, and admitted only after J. S. Woodsworth and others intervened. In December 1928 he was convicted of seditious libel for publishing an editorial which expressed indifference about the possibility that the King might die from an illness he was currently suffering. His appeal failed and he was in prison until August 1929. He was in trouble soon after his return to Sudbury, where he was editor of *Vapaus* and a stalwart of the Finnish Organization of Canada. In 1931 he was arrested for a May Day demonstration and various free speech activities; the authorities kept tabs on *Vapaus* and accumulated other articles that they thought might be seditious. Vaara was adjudged to be a "particularly clever individual . . . particularly dangerous. He is a menace to Canada and to the existing economic and governmental structure of this country." He was deported 17 December 1932.[45]

John (Toivo) Stahlberg (aged forty, married to a Finnish citizen), was born in Finland and had come to Canada in 1910, but had gone on to the United States where he had worked for ten years and acquired citizenship in 1917. He was a trained blacksmith, but after his return to Canada he worked as a steamship agent and as business manager for *Vapaus*. He was also involved in the Finnish Organization. He was deported to the United States in December 1932.[46]

Gottfried Zurcher, a Swiss citizen (thirty-two years of age), had been in Canada since September 1927. After working on a friend's farm for nearly a year, he became a welder in Winnipeg. He eventually settled in Vancouver. Active in the Communist Party from his early months in the country, at the time of his arrest he was Secretary of the CLDL. In addition to Sergeant Leopold's testimony, the Department used the testimony of two Mountie spies who had witnessed Zurcher's speeches and activities at various meetings and demonstrations. In particular, Constable Upton had been a fellow member of the Vancouver branch of the National Unemployed Workers Association. Immigration and the Mounties regarded Zurcher as an "active and dangerous" communist. He and his wife (who had come from Switzerland to marry him in 1928) were ordered deported, and departed 1 January 1933.[47]

By comparison, Stefan Worozcyt of Montreal was small potatoes. Single, aged thirty, he had come in 1926 as a farm worker through the CPR, to a job in the West. Instead, he went to Hamilton and next to Montreal where, at the time of his arrest, he worked as a window cleaner. He was involved in the ULFTA, CLDL and Ukrainian patriotic associations (Society for Assisting the Liberation Movement in Western Ukraine).

Although he was not high up in the Party, and "possibly of a lower grade of intelligence" than the leaders (in the view of the Department), he was still a prime candidate for deportation. The Department saw two reasons to deport him: he had "failed to comply with the conditions of entry when he came to Canada" by skipping out on farm work, and he had "obviously associated himself with a class who are a menace to the accepted government structure and institutions here." He was deported 23 January 1933.[48]

Although the Department preferred that the Halifax Ten (as they came to be known) never saw the inside of a courtroom, the CLDL did its best to get the case into the courts. Their first attempt failed: the Nova Scotia court under Justice Carroll refused to consider an application for habeas corpus under the provisions of the Liberty of Subjects Act of Nova Scotia. The CLDL appealed this refusal and got a hearing before Acting Chief Justice Renfret and his colleagues in the Supreme Court in October 1932. Technically, the issue was the lower court's refusal to hear the habeas corpus application, but the Ten's attorneys challenged the validity of the entire deportation proceedings.

The discussion centred on the issue of the Supreme Court's authority to review the evidence considered by the Boards of Inquiry. The men's lawyers argued that due process had not been followed, that "full particulars" of the charges (as required by the Immigration Act) had not been given, and thus the arrests and hearings were unfounded. Moreover, the charges were so vague that the men did not know of what unlawful actions they had been convicted. Besides which, the applicants had been charged with advocating the overthrow by force or violence, and their advocacy had not been proven.

The Justices accepted the argument that "full particulars" had not been given. They were not swayed by most of the points put forward by the Department of Immigration's lawyer who claimed that: it was too late to challenge the validity of the composition or activities of the Boards of Inquiry; a provincial tribunal could not judge the activities of a federal tribunal or question the extent and nature of the powers of the Minister of Immigration in relation to the cases under consideration. But in the end, in November 1932, the Supreme Court dismissed the appeal. The Minister of Immigration did the same in December.[49] Despite much agitation and a veritable flood of letters, petitions, telegrams and other documents attempting to avert the deportations or alter the destinations, as soon as arrangements for documents and transportation were completed, the men were shipped out.

The most important source of protests against the deportation of radicals in the 1930s was the Canadian Labor Defense League.[50] It was a Communist Party front, established to raise funds in aid of striking miners and their families in the mid-1920s. It was modelled on International Red Aid which carried out diverse support activities, including supplying fake passports and safe passage to the U.S.S.R. for radicals who were being deported to unsafe countries. With the intensification of political repression in the late 1920s, the League refocused its activities from fund raising to organizing protests and providing legal defense for arrested radicals. It defended eighty-eight Toronto cases alone between January 1929 and February 1930. In 1930 the CLDL began a major membership and fundraising drive to increase its skimpy resources. It was heavily dependent on its 130-odd branches, most of whose members were non-British in origin. The Finnish and Ukrainian organizations were particularly important. By 1930, deportation of the unemployed and of radicals were the major issues with which the League was dealing. After 1931, as the authorities increased their crackdowns on the communists, the CLDL began to campaign for the repeal of Section 98 and the reform or abolition of deportation procedures.

The campaign for repeal was played out against a background of intense anti-radical paranoia. Anyone speaking out against persecution of radicals risked being labelled a communist. In some cities, more than a label was at stake. In Toronto, for example, businesses stood to lose their licenses if they allowed communists to use their premises. The men and women going bail for Buck et al. in 1931 risked losing everything they had put up if Buck et al. were convicted, as Section 98 provided for the seizure of property of communists, and large fines. Anyone willing to put up bail was a de facto communist.[51]

Not everyone was intimidated by such a climate. Although most of the protest generated by the League was from communist affiliated organizations, a good part of it was not, especially on two issues. The first was the free speech issue in Toronto. When the city police moved from communist-bashing to an attack on the Fellowship of Reconciliation, a religiously based liberal group of pacifistic leanings, the respectable middle classes were affected and a certain measure of indignation was aroused. When sixty-eight professors from the University of Toronto took on the redbaiters, the ensuing furor at least had the effect of showing the importance of the free speech issue as a civil liberties question of much broader importance than the quashing of radical dissent and disorder.[52]

The second and more significant instance of broad support for a CLDL campaign was that for repeal of Section 98. Mainstream farm, labour, church and social groups worked for repeal. J. S. Woodsworth, who had opposed Section 98 from its passage (as Sections 97A and 97B) in 1919, made numerous attempts in the Commons to have it repealed or revised. Eventually Mackenzie King agreed to support repeal and when he was elected in 1935, he repealed Section 98 the following year.[53]

Among its many activities the League published a pamphlet entitled *Deported!* which contained a succinct and accurate analysis of the activities of the government in deporting radicals, activists and the unemployed.[54] The adjectives may have been extreme, but the League's understanding of the mechanisms and purposes of deportation was quite sound:

> The Immigration Act as a whole is essentially a legal carte-blanche for the brazen skin-game of importing labor, using this labor as a lever against both the native Canadian and the imported labor itself, forcing every possible dollar of profit out of it and throwing it on the scrapheap, ready for deportation.

Oscar Ryan, the author of *Deported!*, compared Section 98 of the Criminal Code with Section 41 of the Immigration Act, pointing out the essential sameness of the offences described in each. Except for the critical flavour of his description, that section of the pamphlet could have been taken from a Departmental memo describing the legislation. Ryan concluded that it was easier for authorities to rely on Section 41 for political deportations, because such a procedure "dispenses with the bother of a formal Section 98 charge and the routine of court procedure."[55] This was in fact a view shared by authorities.

The CLDL claimed that large-scale protest could stop deportation of activists – at least in some cases. Ryan described the case of Dan Malone as an inspiring example of what could be done. According to an account in the *Canadian Labor Defender*, Malone, his wife, and several others were driving to a meeting in Ottawa when they were stopped by the RCMP brandishing guns. After allegedly attempting to plant a gun on Malone (the planter admitted at the scene that it was his own gun, said the CLDL; the account was confused), the RCMP searched and eventually released all the travellers. Five days later, two officers from the notorious Toronto Red Squad arrested Malone, charged him with vagrancy and accused him of being an IRA terrorist. The CLDL organized mass protests. In the next few days the police case did not advance, and on 8 August Malone went to court on vagrancy charges alone. Although the papers of 5 August had reported that the RCMP had ordered Malone's arrest in relation to a plot to assassinate J. H. Thomas, a British delegate to the Imperial Conference, the Toronto police did not lay any such charges. Before Malone went to trial, it was announced by the Department of Immigration that Malone would be deported as a public charge: he was unemployed and had received some relief money.

Meanwhile the CLDL was publicizing the cases as widely as possible and organizing protests. On 12 August the League claimed that it had found a stool pigeon called Kusack, who had been responsible for initiating the accusations of terrorism (no motive was suggested). Malone went to trial 13 August, and the vagrancy charges were dropped. He was free, insofar as the criminal justice system was concerned, but still under threat of deportation. The next day a large meeting was held at the Labor Temple to protest his deportation, and on 18 August the Department announced that his deportation "would not be effected".[56]

On the face of it, the protests had influenced the course of events. By the summer of 1932, the CLDL had become an old hand at protests. But just how effective were they? Did the CLDL succeed in more than a few scattered cases? Certainly it was active. It got thousands, tens, and in some cases hundreds of thousands of signatures on petitions; it got hundreds and thousands of letters and resolutions against deportation sent to the government over the years. It provided legal defence for many hundreds of court cases, and sometimes – when the cases were shaky, the actions of the authorities particularly unconscionable, the defendants clearly victimised, and the judge fair – the defence was successful. Noisy publicity about unsavoury practices by the authorities was awkward; protests probably helped in some circumstances. Petryshyn, who certainly knows more about the CLDL than anyone who was not a participant in the organization, believes the CLDL was an effective force in at least slowing down the deportations.[57]

The files of the Department of Immigration tell a different story. The Department was eager to avoid informed criticism by the public, press, politicians or the courts – partly because its practices were often illegal or at least unpalatable and would not stand scrutiny. Fortunately for the Department, few people ever understood that deportation procedures violated cherished traditions of British justice and fair play. Those who realized this were rarely powerful enough to bring about more than cosmetic changes. Fear of publicity aside, when Departmental officials were assured that they had the support of the government, the public could go whistle, and especially the radical public. This is quite evident in the Department's response to substantial protest against the deportation of communists. Tomo Cacic's case is a good example.

Cacic was not a big fish. He was only picked up in the 1931 raids by chance. He had spent many years in North America, had worked seasonally in the United States and in British Columbia for several years before and during the First World War, and then had returned home to Yugoslavia. After a spell in jail for his political activities, he came to Canada as an immigrant in 1924. He had not applied for Canadian citizenship (and probably would not have been granted it, in any case). At the time of his arrest he had just returned to Toronto from an organizing trip through Sudbury, Timmins, and Kirkland Lake. He worked primarily in unions and ethnic organizations for the Party. On 12 August, he was at the Workers Unity League office arranging to have some pamphlets shipped, when the police burst in.[58]

His deportation hearing was held early in 1933 at the Kingston Penitentiary by a one-man Board of Inquiry. Officer Reynolds acted under strict instruction by his superiors, who foresaw weaknesses in the case and wanted to avoid problems. Cacic had been in Canada long enough to acquire domicile; Reynolds was to be sure to establish that Section 41 nevertheless applied because as a member of the "prohibited or undesirable classes within the meaning of Section 41 [Cacic was not] capable of acquiring Canadian domicile."[59]

As Cacic's deportation date grew closer, his case was made a focus of protest. Radical groups from all over the country sent in resolutions, petitions, letters, and telegrams, urging the government to cancel the order, or failing that, to change Cacic's destination. By the fall of 1933, there was a furor over the conditions of Cacic's imprisonment (which were unusually punitive, if the records can be believed), as well as his imminent deportation.[60]

Protests were futile. Not only the bureaucrats but also the politicians – including the Prime Minister – were determined that Cacic's deportation would be carried out. Just as the protests were heating up, the Yugoslav Consul wrote to the Department of Immigration: "As one of the leaders of the Communist Party in Canada and . . . of very dangerous influence upon our nationals in this country, this Royal Consul would appreciate very much if you would proceed with his deportation.'' Such requests were treated seriously by the Department (while protests against the deportation of public charges by other consuls often were not). A Departmental official wrote and twice underlined "VERY IMPORTANT", in red ink, upon the consul's letter. The Department's reply was reassuring: a number of protests had been received but "it is not our intention to favourably entertain these requests. The Department fully appreciates your desire to have Cacic removed on account of his very dangerous influence upon his fellow-countrymen in Canada.''[61]

Although the Department was determined not to accede to demands to cancel Cacic's deportation, there were a number of practical problems to be solved. The Department frequently could not arrange to collect prisoners on the day of their release and to take them to a port for deportation. The usual solution was to detain them (illegally) in the prison until shipping arrangements could be made. This avoided the bother of timing a re-arrest by Immigration officials, and lessened the pressures on the Department's already-overcrowded detention facilities. Of course there were protests against such practices, but the Department had decided that it could usually afford to ignore them.

When the stream of protests became a flood and Cacic's case threatened to become a cause célèbre, the Department could no longer carry out business as usual. The publicity would do its reputation no good, and by late 1933 it was already under fire for its deportation activities. When the Hungarian Workers' Club wired that it was determined to "free Cacic and stop his deportation," the implied threat was the last straw.[62] The Department was caught between two unpleasant alternatives. Holding Cacic past his release time might invite court intervention and rescue by legal means. Releasing him might make it possible for some sort of home-grown Red Aid attempt to smuggle Cacic to safety, to secrete him who-knew-where.

There was pressure from the Prime Minister. Bennett had been at Minister of Justice Guthrie after Guthrie received the threatening telegram. Guthrie in turn sent an alarm to Gordon at Immigration who passed on the substance of Guthrie's memo to Commissioner of Immigration Jolliffe. Identifying Cacic only as "one of the Tim Buck crowd," Guthrie had said, "I do not know this chap's name but the Prime Minister made it clear that he desired great care taken in connection with the holding of the Board on this man to see that it is conducted strictly in accordance with the law.'' Gordon told Jolliffe to have the Department of Justice go over each step of the case to be sure it was legal, so that there would be no repetition of a "previous unfortunate case" where the government had bungled a deportation and the prisoner had been released.[63]

Jolliffe wrote reassuringly to Guthrie. Radical elements might indeed "seek to obstruct the process of law by legal action or other methods which may tend to cause embarrassment." Immigration would take "every precaution . . . tending to ensure of his safe delivery." The Assistant Commissioner of Immigration would personally oversee sailing arrangements.[64]

Not too surprisingly, Justice found that the case was shaky. The only evidence given at the Board of Inquiry that Cacic had advocated the overthrow of government by force was his conviction under Section 98 of the Criminal Code of being a member and officer of an unlawful association. If a habeas corpus application were made, likely the court would hold that this was "not evidence of the conduct described in Section 41 of the Immigration Act, which renders the immigrant undesirable." Justice suggested holding a second Board of Inquiry with a fresh complaint and a new Ministerial Order, and adding to the evidence a certified copy of the transcript of Cacic's court trial. The trial evidence would probably satisfy the requirements of Section 41 and safeguard the Department from the courts.[65]

A new Board of Inquiry was held, following procedures carefully specified by high-level Justice and Immigration officials. Nothing was left to chance. Sergeant Leopold was brought in as a witness to repeat his testimony that, regardless of Cacic's personal views, as a Party member he was committed to carry out Party policy supporting the overthrow of government by violence. As the hearing continued, Leopold's testimony broke through Cacic's resignation. Defending the ethnic organizations as teachers of "geography and the everyday life of Canada to . . . illiterate immigrants," Cacic burst out at Leopold, "You are a paid agent who appeared in court against myself and comrades, swore their life, through nothing else but reading pamphlets and trying to establish a Red scare. I really do not expect anything else from you."[66]

As far as the authorities were concerned, everything was now ready. They geared up for final arrangements. Guthrie wrote privately to the Commissioner of Immigration to make sure that everything was properly arranged. None of the casual illegalities so much a part of deportation must be permitted for Cacic. Guthrie told Jolliffe to "take such steps as may be necessary to take charge of him upon his release.

In my judgement it will not be possible to hold this man in the penitentiary after the [end of his sentence] . . . . This letter is for personal
information and not for your fyles."[67]

Cacic appealed. The Department reluctantly decided to release
relevant documents to Cacic's CLDL lawyer on an eyes-only basis. Justice
had carefully double-checked the second Board of Inquiry, so that
Immigration had little to fear about the outcome of the appeal.[68]

Cacic's lawyer was afraid that his client would be hastily removed
from prison and deported. He need not have worried. Justice had cards
up its sleeve. Cacic was to serve every single day of his sentence – none
of the usual time off for good behaviour. Further, it might be possible
to hold him beyond the late December expiry date until the first of
March 1934, under Section 72 of the Penitentiaries Act which provided
that a convict could request to stay in jail from December to the end of
February.[69] How Cacic would be induced to make such a request was
not discussed.

While Justice plotted and Cacic's fellows protested his imminent
deportation (to prison or death, they feared), the Department methodically
arranged for Cacic's shipment. The day after the appeal was refused, all
procedures were in place. Deportation Officers Howell and Souillard would
pick up Cacic, take him on the train from Brockville, Ontario ("take great
care to avoid publicity," the Officers were told) to a remote stop in Quebec,
where they would be met by car and driven to a police station to wait
for the Halifax train. At Halifax they would take him directly to the
Immigration Inspector-in-Charge who would oversee boarding the ship.
Ordering the officers to take the "greatest care . . . overlook no details,"
their superiors made it clear that this case must go off perfectly. "It is
absolutely essential that the law should take its course in this particular
instance."[70]

Far from masterminding a rescue plan, the CLDL almost missed
its chance to make a last-ditch legal plea; they only indirectly learned
that Cacic was about to be taken East. By now the CLDL was resigned
to Cacic's deportation. Now their tactic was to try for a change of destination. If they could get him to the U.S.S.R., he would be safe. The CLDL
and Department lawyers fought it out in the Halifax courts. Justice Doull
refused habeas corpus; so did the Full Court on appeal. The *Montcalm*
sailed at 4:30 a.m. New Year's Day, 1934 with Tomo Cacic aboard.[71]

Did the Department believe that it was sending him to his death?
Probably not, but it seems unlikely that Immigration officials truly had

no idea that radicals deported to their native countries might be in danger. Even if Immigration officials rejected as excessive the alarms raised by the left (and there were thousands of these warnings), they had information from more palatable sources. For instance, in 1930, Commissioner Cortlandt Starnes of the RCMP, a much-relied upon and consistent source of information on the Red menace, passed on reports from a British source that a "fascist" takeover in Finland featured persecution of communists.[72]

The man who usually made crucial Immigration decisions (then instructed the Minister, as well as his own subordinates) was the type who allowed his head to rule his heart. Frederick Blair had joined the Department by the turn of the century; in 1905 he became an Immigration officer and moved up rapidly. After a spell as Secretary, he became Acting Deputy Minister, and in 1936, Director (equivalent to Deputy Minister in rank). He was a wonderful bureaucrat, which was particularly easy because he had determined most of the rules under which he operated. He was anti-Semitic, anti-radical, anti-East Indian, anti-Eastern European, and anti-Southern European – a typical churchgoing English-Canadian civil servant, exemplifying much of the worst of Canadian society of the time. It was Blair who played a major part in refusing entry to and deporting Polish Jews around 1920, and who held the line (even in the face of occasional rebellions by his Minister) against European Jewish refugees in the late 1930s, even after he began to realize that they were going to be killed in Europe.[73] Blair was perfectly capable of knowingly deporting communists to prisons or worse.

It was not just Blair. Discussions of this issue in the files of the Department reveal a punitive attitude. Assistant Commissioner Munroe commented to RCMP Director of Intelligence Charles Hamilton that he hoped deported radicals would "appreciate the laws and conditions which prevail [in their own countries] better than those which we have in Canada and which they decry so violently." The RCMP Commissioner wrote Jolliffe about two Yugoslav radicals who had escaped in Germany during their deportation, picked up clothes and false passports, and fled to the U.S.S.R. If they had gone to Yugoslavia, it would have meant their deaths, said Starnes. The response of Immigration was to tighten up procedures to prevent more escapes.[74]

Publicly the Department denied that there were any risks. Concerning an "alleged danger to those men following deportation," it wired the CLDL, "they will unquestionably have the full protection

of the laws of their native countries to which they are being returned.''
During December 1932 when arrangements for the deportation of the
Halifax Ten were being completed, there were massive protests sent to
the Department about the dangers awaiting the men in native countries
now under repressive governments. Arvo Vaara and Martin Parker, for
example, were to be sent back to Finland, where the Whites had been
in power for more than a decade (which they had initiated with concentration camps and executions for Reds) and were busily carrying out anti-
radical campaigns of their own through the agency of fascist thugs.
Immediately after receiving strong warnings of dangers to Vaara and Parker
in Finland, and pleas to let them go to the Soviet Union instead, the
Department ordered extra guards and arranged particularly tight security
to ensure their delivery to Finland. Perhaps the best that can be said about
the Department officials is that they did not take the warnings seriously,
even those given by the RCMP. They hid behind the law, which said that
deportation sent immigrants back whence they came; if there was any
reluctance in this choice, it is not evident in the records. As Guthrie said
about the protests, he received too many to acknowledge. ''I merely hand
them over to the Mounted Police in order that a record may be kept of
the names and addresses of the people who sign them and I make this
statement so that the petitioners may know what I do with them.''[75]

What is evident, and perhaps more to the point, is the importance
of links to overseas security organizations. If overseas governments were
anti-communist (and this was characteristic of fascist and pro-fascist
governments in Europe), then their law enforcement agencies would treat
communists as enemies of the state; appropriate information would be
shared with fellow law enforcement organizations, usually through
diplomatic channels. Canada was especially reliant upon the British who
were only too happy to co-operate with anti-communist authorities in
Europe.

There are many examples of the Department of Immigration being
fed such information. In 1926, before the extreme crackdowns in Finland,
a communist newspaper celebrated its third anniversary by printing
congratulatory messages from a number of Canadian Finns, whose names
and addresses were published. A copy of it was sent to Commissioner
Starnes of the RCMP who sent it to the Deputy Minister of Immigration
for action. As the Finnish government stepped up its anti-communist
activities, the RCMP was kept informed. In 1928 it passed on a list of
communists purged by the government, obtained from a confidential

source; later, photographs were sent and distributed to Immigration officers, in case any fugitives sought refuge in Canada.[76]

Acting on another RCMP tip in 1932, Immigration told its agents to "closely examine" persons returning from Russia, "irrespective of the documents they present in the nature of passports or citizenship papers." (Canadian citizens were by law not subject to re-entry examination. Once Immigration determined they were citizens, it had no legal right to examine them.) In 1934, the Department issued a general order to be on guard for Canadian Finns who had "confessed" to the Finnish police that they were spies for Russia. In fact, these people had fled the dreadful conditions of Karelia, a Finnish socialist colony in Russia. The source of the report on the "spies" was the British Consul in Helsinki, whose report was forwarded by the British government to Canadian authorities.[77] The validity of such information, or the conditions under which it was obtained, are nowhere questioned.

Similarly, the RCMP regularly sent on the Immigration secret circulars from the Home Office consisting of a series of cards giving the name, date of arrival in the United Kingdom, and passport details of various radicals. British Immigration also communicated directly with its Canadian counterpart, sending on its "suspect index" of people to be rejected or detained. This information was considered to be sufficiently confidential to order previous editions burned upon receipt of updated editions.[78]

American sources were also utilized. Canadian authorities kept abreast of U.S. crackdowns on Reds, of course. As well, Canadian Immigration regularly received a "lookout list" for American "Reds" who had been active in "riots" and the like – in other words, had been involved in organizing workers or the unemployed, free speech movements, and other social protests most of which were not illegal. Such exchange of information was not a phenomenon of the Depression. Similar channels had been in existence for decades. They were without question acted upon by Canadian Immigration authorities.

Officers of the Department must have found it frustrating when, despite their best efforts, subversive foreigners kept slipping through the net and popping up in Canada. Officers of the RCMP must have been even more frustrated. The head of the RCMP in Vancouver wrote to his chief in Ottawa pleading for changes to the Immigration Act to reduce protection against deportation; as it was, he could not do his job. The Vancouver area was a hotbed of "foreign agents", as he called radicals. "Deportation is the one effective weapon against foreign agents and one of which they are in continual fear." But a recent ruling by the Commissioner of Immigration was creating problems for the Mountie.[79]

Fearing court intervention, Jolliffe had ruled that communist deportations had to be based on evidence of active (as opposed to nominal, former, or alleged) involvement with the Party. And the only way to provide the necessary evidence was to have a Mountie spy testify at the Board of Inquiry. "Uncovering a secret agent" ended that agent's usefulness. Alas, agents were hard to replace. The high level of commitment among radicals in the vicinity made it hard to recruit agents from radical ranks (because there were so many "foreign agents" around, argued the Mountie).[80]

Political deportation relied heavily on RCMP spy reports. The best-known example is the testimony of Sergeant Leopold, who not only identified the official functions of suspects, but provided the evidence of centralized control and universal applicability of Party discipline that was necessary to declare the Communist Party an illegal organization. Leopold's testimony was supported by documents seized from Party offices and members' homes. Other RCMP sources relied less on evidence, documentary or otherwise. Some like Secret Agent #125 Tatko or Constables Upton and Bordeau were regular RCMP officers. Others were disaffected radicals, anti-labour or anti-radical informers, and less savoury elements not noted for their integrity or intelligence. An RCMP Crown witness against radical Allen Campbell in Vancouver claimed the alphabet had thirty-six letters.[81] He was far from the worst.

In addition to the paid agents, there were public-spirited citizens only too pleased to turn in their neighbours. For example, the Reverend Thomas Jones from Sudbury was responsible for Arvo Vaara's 1929 sedition conviction. It was Jones who got a Finnish fellow missionary to translate Vaara's "seditious" editorials, then took the translations to the Sudbury *Star* for publication. The town was duly stirred up, the Legion passed resolutions, the local Crown Attorney stepped in and brought the wrath of His Majesty's Government on Vaara's head. Jones was certainly a patriot. Nonetheless, as Betcherman points out, he had a few grievances against Vaara. The success of the Red Finns and *Vapaus* was a serious hindrance to Jones' missionary work. *Vapaus* made fun of the missionaries. Equally bad, *Vapaus* was campaigning to organize a union for the Northern Ontario miners. The timing was inopportune; two major nickel companies were negotiating a merger. Queen's Park, ever a friend of the mine owners, would not have approved of any hitches.[82]

By 1934, public opinion was beginning to change. It was no longer merely the communists who objected to mass deportation, the curtailment of civil liberties, and Section 98. Mackenzie King had found it expedient to oppose the worst of Bennett's Iron Heel policies. He had promised that if elected he would repeal Section 98 and, by implication, stop the abuses. The Co-operative Commonwealth Federation (CCF), whatever support it mustered, also opposed mass deportation and Section 98 as violations of civil liberties and common decency.[83]

Many people, who were untroubled by the summary deportation of radicals, were not so sanguine about wholesale deportation of the unemployed. Challenges in the courts had combined with public opinion to cause the Department of Immigration to become slightly more circumspect in its activities. By 1933, the Department had to tighten up on irregular or illegal practices. As the Commissioner of Immigration noted in a directive, the courts were increasingly reviewing deportation cases upon habeas corpus applications by the prospective deports. When courts found procedural irregularities, they were empowered to order the release of the appellant. Any departure from strict legality could destroy a case, and lead to "an adverse decision with embarrassing consequences and complications."[84]

The excesses of some local authorities had begun to come under fire. The Toronto Police's Red Squad had been under criticism for some time, because of its heavy-handed and arbitrary actions: beating up suspects, seizing papers, almost at Red Squad leader Nursey's whim. Whims were no substitute for good judgement or legality. Lawyers and judges began to express concern. In the fall of 1933, the Toronto Police Commission (its two most rabid members had retired) told Nursey that henceforth he could only raid meetings that were clearly in violation of the law.[85] That cooled down Toronto considerably.

After 1934, the worst was over. That year was a turning point. The most spectacular event was the arrest and trial for sedition of A. E. Smith, the head of the CLDL. It all began with a play called *Eight Men Speak*, put on by the CLDL in Toronto in December 1933. It castigated prison conditions, the shooting of the Estevan strikers, and the attempted shooting of Tim Buck, allegedly on orders from high authority. The play was quickly closed by Toronto police.

Bennett was furious about the play. He hated Smith and had been seeking a way to silence him. Two weeks later Smith publicly accused

Bennett of giving the order to shoot at Buck.[86] Bennett ordered Smith charged with sedition.

This time Bennett and his men had gone too far. They were criticized in the press. Support for Smith came also from mainstream labour and church groups. Then the trial revealed that the Crown had no case against Smith; he was found innocent. And if he was not guilty, other sedition cases were cast into doubt. A few months later, all of the remaining Kingston communist prisoners were set free, save Buck who was held until November. Bennett had backed down.[87]

The Department of Immigration still carried on. It scoured the jails periodically to find those ''convicted as a result of identifying themselves with riots, or disturbances of a communistic nature.''[88] But when the country-wide crackdown against Reds lessened, so did the supply of radicals in the jails who could be deported for their political activities. When King repealed Section 98, early in 1936, the authorities lost their strongest weapon for political deportation. Immigration still had all its apparatus intact; it merely had to return to a more discreet style of operation, relying on other methods and other charges for deporting immigrants judged undesirable.

Deportation ultimately depended on a network of referrals from criminal justice, relief, medical, and political authorities. When such referrals became inexpedient, deportation diminished. There were limits to what could be accomplished by administrative fiat from the top down. The limits had been reached. After 1935, deportation declined to ''normal'' levels.

"Shovelling Out" the Redundant, 1930-1935

The deportation of the unemployed in the 1930s continued well established practice, but at the same time intensified to such a degree that it became a change in kind. The tradition of expelling immigrants who had become public charges had been established some fifty years earlier. The unemployed who had gone on relief were the main target group for the Department of Immigration during the Depression. Just as unemployment became a mass phenomenon, the response of the Department to it was the mass production of economic deportation.

The Department had claimed, during an earlier period of high unemployment, that it was not its policy to deport the unemployed, unless there were other factors that would make these people unlikely to succeed in Canada. The Department's claims were necessary to balance the conflicting interests of the transportation companies and the municipalities. It was usually the companies who had brought in the immigrants and who would be asked by the Department to pay the costs of sending deports back whence they came. It was the municipalities who had to pay the costs of maintaining immigrants who became public charges. Except in times of economic crisis the Department had been able to balance these conflicting interests. One of the most important tactics used by the Department in this balancing act was the claim that it did not automatically and arbitrarily ship out the otherwise desirable and fit immigrants who had fallen on hard times. Such a claim helped the Department to avoid political controversy.

Despite the attempts of the Department to argue that it deported the unemployable rather than the unemployed, the mass deportations of the 1930s aroused a good deal of controversy. Leftwing and liberal public opinion (from the Communist Party to the Co-operative Commonwealth Federation to the churches, for example) attacked the Department for "shovelling out" the down and out. The municipalities were caught in a severe financial squeeze, as they were overwhelmed by spiralling relief costs. Neither the provinces nor Ottawa were willing to contribute anything substantial to the high costs of relieving immigrants. The municipalities attacked immigration policies, accused the federal government of importing undesirables, and demanded stronger action. Canadian nativists demanded that the "foreigners" be sent back home so that "white men" could find jobs. None of this was unique to the 1930s, but the scale of the problem was unprecedented.

The official position of the Department of Immigration during the Depression was that it did not systematically deport the unemployed. The records do not support that claim. The general policy of the Department in those years was to deport those unemployed immigrants who had gone on relief. Within that general policy there were some slight deviations. During 1929 and the first six months of 1930, the Department balked at a very few requests for specific deportations. From the summer of 1930 to the fall of 1935, the official policy was one of automatic deportation of the unemployed, while claiming that they were unemployable and undesirable. By 1932, certain ameliorative practices were developed, mostly in response to public outrage and pressure. Most of these practices were related to suspending deportations. Reliefers who found work might have their proceedings put into abeyance; Britishers might be ordered deported but the order never carried out.

These years were noteworthy for a concerted effort by the Department of Immigration officials to conceal, deny, or justify their practices. Spurious or misleading statistics were cooked up and purveyed, editors regaled with letters and rationalizations, statements made in Parliament, in public, and in private. In some instances, the Department representatives misled; in others they lied.

By the fall of 1935, the worst was over. The economic situation had bottomed out and was slowly improving, but it was the changes in the political climate that were crucial. The new Minister of Immigration,

Thomas Crerar, was wishy-washy, rather than determined to "shovel out" all of the unemployed. Large numbers of the general public, many Members of Parliament, and perhaps most importantly, numbers of municipal councillors, had condemned the deportation of the unemployed. Even with a compliant Minister (and most of them had little real understanding of what went on in their Department), it was no longer possible to "shovel out" vast numbers at the rate of previous years.

Not that the Department stopped; rather, it retreated. Circumstances directed public attention elsewhere, while the Department continued its usual activities on a scale diminished in comparison to the heyday of the early 1930s, but still higher than in previous decades.

By the fall of 1929, there were already sizeable numbers of unemployed immigrants to be shipped out as public charges. The Department had already begun to send back large numbers of young British men who had come over earlier that year as trainees under the auspices of the Ministry of Labour. A special procedure was set up: the men would be received at the Immigration Building at Montreal, thus qualifying as public charges, then face Boards of Inquiry at which they would be ordered deported as public charges, "they of course refusing farm work." Deporting these men was enough of a political embarrassment, but the special procedures adopted had the potential to create a worse one.

The problem was that many other able-bodied unemployed Britons did not see why they too could not be promptly received and deported. In Montreal, the alternatives for the unemployed were very grim. The Immigration Building meant food and shelter. But the Department argued that these men could find work if they wanted it. While it would be simple enough to hold Boards of Inquiry and deport these unemployed immigrants, the Eastern Division Commissioner of Immigration predicted that if this were done, there would "be a rapid increase in the number of cases the Division will have to deal with and we will develop more or less into a booking agency."[1] That would not only be politically awkward, it would swamp the Montreal Agency with bodies and papers. Neither the staff nor the building could stand the extra load.

The Commissioner of Immigration in Ottawa concluded that the Department of Immigration must take a firm stand to discourage immigrants who were unwilling to work, in anticipation of "quite a number of these cases." Men who were unemployed and refused farm work were to be told, "they will have to make their own way" back home. The

Montreal Agency was told that no special procedures would be permitted to those who applied.[2]

By the following spring, municipalities were clearly using deportation as an alternative to relief. The regional office of the Department in Winnipeg was receiving deportation complaints against immigrants who had received miniscule amounts of relief. Single unemployed men who had gotten payments of $2 to $4 had been labelled as "public charges". Ottawa balked: immigration was willing to "co-operate" with the municipalities, but not to "extend facilities in the matter of deportation on such slim grounds" if there were no other reasons than unemployment. Immigrants might stop trying to find jobs and "adopt the line of least resistance, which means a free trip home." If the municipalities wanted to deport these people, it was up to them to show that "whoever is involved is a misfit or a type who cannot become established."[3] In other words, the cases had to be somewhat differently constructed and presented. Relief payments of $4 were not in themselves sufficient grounds for deportation in May 1930.

The following month, the Deputy Minister told the Winnipeg Division Commissioner to pass the word to Calgary municipal officials that Immigration would not issue deportation orders against a group of immigrants who had received relief payments ranging from $1-3 for individuals, to $11 for a family. "Unless there is an unfavourable history behind each one of these, they should be given a chance to make good," he wrote.[4]

By 1930 there was intense pressure from the municipalities to deport public charges. Relief costs had begun to escalate. In Winnipeg, for example, relief costs for 1927-28 had been $31,394; for 1930-31, they rose to $1,683,386. In March 1930, representatives from British Columbia, Ontario, and Prairie provincial governments and a number of Western municipalities had presented to Cabinet figures outlining the financial costs of high immigrant unemployment, in an unsuccessful effort to force the federal government to pay these costs. The federal government's alternative to paying immigrant relief costs was to order deportation of the unemployed. A directive to that effect was issued in the summer of 1930.[5]

Drastic enough, such a policy was conservative in comparison to what had been proposed by Minister of Immigration Charles Stewart. The municipalities had sought sterner measures. While on a visit to the West, Stewart was persuaded to wire his Department to bypass legalities and ship out the unemployed en masse to clear the relief rolls. His staff reacted with dismay to this politically explosive proposal. Deputy Minister William Egan wired Stewart that certain steps could not be bypassed. "Summary returns impossible unless Department pays all transportation costs both rail and ocean." Because so many of the unemployed were British, Egan feared that "following procedure [outlined] your wire yesterday means those returned would be mainly British and the effect would be disastrous once this becomes known as it will the moment movement begins." Egan suggested instead that the Department stick to a formula of "50% British, 50% foreign and handle all by regular procedure. This only safe course. Using telegraphic warrants will facilitate action. Will act immediately on your reply." And such remained the policy of the Department for a substantial period.[6]

Although it was at the request of a Liberal Minister that "shovelling out" the unemployed was intensified, the policy continued after the July 1930 elections. The new Tory Minister of Immigration, Wesley Gordon, was briefed by his staff that August. He was told (on Egan's orders) that it had been and should continue to be the policy of Department to deport unemployed reliefers as a matter of routine. Although harvest work might take the burden off Western cities for a time, by winter most of the unemployed men would return to the cities. Either because they would be "determined not to help themselves" (that is, take winter farm "jobs", usually for little more than room and board) or because "they cannot obtain employment," these immigrants would be "public charges at least through the winter," reasoned Department bureaucrats. The new Minister should be acquainted with these facts and his permission asked to continue deportations of the unemployed.[7] He apparently did not object to his staff's proposals.

Despite the fact that Egan had insisted to Stewart that it was necessary for the Department to follow legal and routine procedures, the Department regularly used illegal shortcuts. Telegraphic warrants, for example, were not illegal in themselves, but "Minister's Orders" for examination were supposed to be issued only after certain basic facts of the case had been sent to Ottawa for perusal. These niceties broke down under the load of public charge deportations. By the summer of 1931, several cities in the West had hundreds of complaints backlogged. The Winnipeg regional office was overwhelmed and unable to process them. Up to May 1930, Ottawa Immigration officials had been sending telegraphic warrants after receiving lists of immigrants' names by nightletter telegram, without knowing the facts of each case. The Commissioner of Immigration had ordered this practice stopped. But a year later, being swamped under work posed the greater danger. Ottawa agreed to resume the illegal practice of sending warrants in response to wired lists of names. The documentation would be sent to Ottawa after the cases were heard by Boards of Inquiry and deportations ordered.[8] The Immigration Act set out clearly the procedures to be followed, and violations were knowingly tolerated for years at a time for the sake of convenience. Such illegalities were usually well concealed in internal documents and seldom uncovered by the courts.

The Department of Immigration played a key role in the early part of the Depression. Worsening economic conditions and widespread unemployment meant heightened social unrest. Powerful interest groups such as employers' lobbies and corporations wanted industrial and social peace at any price, so long as they did not have to pay for it. Municipal governments (and taxpayers) were frantic about relief costs. There were political as well as financial limits to municipal sources of revenue. Local elites were determined to keep the lid on. Angry citizens and all manner of protest groups, from fraternal organizations to veterans' associations, blamed immigrants for taking jobs away from Canadians.[9] The Department served all these and the government as well, by shipping out the unemployed; none were satisfied and all wanted increased service.

On the other hand, there was a storm of criticism in the press and from a variety of organizations and associations – including some churches, unions, and the moderate and far left – and from foreign governments. Complaints about the deportation of ''foreigners'' could usually be dismissed or sidestepped. More worrisome was the furor in Canada and Britain about the deportation of unemployed British immigrants. Many of these had come in the 1920s through the Empire Settlement Act. They had been wooed and subsidized as highly desirable settlers. Now unemployed and on relief, they were labelled as ''undesirables'' and shipped back home.

Their arrival in Britain often caused howls of protest. His Majesty's Government made inquiries. Memoranda were exchanged. A few scandalous incidents were discussed in the Canadian and British press. Two particularly outrageous deportations were condemned: Miss Alice Barton, an epileptic who had been resident in Canada for seventeen years, and Mrs. Arnsworth, here twenty years, also an epileptic and an inmate of a hospital for the insane. Despite their long residence, they were deportable; as members of the prohibited classes they could never legally obtain domicile. These two cases created such controversy that Immigration Minister Gordon ordered that all proposed mental or epileptic deportation cases of immigrants here more than five years were to be submitted for Deputy Ministerial review.[10] Such matters were handled more cautiously thereafter.

Most criticism was directed at public charge deportations. As unemployment and hence public charge deportations increased, so did criticism. By the end of 1930, the Department had decided to take the offensive. The Minister and his staff initiated a campaign to conceal their policies and justify their actions. The campaign took three main approaches. First, it attempted to build up a case that deports were not just the unemployed but rather the unemployable, because they were unable or unwilling to work. Second, it attempted to create and display evidence that the majority (the figures vary) of the deports did not mind being deported and in fact were eager to go home. These were referred to as "voluntary" deportations. Third, the Department tried to conceal the true nature and extent of the deportation of unemployed immigrants who had become public charges, both by misleading statements about its policies, and by publishing figures based on statistics compiled to buttress the "unemployability" and the "voluntary" claims. Such a public relations exercise was to preoccupy Department officials for the next several years.

The campaign began with carefully aimed letters. Deputy Minister Egan, who was fully aware of the Department's policy, wrote to the Council for Social Service of the Church of England in Canada, claiming quite falsely that "we have not . . . adopted any policy of sending people back home in any numbers merely because they are in temporary distress through unemployment." Egan pointed out that the Minister of Immigration had stated publicly that he was not in favour of mass deportation.[11]

Gordon wrote explanatory letters to the editors of daily newspapers, hoping to improve the Department's publicity. By January he was citing case studies and analyses based on Department statistics. He claimed that deportation had "affected approximately only one half of one per cent of the immigrants who came to Canada since the commencement of the century."[12] He circulated to editors an analysis of the deportation cases of immigrants on a recent sailing of the *Ascania*, of which there had been much criticism. The analysis purported to justify these deportations on the grounds that each one was necessary, not just the result of a policy of "shovelling out".

The analysis was not particularly convincing on the face of it. The *Ascania* contingent had consisted of 72 men and women ordered deported, 37 of whom were accompanied by their families, including 6 Canadian-born children. Of the grounds for deportation, five were due to physical problems (three men were public charges, due to unemployment, and claimed they could not work because of physical disabilities, even if jobs were available; one man was tubercular and ordered deported under Section 33b as a member of the prohibited classes; and one woman, a domestic servant, suffered from pleurisy which the Department regarded as a tuberculosis case). There were four female domestic servants deported as public charges, but in addition these had "unsatisfactory records", meaning that three were unmarried and pregnant and one was accompanied by her illegitimate child. Five of the men had been convicted of unspecified crimes. (A vagrancy conviction, followed by a brief prison term, was an oft-used method of deporting unemployed immigrants as criminals.) Fifteen men were public charges allegedly unwilling to take farm work. Twenty-nine claimed that they were unable to obtain any kind of work. By the Department's own description, a substantial proportion of these people were being deported for unemployment alone. But the Minister claimed in his analysis that "not one of them was deported because employment could not be found for them on the land."[13]

Justifications such as this may not have been entirely convincing, but without inside information on the methods used by the Department to compile such data, little real criticism could be levied. Few daily newspapers questioned the Department's assertions, however little they liked the situation. The Ottawa *Citizen* was one of the exceptions. Editor Charles Bowman did not believe that the Department deported only the unemployable. "What about the other 200,000 unemployed in Canada? Are they similarly unemployable?" demanded his editorial.[14]

Not surprisingly, statistics normally kept by the Department were not particularly useful for its public relations campaign. They tended to damn rather than justify the Department's actions. By February 1931 the bureaucrats were creating new evidence. In order to show that British immigrants were only too pleased to be sent back home, Immigration officials were told to obtain written statements from any Britons requesting or agreeing to deportation.[15]

Not only were officers supposed to produce written evidence that deportations were voluntary, they were also given specific instructions to try to have immigrants say that they would refuse work if offered, and did not want to "become established" in Canada. By combining these techniques, the Department attempted to argue that "in every case they wanted to be sent home" or, alternatively, even though the statutory cause for deportation was "becoming a public charge", the real reason for becoming a public charge was "something more than unemployment."[16] The unemployed were thus the unemployable, and the blame shifted from the economy to the individual who was to be deported.

The system of obtaining "evidence" was applied with a vengeance. In short order the practice of having some willing British immigrants sign written requests for deportation rapidly expanded to the point where it was applied to all British subject deports. Such zeal could be troublesome: in May 1931 Division commissioners were told to have their officers return to the practice of obtaining handwritten statements from those immigrants who had asked to be sent back. They were no longer to require all those who had been reported for deportation investigations by municipal authorities or other sources to sign forms attesting to their voluntary deportations.[17] Department officials may have stopped extorting signatures; municipal officials continued the practice and applied it to more than the British immigrants. This issue would blow up in Winnipeg and other cities within a short period of time.

Other means were used by the Department to collect evidence that immigrants were volunteering to be deported. Boards of Inquiry were repeatedly instructed to have immigrants agree that they would not take a job, did not want to become established in Canada, and wanted to go home. High-level officials in the Department insisted that these instructions be carried out. They sent pointed reminders. "These instructions were issued with a definite purpose and a rather awkward situation has arisen through failure . . . to carry out the instructions," scolded one missive in November 1931.[18]

By this time Canada's deportation policy had become an Imperial issue. The British Secretary of State for External Affairs had told Bennett that not only had British public opinion been aroused by the large number of public charge deportations from Canada, but the issue would be taken up by Parliament and the press if the numbers continued high during the winter. This could be especially awkward in view of the upcoming Imperial Conference in Ottawa. The U.K. government was unhappy about the deportation of Britons for problems "beyond their control." Australia treated its British immigrant unemployed as Australians, and Britain wanted Canada to do likewise. More than ever, the Department needed evidence manufactured at Board of Inquiry hearings to "prove" that its victims wanted or deserved deportation. "I wonder if you can put your hands on any cases where Britishers or others have smashed windows or done something of that sort in order to get deported?" asked the Deputy Minister. The answer is not recorded.[19]

The Department seized on any local improvement in the labour market as evidence that immigrants who remained unemployed did so by choice. Seasonal farm jobs were golden opportunities which the Department insisted lazy immigrants threw away. Departmental officials in Ottawa urged their regional subordinates to send them examples of such stubborn refusals to give up the posh life of a reliefer. In June 1932, for example, a circular to all Immigration offices discussed the inexplicable increases in public charge deportations despite the chances for farm jobs offered by the coming of summer. Blame for continued unemployment must "to some extent be attached to the individual who is unwilling or refuses to accept what is available, as well as to labour conditions generally . . . . The Department is anxious to have definite evidence . . . where deportation is ordered solely on the public charge ground . . . which will indicate whether or not the individual concerned is prepared to accept work, or refuses to do so."[20] The implication was clear: if such evidence were lacking, it was because of the failure of the Boards of Inquiry to produce the hoped-for statements.

Some small concessions were visible, usually as a result of widespread criticism of the Department's practices. For example, some Immigration offices had been requiring recently employed immigrants to leave their jobs in order to attend their Boards of Inquiry for public charge deportation based on their previous receipt of relief. In June 1932 local offices were told that they could no longer do this unless the immigrant were undesirable for reasons in addition to previous unemployment.[21]

This was a political rather than a legal decision. The legalities were confused. The Department of Justice had ruled in 1926 that anyone who "is" or "has been" a public charge before acquiring domicile was legally liable for deportation, even if they were no longer a public charge at the time the deportation concluded. On the other hand, an April 1927 Department of Immigration memo had ruled that if someone ceased to be a public charge between the time the deportation complaint was received and the Board of Inquiry held, they were not deportable under Section 40 as a public charge. This ruling was not generally applied in the early 1930s; the tendency was to follow the older Justice ruling. In 1933 the Department of Justice ruled that if a family received relief for a brief period and subsequently became self-supporting and paid it back, they probably should not be deported as public charges.[22] This ruling would not have greatly affected deportations, because few families would go on relief (or, for that matter, be granted it) if they had any other resources. Few could hope to remain only briefly on relief, find work paying enough to repay it, and thus escape liability to public charge deportation.

In practice, going on relief usually meant a one-way ticket home for single or family immigrants. In some cases, family ties to a reliefer were sufficient grounds for deportation. For example, if a husband were ordered deported, his wife and children were usually included in the order, whether or not they were living apart from him. In many cases, Canadian-born children who were not legally deportable were sent along as "accompanying" rather than being listed on the order. Even if the wife were self-supporting, her legal ties to the husband might be sufficient grounds to include her in the deportation order. Admittedly she might not actually be sent with him when the time came. It depended on individual circumstances, and on the discretion of the Department.[23]

The municipalities were essential partners in the enterprise of "shovelling out" the unemployed. Public charge deportations were initiated at the request of municipal officials. Most cities were eager to remove reliefers. On the other hand, elected officials had to pay some attention to public opinion. By 1932 the situation was desperate in many Canadian cities. In Sudbury, for example, the city was running out of money. In the spring of 1932, Sudbury City Council had asked Immigration officials to deport all undesirables. By the end of that year, the definition of undesirability must have expanded somewhat. The city was spending $1,700 daily on relief: $5 a week in food vouchers for a family of two adults and four children. City Council had initiated money-saving measures. Civic workers' wages were cut and their hours reduced to three weeks per month for married, one week for single. Notices were placed in newspapers that a year's residence was required for relief eligibility. Couples married less than six months were ineligible. Property owners receiving relief had a lien placed against their property. Reliefers who were residents elsewhere were cut off and sent back home. Some reliefers were sent directly overseas to get them off relief: one family was sent back to Norway. Deportation was even better: someone else would pay the shipping costs. Council told the municipal relief committee to compile lists of all non-citizen reliefers so that they could be considered for deportation.[24]

Routine reporting for deportation of all immigrants who had become public charges was the rule in a number of cities. In Montreal, for instance, there was much unemployment, resources were scarce, and relief hard to get. Large numbers of immigrants were reported destitute and on the verge of starvation. The City reported them to the Montreal Immigration Office for deportation. The local agent said that the office was "filled daily" with public charge immigrants who had been ordered deported, and who wanted to know what would happen to them. He said that they seemed to him to be eager to work, and regarded deportation as a last resort. Edmonton likewise reported all immigrants on relief. The Oshawa City Council had passed a similar policy. In Sault Ste. Marie, immigrants had to sign a request to be deported, before they could obtain relief.[25]

Traditionally a gathering point for the unemployed, Winnipeg was particularly hard hit. By 1932, Winnipeg's percentage of unemployed was the second highest in Canada. Since 1930, the city had been borrowing to pay its relief costs. In June 1930 the Winnipeg City Council passed a motion to deport all immigrants who were public charges.[26] Council was always on the lookout for ways to cut costs or find more money. Councillors seemed unaware of the human costs of such measures. But after a few years of the Depression, some Councillors began to evince a different attitude.

In June 1930 there had been no dissent to the motion to deport all public charge immigrants; in fact it was initiated by two pro-labour Councillors. But by January 1932, a request by the City of Montreal to join in a scheme for "voluntary repatriation to their native lands" of all unemployed aliens was only narrowly passed (nine "yes", eight "no" votes).[27] Later that year, deportation was to become a contentious issue in Winnipeg municipal politics.

The reaction of the City of Winnipeg to the deportation issue illustrates several significant factors: the point of view of the municipalities; the development of deportation into an issue in civic politics (both partisan and across party lines); the roles of elected city officials (as opposed to city bureaucrats) in deportation; the legal and political ramifications for the municipalities and the federal government of the Immigration Act provision for city officials to report public charge deportation complaints;

the response of civic officials to public outrage (and to a certain extent their own) when the facts were revealed about their complicity in the policy of "shovelling out" the unemployed.

In the absence of studies of other municipalities it is unclear to what extent the situation in Winnipeg was representative. In terms of the local arena, certain tentative conclusions can be drawn. It seems evident that most members of Winnipeg City Council did not know in 1932 that their own City Relief Department was forcing immigrants to sign deportation requests in order to obtain relief. Nor did Councillors know the extent of relief deportations, that is, that the Relief Department was routinely reporting for deportation all those who went on relief after less than five years in Canada. This ignorance was reinforced by the lies about procedures and policies told early in 1932 by Fraser, the Director of the Relief Department. It was not until late 1932 or early 1933 that sufficient evidence had accumulated to convince the majority of Councillors that improprieties and injustices were the norm rather than being caused by oversights, happenstance, and exceptions to the rule.

In Winnipeg it was for the most part the Labour rather than the Citizens faction on City Council who questioned deportation practices. Ed Rea has noted that Winnipeg politics have operated along class lines drawn in the 1919 strike. Winnipeg City Council has long been split between the descendants of pro-striker (Labour) and anti-striker (Citizens) factions. (Although Council's positions on deportation did not always follow the usual patterns, Rea's analysis remains helpful.)[28] The Citizens representatives, who were the budget-conscious spokespersons for the Winnipeg political and economic powers-that-be, were only briefly recruited to the anti-deportation side. They were likely drawn there by dismay that British principles of fair play and justice had been betrayed, and the shrewd calculation that it was politically unsound to support a practice widely regarded as morally reprehensible and possibly legally questionable. What none of the Councillors realized was that British justice and fair play had no part in the deportation system, Depression or no. After the mists cleared from their eyes, Councillors found themselves blackmailed by the Department of Immigration. Mounting relief costs and pleas from a few immigrants to be deported, combined with Ottawa's blockade on all public charge deportations (as opposed to the unemployed public charge deportations to which Councillors had objected) eventually led to sober second thoughts about their refusal to report reliefers for deportation. After seven months of standoff, a morally and politically palatable compromise was developed. Desirable unemployed immigrants would be safeguarded and not reported for deportation; the "unfit" would be liable to deportation without their consent. Council got itself off the hook with this policy and the deportation machinery was set into motion again.

Deportation became a public issue when early in 1932, Winnipeg began to cut off relief for some people. There were public protests not only about access to relief but about deportation of reliefers. In February a large demonstration in front of the Legislature complained that one W. Musali had been cut off relief because he "refused to sign for voluntary deportation."[29] Other demonstrations protested wholesale deportation of the unemployed. City Council began to look more closely at the relationship between relief and deportation.

Shortly after these demonstrations a Labour Councillor moved that the Unemployment Relief Committee should not report for deportation those immigrants who were on relief solely because of unemployment (unless they had asked to be deported). A Citizens Councillor countered with a motion to tell the Unemployment Relief Committee to request the deportation of all those eligible. The heated debate which followed posed the argument that the deportation of the law-abiding unemployed was "unhuman", against the fear that Winnipeg would become a relief haven. Eventually the matter was turned over to the Committee to consider. The debate revealed splits on Council over the deportation issue. More importantly, it revealed that Councillors had little information about the actual deportation practices of the city. Some Councillors were beginning to wonder if there were not something wrong with the situation. Indeed there was. At this time, Manitoba's per capita deportation rate was higher than Ontario's, which deported the greatest number of immigrants during the Depression.[30]

Winnipeg City Council was drawn more directly into the issue in June 1932 when the Consuls of Germany, Sweden, Hungary, Norway, Poland, and Denmark wrote wanting to know why so many of their nationals had been deported as public charges. They asked three questions: 1) What city regulations provided that immigrants resident more than twelve months were deportable for being on relief due solely to unemployment? 2) What were the regulations for those resident longer than twelve months? 3) Many of their nationals had appealed deportation, yet the Consuls had been told that Winnipeg deported only if the immigrant so requested. Was there a city regulation that reliefers who were willing to work could be deported only voluntarily at their own request?[31]

Winnipeg City Council asked J. D. Fraser, head of the City Relief Department, and City Solicitor Preudhomme, about the city's procedures. Fraser's report (which may have been drafted by one of his staff) misrepresented the actual practices and policies of his Department. Whether or not it was Fraser who wrote the report, he sent it on to Council as his, and he continued to misrepresent his Department's practices on subsequent occasions.[32]

Fraser's memo is worth citing in detail for what it reveals about the rationale of municipal bureaucrats (as opposed to elected officials) for relief deportations. The memo stated correctly that there was no city bylaw governing deportation: the federal Immigration Act said that anyone not a citizen or domiciled (then five years' legal residence) could be deported if they became a public charge. The deportation was set in motion by complaint from municipal officials. Cases were handled ("thoroughly gone into") by Boards of Inquiry which had some discretionary powers. About the issue of voluntary deportations, he said only that the Immigration Act did not require that immigrants apply for their own deportations. Nonetheless, his Department provided a form for that purpose. "Last year we had many letters from persons on relief asking for deportation, and as a matter of convenience to them and for the purpose of having a uniform application form for deportation, the present form in use was adopted." Fraser did not mention that it was not necessary to apply for deportation to be sent back. The city often paid for all or part of the trip in order to remove people from the relief rolls. There are numerous such examples in the minutes of the Unemployment Relief Committee.

Fraser's memo concluded with a statement that was blatantly misleading. "The City of Winnipeg does not propose deportation other than in cases where the same has been voluntarily asked for except in exceptional cases, and then only for good cause." The Relief Department had "no fixed rules or regulations" on deportation. When an "application for deportation" was received, the Department obtained from the "applicant" information about birth, residence, immigration, kin, and so on, to determine if they were a "bona fide resident". The information was sent on to the local Immigration officer, who would decide the next step. The "applicant" could have legal counsel at the deportation hearing. Unless Immigration asked for further information (such as a change of address or the "amount of relief . . . obtained from" the city), Fraser concluded, his Department had no further interest in the case.[33] This memo reveals what Councillors knew officially about the deportation practices of the city.

City Solicitor Preudhomme's memo to Council was similarly detailed, legalistic, and repeated much of what Fraser said. Preudhomme explained that unemployment relief was managed by the Unemployment Relief Committee under the control of three levels of government. Since the city had only one-third of the seats, it was not solely responsible for the Committee's regulations and actions unless these had been separately approved by Council. Council had not passed any regulations or officially "taken any action" about deportation; it was a federal matter governed by the Immigration Act which was a Dominion statute. Moving to the city's procedures, Preudhomme discussed the record keeping practices of the Relief Department. Obviously he had been talking to Fraser or a member of Fraser's staff.

> The form which is being used by the Unemployment Relief Committee is something which, I take it, has been adopted purely for keeping on record the fact that individuals making voluntary applications to be deported have done so to the Unemployment Relief Committee, so that this committee can have on record the names of persons who have been on relief and should be on the nominal roll of the Committee and may in consequence or deportation be removed therefrom. I can see no other reason for the matter going through the Unemployment Relief Committee.[34]

Preudhomme apparently understood little about the procedures used in deportation. He was also confused about the difference between the Relief Department and the Unemployment Relief Committee. The latter was dominated in numbers by Council members but in practice and policy by the provincial representative, Public Works Deputy Minister Arthur MacNamara. The sole federal representative seldom interfered, although he did occasionally find some federal money. The committee in fact did not oversee all deportation cases. Moreover, it seems likely from the records that the Committee was not aware of the specific procedures used by the Relief Department. The Committee did hear appeals from people who were refused relief, wanted reinstatement or, infrequently, requested deportation proceedings be halted. There is no evidence in the minutes, however, that the Committee's knowledge went beyond the tip of the iceberg. After 1932, Fraser was the Secretary of the Committee, and would have had control over how much and in what form information reached the Committee, which in turn was dependent on Fraser for information about the concerns of the Relief Department. There were frequent complaints about Fraser, his staff, and his methods, but most of these were dismissed after superficial investigation. Despite occasional and usually veiled criticism of Fraser by Committee members and others, he easily retained control of his Department and had virtually unchallenged power over relief matters during the 1930s and beyond.[35]

On the basis of memos received from Fraser and Preudhomme, Council told Preudhomme to draft a letter to the Consuls. The letter was quite misleading, but is useful for what it shows about the city's official views on deportation (assuming that Preudhomme's statements were sincere). Under the British North America Act, he said, the City of Winnipeg had "no power to propose deportation on any grounds; but of course, if any resident appeals to the officials of the city to be voluntarily deported, then the only thing the City Official can do is to submit the appeal to the proper authorities of the Dominion Government." Preudhomme repeated Fraser's version of the procedures followed by the Relief Department, and his own description of the structure of the Unemployment Relief Committee and the city's consequent lack of responsibility for the Committee's actions and policies. In any case, he concluded, misleadingly, "the Unemployment Relief Committee cannot take any effective actions towards deportation. The matter is an entirely Dominion matter . . . the City does not propose deportation and cannot decide on what grounds deportation will be ordered."[36]

Both Fraser and Preudhomme had mentioned "forms". Anyone applying for relief had to fill out numerous forms. They had to record the length of residence in Canada and in Winnipeg. Immigrants eligible for deportation could easily be identified. When Council found out more about deportation, it would oppose collecting such information. City officials elsewhere had already balked (in Toronto in March 1931, for example), but such obstreperousness usually came to naught. There were other forms to be completed when applying for relief, about which Council was informed; for example, a form promising to repay any relief money granted on penalty of seizure of property. Council had passed a motion to authorize this policy shortly after learning that the 1931 relief bill was $2,408,474 (of which $788,728 was paid by the federal government).[37]

Council did not know that the Relief Department was also forcing immigrants to sign a form requesting deportation, as a condition to obtain relief.[38] Other city officials outside the Relief Department probably did not know of this, either. The strongest evidence for this ignorance is provided by Preudhomme's fury when he found out about this practice.

Sometime in January 1933, Preudhomme came across documents showing that the Relief Department had forced reliefers to sign a voluntary deportation form. The Department had been using these forms to extort repayment of relief: pay up or be deported, in effect. As well, the form was used to initiate deportations. In the cases which came to Preudhomme's attention, the Relief Department had asked the Department of Immigration to suspend deportation proceedings against two immigrants who had begun to repay the money that they had received in relief. Preudhomme was furious. He exploded (in a letter marked *Confidential*) to Fraser,

> It is very startling to see that this contract was made, and perhaps some of the aldermen would be astounded to know that the facts as set forth in this contract have occurred. This question of deportation has come upon the floor of the council on several occasions and charges have been made and denied that the Unemployment Relief Department has taken any action whatsoever in deportation proceedings. The agreement in the very first recital states that the Unemployment Relief Department is "minded and disposed to enter a stay of action in the deportation proceedings" . . . clearly indicating that the city of Winnipeg did take proceedings for deportation and was in a position to stay these proceedings . . . .[39]

Preudhomme warned Fraser against continuing the practice and advised that the Unemployment Relief Committee (which he presumed had directed Fraser – an assumption not wholly supported by the records) should be guided by policy established by Council. Preudhomme sent copies of the letter to the City Clerk and to Councillor Andrews who was Chair of the Unemployment Relief Committee.

There is no evidence in Council or Committee records that Councillors or Committee members saw the letter or knew the complete details of the situation. The Committee did discuss the two cases to which Preudhomme referred, and decided to press for repayment without legal action, but the issue appears in the minutes as a routine and brief matter. There is no hint of controversy, no hint that the issue raised questions beyond how to collect relief repayments from these two individuals. Fraser, as Secretary, wrote the minutes; he probably also prepared the agenda and presented the matter as he thought wise. There is no evidence that anyone but Fraser saw Preudhomme's letter (City Clerk records are missing; Council records contain no comment at all). The absence of a recorded reaction to the letter suggests that no one on Council was shown it by Andrews, who must himself have seen it unless his copy was directed to the Committee. In that case Fraser might have opened it. The City Clerk's copy is probably the only one existing in the files.[40]

The issue of deportation arose in Council two months after Preudhomme's angry letter was written. Why, and why then? Crucial documents are missing, existing records reveal little. Did members of Council or those on the Unemployment Relief Committee hear privately of Preudhomme's letter? Did the Labour group (which had three seats on the Committee in 1933) hear about it from Preudhomme, or Andrews, or some other source in the City Clerk's office? Or was it simply that the stories told by frightened immigrants or occasionally reported by the press added up to a pattern that could no longer be explained away as exceptional instances of unfairness or injustice?

A precipitating factor was certainly the flood of deportation complaints sent by the Relief Department to the Winnipeg Immigration office in the spring of 1933, to remove many reliefers who were about to gain domicile. Councillors heard stories about these people, and some decided injustices were occurring. Councillor Andrews, head of the Unemployment Relief Committee, had come back from a national conference on unemployment spouting spurious statistics created by the Department of Immigration to conceal its actions in "shovelling out" the unemployed. Andrews denied that deportation was being abused. He repeated Ottawa's claim that 2,153 out of 5,532 public charge deportation cases between 1 November 1931 and 31 October 1932 had requested deportation, and only six per cent of all immigrants ordered deported had appealed (fifteen per cent of the "foreign-born" or non-British immigrants).[41]

Such claims were no longer believed by leftwing Councillors from immigrant wards who were being "beseiged" by people under orders of deportation. The issue came to a head in June 1933 when over 1,000 people marched on the Winnipeg Immigration office in a demonstration organized by the Canadian Labour Defense League, the Neighbourhood Council Movement, the Unemployed Ex-Servicemen's Association, and the Committee of the Single Unemployed. The group protested the city's practice of forcing the unemployed immigrants to sign voluntary deportation request forms before receiving relief, and demanded that the Department of Immigration put an end to this practice.[42]

When the local Immigration official sent the protest to his superiors in Ottawa, they denied that such a practice was in force. The Winnipeg man called on the Relief Department and got a copy of the form in question (the same form Preudhomme had enclosed in his angry letter to Fraser), as well as an admission that the form had been ''in general use'' through 1932. He also got a string of limp excuses: it was only for those who wanted to be deported, and anyway it was no longer used and the man (not identified) who had put it into use was no longer with the Relief Department.[43]

It is possible that the local Immigration officer had been unaware of some of the procedures followed by the Relief Department. He continued to check out the legality of Relief practices in his correspondence with Ottawa. For example, he wrote asking if a promise to repay ''on demand'' the full amount of relief received (which relief recipients had been forced to agree to, since January 1932) were a legal promissory note. Was the person signing such a promise legally deportable for failure to honour it? The reply of Immigration officials in Ottawa is not recorded. Nonetheless, reneging on such an agreement could be construed as evidence of undesirability. Preudhomme had said that such agreements were illegal and unenforceable as contracts, and that the Relief Department had no authority to enter into or act upon them. Yet it is clear that the Relief Department, and the Hospital Commission, and possibly other city bodies, were routinely using such agreements extralegally to blackmail immigrants into repaying, by threatening them with deportation.[44]

By the fall of 1933, the Immigration official in Winnipeg had pieced together enough information from gossip, hard luck stories, and press reports to make some shrewd guesses at what had been going on behind the scenes in municipal politics over the last few months. He thought the Relief Department had been trying to use the Department of Immigration as a buffer between itself and some of the City Councillors. Pressure from some Councillors opposing deportation had caused the Relief Department to refrain temporarily from its usual practice of sending over deportation complaints for all immigrants on relief. By the spring of 1933, the Relief Department had a backlog of immigrants who were about to acquire domicile. Delay was impossible: the Relief Department sent over a long list, the stories became public, and hence the uproar.[45]

By December, deportation scandals were featured in the local press. City Councillors began to give names; for example, four Britishers who had been in Canada nearly five years, were told that they were going to be deported because they were on relief. None had committed any other offence. The Winnipeg Immigration officer fanned the flames by telling the press that no one was ever deported solely for being on relief. He labelled as "fantastic" the charge that the Department of Immigration wanted to deport all reliefers, and claimed that in only five per cent of cases was deportation actually carried out. In any case, he said, deportation originated in written complaints from the city. His Department only carried out deportation, it did not initiate it.[46]

Such claims about suspended deportations can only be regarded with skepticism. Figures are not available on the actual number of suspended public charge deportations, but the Department claimed to have suspended (that is, ordered but not carried out) fourteen per cent of cases for 1932-33. The memo in which this claim was made, however, contains a number of demonstrably false statements, so the figure is not reliable. It may be based in part on deportations which were never completely processed and ordered. For example, in the spring of 1932, the Winnipeg office reported that if an immigrant who had received only a small sum of relief got a job and got off relief, the office usually suspended deportation proceedings. According to other documents it was not until several months later that the Department began routinely to suspend some British public charge deportations.[47] The claim that ninety-five per cent of public charge deportations were suspended is simply ludicrous.

All of this erupted in a tumultuous City Council meeting in mid-December 1933. There were three issues: the deportation policies of the Department of Immigration; the practices of city officials; and the legal position of the city in regard to deportation. The crux of the first issue was whether or not the Department of Immigration was routinely deporting otherwise desirable immigrants who had gone on relief solely because of unemployment. Debate on this question became so heated that the second and third issues were not much discussed. At the outset, some Councillors reiterated the Department of Immigration's oft-repeated claim that it did not deport people merely for being on relief. McKerchar, dubbed "watchdog of the treasury", piously reminded his colleagues that Mayor Webb had said "again and again that no one was being deported for being on relief alone." Such statements rang hollow in the face of mounting evidence to the contrary.

Thirteen people on unemployment relief had come to Councillor Flye for help: they were being "badgered and harried" and had been ordered deported. J. S. Woodsworth had confirmed to Flye that such cases were common, and that other municipalities were pushing for deportation. Flye spoke of one Winnipeg family he knew who had gone off relief after being threatened with deportation, and were being kept from starvation by the charity of neighbours, until their five years were up and they would be safe from deportation. Blumberg told his colleagues about an English family who had been in Canada for four-and-a-half years. They had arrived with $5,000 in cash, but had gradually been forced to use up their capital, and eventually had to seek partial relief. They had been ordered deported. The family was devastated, the wife "nearly crazy with worry." Blumberg insisted that it was not an unusual case, and that people in such circumstances were often "driven to desperation." The example of this family showed why relief deportations had to be stopped, he said.[48] Other Labour Councillors added to the evidence.

Such accounts may have swayed skeptics on Council. Their skepticism began to turn to shock, and finally to outrage, when irrefutable documentary evidence was presented. Flye passed around a sheaf of Department of Immigration documents and correspondence given to him by people appealing for help. Simpson read out an actual deportation order. Councillors began to react. Lowe said that he now believed that it was true that the Department of Immigration was trying to send out as many of the unemployed as possible; this was a "blot on the good sense of Canada and the officials responsible for a policy of this kind." Lowe's reaction is not surprizing; he was an Independent Labour representative who usually sided with the left on Council, who were leading the attack on deportation. But Lowe's moral outrage was echoed by other less likely allies. Rice-Jones, who probably spoke for a number of the Citizens faction, expressed "alarm" over injustices, saying that the policy was "almost incredible"; he could not understand "how any government could get away with that policy!"

The outcome of the discussion was twofold: first, a demand that the Minister of Immigration declare publicly that nobody would be deported solely for being on relief. Second, the Council would try a course of "passive resistance." This position was not unanimous, nor easily reached. Originally, Flye and Lowe had wanted Council to tell Immigration to stop proceedings in all cases where no criminal charges were involved. Councillors Andrews and Gunn, concerned with possible legal consequences of a refusal to report deportable immigrants to the Department of Immigration, wanted some reassurances. It was their idea to ask the Minister to make a public statement on Department policy; they also wanted to ask him to relieve the city of its legal obligation to report. Their proposal passed only when Acting Mayor McKerchar broke the tie by voting with them. (The split was along predictable class lines.) Next, Council agreed without much heat to tell the Unemployment Relief Committee to eliminate from their relief forms any questions on length of residence in Canada. Similarly smooth in passage was a motion that Council was opposed to deportation of reliefers with no other charge against them.[49]

Local evidence based on direct testimony from people ordered deported strongly contradicted official statements from Ottawa. By Christmas 1933 the Department of Immigration had been claiming to whomever would listen that between 1 November 1931 and 21 August 1933, 48 per cent of British and 28 per cent of foreign-born deports had "applied for deportation . . . [and] during the Board of Inquiry, a further 43 per cent of British and 56 per cent of foreign-born" had asked to be sent home. In the calendar years 1932 and 1933, a total of 8,758 persons were deported as public charges, and hundreds more not counted in the official figures were sent back as "accompanying persons". In this same period deportation for other causes brought the total deported up to 12,785 with 1,130 accompanying persons. Of these, 7,586 deports were British (59 per cent).[50]

In a similar statement, the Department claimed that in 1932-33, of the 8,758 public charge deportations, 41 per cent of the people said that they wanted to go home, 23 per cent refused to consider further employment, 8 per cent demanded impossible wages. In a very considerable proportion of public charge cases, the Department said, these individuals had been admitted to Canada to do agricultural work, but many had worked only briefly on farms, then had gone to the cities for industrial work. Others had never worked on a farm at all. "In a number of these cases . . . the men were anxious to join their dependents" at home and glad to be deported.[51]

Internal documents of the Department leave no doubt that these statistics were unreliable, misleading, and sometimes patently untrue. These figures were derived from charts with such headings as "desire for deportation expressed", or "desire for deportation not expressed"; "applied to be deported", "refused to consider employment", "demanded impossible wages or working conditions", "illness", "anticipated employment in native country". They also tabulated "appeal dismissed" and "would consider employment but did not appeal".[52]

Spurious deportation requests were produced by various methods: words of testimony before Boards of Inquiry were twisted; immigrants were forced by municipalities to sign deportation requests. There were manipulative questions asked at Boards. Immigrants who had been assured that they would be deported were asked if they looked forward to seeing their families and friends; if they agreed, the response was counted as a request to be deported or a desire to go home. The Department included numbers of those who "did not appeal" in its voluntary deportation figures. Similarly, if during the Board of Inquiry immigrants made any statements indicating a lack of enthusiasm for a specific job or work experience (such as saying they preferred an industrial job they once had, to farm work, because the former paid better) or a field of work, or even if they expressed discouragement about their ability to find a job, the Department made use of such statements in their statistics showing that public charge deports were unemployable, unwilling, or undesirable. There are cases on record where the Department stated in its memo on the appeal that the immigrant had refused farm work, when in fact the Board of Inquiry transcript showed the opposite.[53]

Labour Councillors in Winnipeg had reached much the same conclusion. After the New Year they served notice that they were not going to let the deportation issue rest. They presented further information about federal deportation policy and practices, and pressed for action. The local Immigration officer took note of this and wrote to Ottawa suggesting relief cases no longer be processed. If the policy was in truth not to deport immigrants on relief because of unemployment, as Ottawa had been claiming, then those deported as public charges were labelled as undesirable without ever being charged or examined as such, he pointed out. Such cases, even if suspended, were politically dangerous; people treated like this became "centres of propaganda very unfavourable to Government."[54]

Ottawa did nothing. Council had to act. Public opinion had been aroused by hard luck stories of struggling, respectable families. The press raised embarrassing questions about the deportation of the unemployed, about the Relief Department and its Director, and the responsibility for and substance of orders under which he may have been acting. The increasing ire of the respectable lent weight to that of the radicals, the unemployed, and the "foreigners". As well, the new Council had equal numbers of Citizens and Labour representatives, with the election of Jake Penner for the Workers Unity League.[55]

At the end of January 1934 Council decided that unless they were officially notified that they must do so, the City would cease to report for deportation any cases of public charge solely because of unemployment. Locally, the decision was applauded. The *Tribune* spoke of the previous policy of automatic reporting and deportation of the unemployed as an abuse and misapplication of the deportation clause in the Immigration Act, and expressed particular concern that nearly ninety per cent of the relief deportations of the last few years had been British immigrants. (In fact, automatic public charge deportations were perfectly in accord with the provisions of the Act, but few people outside the Department of Immigration ever understood that.)[56]

The response from the Department of Immigration expressed concern over potential bureaucratic difficulties, irritation at the persistence of the issue, and a determination that the Winnipeg City Council be given enough rope to hang itself. The federal Department of Immigration gave Council what it had asked for. Commissioner of Immigration Jolliffe wrote from Ottawa that he and the Minister had agreed to discontinue all proceedings; he would not order the city to report relief recipients. In fact, no public charge deportations would be undertaken from Winnipeg.[57] In effect, Winnipeg was to be starved out.

The standoff was by now part of a national issue. Were municipalities required by law to report public charge immigrants to Ottawa? Technically the answer was yes, but the situation was confused by Ottawa's tactics of playing off the municipalities against interest groups. For example, the Canadian Legion had protested to the Department that many municipalities had been threatening veterans with deportation. The Minister of Immigration wrote back denying that veterans had to worry about this. Even if municipalities had been threatening veterans, it was Ottawa, not the municipalities, that had the power to decide who would and would not be deported.[58]

The issue was raised in Parliament. Winnipeg M.P. Abraham Heaps suggested in the Commons that it be optional for municipalities to report, pointing out that the legislation had been framed "before the war, when unemployment was a social crime in the land." But Minister of Immigration Wesley Gordon opposed the proposal, claiming that he reviewed all cases and did not authorize deportation until he was satisfied that the individual could not find gainful employment.

There is much evidence that Gordon's statement that he reviewed all cases was a lie. A 1936 memo described the situation clearly. Under the Immigration Act the Minister was responsible for dealing personally with all appeals, while the Deputy Minister was responsible for issuing warrants and so on. These duties were statutory and could not be delegated (except to an Acting Minister or Acting Deputy Minister). Because of the heavy workload, "it has been the practice for years" for the Deputy Minister to deal with "most" of the appeals. The courts had decided that this practice was invalid (the memo cited several decisions). Immigrants had been released on these grounds by the courts. The Department of Justice concurred with this view and had told Immigration that the Minister must personally review cases as provided by law. As an alternative, Blair (who in 1936 became Director, with Deputy Minister status) had proposed that the Minister would be given only those cases where the Departmental officials recommended that the appeals be refused. In other words, even after strong recommendations that blatant illegalities cease, the Department continued these practices.[59] Other documents make it amply clear that even if it were physically possible for the Minister to review all cases (and it was not), it was not the policy of the Department that he should do so.

Gordon's argument against optional reporting by the municipalities rested on more than his spurious claim that he personally prevented abuses. He argued that it would create a situation in which the law would not be equally and consistently enforced throughout the country. "Control would be transferred from the federal to the municipal" level of government, which was contrary to immigration law and policy. Apparently preferring to see the law flouted rather than changed, Gordon softened his stand by saying that no municipality in Canada was now reporting all its cases of immigrants on relief. Of course this statement raised questions about the motivations and actions of the municipalities. As *Saturday Night* tartly pointed out, if municipalities now reported selectively, civic authorities were actually using discretion, while hiding behind the compulsory reporting clauses and "using the statute as an axe over the heads of unfortunate non-citizens."[60]

The freeze on deportation from Winnipeg meant that the city could not remove any immigrant who had become a public charge. Deportations had stemmed from four sources of complaints. The Municipal Hospital

Commission reported cases where immigrants had unpaid bills for medical treatment or had become inmates of asylums and other institutions at public cost. In theory, these cases could be deported for medical reasons, but public charge deportations were simpler to carry out if the immigrant had been here less than five years. For medical deportations it was usually necessary to prove that the conditions had existed at entry, and that required more documentation and effort than deportation as a public charge. The second source was the Social Welfare Commission which dealt with relief for the unemployable. These were safe targets. In the thick of defending itself over deporting the employable unemployed, the Department claimed that it deported only the unemployable. Few would challenge immigration policy aimed at acquiring settlers able to contribute to the country. The unemployable might be so through no fault of their own, but there was little protest against their deportation. The third and fourth sources of complaints were the Unemployment Relief Committee and the Relief Department, in charge of relief for the employable unemployed. Official records do not indicate the proportions of deportations initiated by each of these sources, but evidence suggests that the Relief Department (unbeknownst to city officials, or at least to Council) was responsible for the bulk of them.[61]

City Council's manoeuvre boomeranged. Council had been reacting to wholesale deportation of the unemployed over which it had little control. It was not necessarily opposed to deportation of the unfit or unemployable. Nor was it opposed to legitimate voluntary deportation cases. By the end of March 1934 a few immigrants on relief had appealed to be deported. The Unemployment Relief Committee or Social Welfare Commission were willing to agree to the requests, but the Council's January decision (and Ottawa's reaction) meant that their "hands are tied," they complained. Council tried another ploy. It authorized Mrs. Stewart-Hay, a social worker formerly the Secretary of the Unemployment Relief Committee, now with Social Welfare, to act as an official City Relief Officer and report to the Immigration authorities all legitimate voluntary deportation cases.[62]

Ottawa refused to act on the complaints. Council tried other tactics. Minnie Watt was a test case. A twenty-eight-year old Scot, she had immigrated in 1929 under the Empire Settlement Act. A linen factory and restaurant worker in Scotland, she had worked in hospital and school laundries in Winnipeg until she became unemployed in June 1933. Soon thereafter she went on relief. Her family had found her a job at home. Officials of the Women's Division of the City Relief Department and on

City Council supported her request. Mrs. Stewart-Hay asked Immigration to arrange Watt's "repatriation".

She was rebuffed. The Department did not "repatriate"; it deported. The transportation companies had to pay for deportations of defective immigrants whom they had brought over, and they would not pay for repatriation. Moreover, the Winnipeg office could not deport Watt because Ottawa had ordered that there be no public charge deportations from Winnipeg. If City Council wanted to reconsider its motion, said the Winnipeg Commissioner, perhaps he would be in a position to act.[63]

Council reconsidered, led by Citizens representatives. A motion for rescinding was defeated. It had been supported by five of the Citizens, but opposed by all the Labour Councillors, augmented by four from the Citizens side. The impasse continued until it was broken by a compromise in July 1934. Carefully selected deportations would be initiated in "isolated cases" by the Unemployment Relief Committee, the Social Welfare Commission, and the Municipal Hospital Commission. The Relief Department was specifically forbidden to initiate complaints unless told to do so by the Unemployment Relief Committee.[64]

After a bit of procedural housekeeping over the next few weeks, the deportation machinery again began to operate. It appears that Council kept a closer watch on the system. Certainly those who sat on the Unemployment Relief Committee did so. They required a written request for deportation before they would hear such cases; they had to be satisfied that the person truly wished to be deported. Individuals usually appeared in person before the Committee. If the Committee were not sure, they investigated.[65]

Not everyone on Council was satisfied with the procedures. There were some attempts by Labour members to make further changes, all of which came to naught. Nonetheless, from August 1934 onwards, Ottawa resumed public charge deportations from Winnipeg. The city's surrender was timely; belt-tightening was in order. In September the city cut off relief to 500 families and 1,600 single men (most of whom were Central Europeans) who had arrived in Canada after 1 January 1929.[66]

Winnipeg City Councillors had been shocked by the procedures of deportation and by the cost in human unhappiness of "shovelling out" the unemployed. If they had known more about the day-to-day realities of the experience of deportation, they would have been horrified, as would have been most Canadians. Despite initial fears expressed by the Department that lazy immigrants would use deportation as a free trip home, deportation was no picnic. As larger numbers of deports over-whelmed the system, conditions which had always been unpleasant became abominable. For example, a trainload of deports sent in January 1933 from central Canada to Halifax complained that the food on the train consisted of sandwiches; they were not given clean blankets; they were not allowed to move freely about the train. They criticized the deten-tion centres: clean sheets, pillowcases and blankets should be provided; Board of Health limits on numbers of children per room should be observed; families should not be separated; the rooms should be clean and sanitary; there should be suitable food for babies and small children (instead of pork and beans); all food should be hygienically prepared; the mentally ill and handicapped should be segregated from other inmates; guards should be cleaner in their appearance and habits and more civil to inmates; there should be no alcohol permitted on duty. These complaints were dis-missed by the Department of Immigration as the work of communists.[67]

In fact, there was good reason for complaints such as these. Departmental files reveal that conditions were rarely good at deportation facilities. By 1932 they had deteriorated until they were disgraceful. The main centre was at Montreal, where immigrants "of all classes and conditions, deports being collected from all over Canada and sent . . . for either embarkation or for transmission to the port of embarkation" were gathered and held.[68] The Montreal Detention Hospital, which was primarily a prison, had been a main deport clearing house since 1907, and for most of those years had been plagued by understaffing, over-crowding, and inadequate facilities. As deportation increased each year (except during the war, but then Montreal was overcrowded with long-term detentions and prisoners of war held for the Militia) the building deteriorated. By the late 1920s there were serious problems.

They ranged from breaches of propriety to dangers to health. There were "nasty declarations" written on the walls of rooms used to hold families and children. It took nearly two months of complaints and a personal visit by a shocked Deputy Minister (who said of the writers "it is a wonder such people are allowed to live") to have them painted over. There was severe overcrowding and frequently more bodies than beds. People slept on mattresses on the floor. There were not enough rooms for families, so men and women were put in one big room; a curtain segregated male and female sleeping quarters. ("Mothers and daughters are amply protected" the Division Commissioner assured his superior after a press exposé.)[69]

There was no way for inmates to have fresh air or exercise, and there was nothing to do all day. They were often kept locked up inside. On at least one occasion seventy people were locked into a dayroom meant for a much smaller number. Verandahs formerly used in warm weather were now forbidden because the floors were rotten and iron bars loose; prisoners escaped, or indecently exposed themselves to passers-by. Only patchwork repairs were authorized: Immigration simply ordered the staff at Montreal to "exercise proper supervision" to prevent such incidents. Perhaps it was to prevent escapes that fire escapes were kept locked. Although it was called a Detention Hospital, medical facilities were inadequate. The doctor's examining room was too cold in winter to carry out proper examinations. If he opened a window for ventilation while examining a tuberculosis case, he could not raise the temperature above 50 degrees Fahrenheit. There had always been something wrong with the heating system. To warm up the doctor's room to 60-65 degrees, the rest of the building would be at 75-80 degrees. There was no proper segregation of the inmates with contagious diseases during the 1930s. Immigrants with tuberculosis or venereal disease, or other illnesses, were mixed with those who were insane, convicted criminals, or ordinary public charge cases.[70]

Things got worse. In 1932 the boiler blew up, and failed again later for six weeks during which there was no hot water, so inmates did not wash. The blankets were lousy and vermin were in plain view in the building. Nothing could be sterilized. The disinfecting machine did not work. Even when the equipment was operating properly, there were still vermin; the building, the bedding, and the inmates were infested. The Department blamed it on the deports. The staff made "every possible effort" to fumigate, the Department claimed. But in fact, their efforts consisted of telling the guards to ask inmates if they had lice; no routine measures were taken. Vermin were brought in "practically every week by deportees," was the excuse of the Division Commissioner. When it got too bad, the Department sent some long-term inmates over to a delousing service run by a City of Montreal refuge.[71]

Although Department officials admitted freely in their internal correspondence that these conditions existed and were improper, they were unwilling to take effective measures for improvement. They decided that deports would have to live with the lice: "it would be impossible and not advisable to adopt a general practice of delousing every deport held over in the building." Officials including the Deputy Minister admitted that the existing Montreal Detention Hospital was overcrowded and a danger to health for the inmates (because of filth, vermin, and lack of segregation of infectious cases). "Proper care cannot be given to detained persons." As early as July 1931 they had concluded that the old building was beyond repair and a new facility was needed. They expected deportation to increase and with it, conditions to deteriorate in the Montreal Detention Hospital. They knew criticism would continue, but expected that it would come primarily from deports. This did not pose a danger to the Department. "We can better face this than justify heavy capital expenditure at this time."[72]

Their predictions were accurate. By 1935 the Montreal Detention Hospital, still the main deport clearing house, was in a disgusting state. It was due only to the secrecy with which deportation was carried out that there was not a major scandal.[73] Luckily for the Department, most "nice" people did not concern themselves with such matters. The Department's dirty secrets were relatively safe.

Although the Department was remarkably unresponsive to criticism, there had been so much trouble over deporting British unemployed who were otherwise desirable immigrants, that by the spring of 1934 the Department was suspending "some" of these deportations. It continued to deny that it had been or was routinely deporting the desirable unemployed. In 1934, the Minister wrote to Member of Parliament Kennedy that it was not "the policy of the Department to effect deportation solely" on account of becoming a public charge because of unemployment caused by generally depressed conditions. "In all cases of deportation on public charge grounds, other factors have been present." Backpedalling behind the scenes, the Department sent out a directive in August 1934 ordering all its offices not to carry out British public charge deportations based solely on unemployment, after they had been ordered. Many of these immigrants were almost eligible for domicile, the directive explained. There were Canadian-born children in these families who could not be legally deported. The directive recalled that many of these immigrants had been regarded as highly desirable when they were recruited and screened under the Empire Settlement scheme. They were now undesirable solely on grounds of unemployment, which in the vast majority of cases was due to general economic conditions rather than individual failings. The Department felt that it was only fair that "if their unsuitability arose out of conditions over which they had no control, we keep them rather than send them back to be a charge overseas."[74]

Such a policy had long been sought by the British government. Local events were also important. The excesses of the Canadian government had led to a sizeable protest against deportation, coming not only from the poor and the radical, but from a broad spectrum including respectable sources: international craft unions, churches, the CCF, the Liberals, and increasing numbers of middle class people. The Bennett Iron Heel policy had become politically awkward. If it now seemed untenable to persecute the communists, how could it be justified to deport the otherwise unobjectionable British unemployed?

The effect of the directive to suspend British public charge deportations is unclear. For the British immigrants ordered deported as public charges, it delayed rather than eliminated deportation. Agents were told to inform such immigrants that it was "extremely unlikely" that their deportations would be carried out; they were to "try to settle successfully in Canada."[75] Such advice must have rung hollow. These people lived under a cloud: if Ottawa deported only undesirables, they were officially labelled as undesirable by the deportation order, carried out or not. As well, they lived under a sword of Damocles: deportations were suspended, not cancelled. They could be reactivated at any time for any reason.

An official policy to suspend the deportations of desirable British public charge cases did not mean that public charge deportations came to a halt. Rather, it meant a shift in the description of cases (other grounds had to be brought forward) and in the nationality of the immigrants deported. The overrepresentation of Britons among the public charge deports had long been a political problem for the Department. Relief deportations still continued. For example, a "Statement showing amounts of relief for public charges deported during the month of August 1934" (when the rate of unemployed deportations had slackened) showed the following average amounts of relief for which people were deported: to Scotland $49; Czechoslovakia $126; Finland $33; France $320; Germany $80; Lithuania $100; Poland $120; Roumania $563; Sweden $510. The average amount was $118. Although deportations continued at high levels through 1935, there were several thousand fewer than there had been in 1934. In fact the number of deportations in the fiscal year ending 1935 was smaller than in any year after 1921 (although the percentage of deports compared to numbers of immigrants over the three years previous was still higher than 1931). Public charge deportations still took place with the same intensity they had in fiscal 1930.[76]

When Thomas Crerar became the new Minister of Immigration after the July 1935 elections, Department bureaucrats had to prepare memoranda to brief him on policy and activities of his new Department. What they told him does not accord in many respects with what unpublished Department documents show to have been happening. His staff told Crerar that "over a period of three years an effort has been made to determine the attitude of individuals to deportation." The Department's research led one top official to say "I think it is quite correct to say that at least 90% of the British public charge cases dealt with wanted to go home." They told Crerar that between 1902 and 1934, 27,185 immigrants had been deported to all countries as public charges. Immigrants had become public charges for a variety of reasons: illness in the family, death of the breadwinner, unemployment, criminality, insanity, and so on. But the most important reason, especially in the last few years, had been unemployment, "sometimes due to the inability or unwillingness of the immigrant to accept or undertake the sort of work that may be available." The Immigration Act provided that immigrants who became public charges were to be deported, and this had been done until the spring of 1934 when the Department began to suspend some British public charge deportations. Later that summer, these deportations were generally suspended. The Department's practice was not consistent with the law "as it stands", they told Crerar. One of his first decisions as a Minister concerned this issue. Should the Department carry out the deportations of British immigrants who had become public charges solely because of unemployment?

The Minister's reply was consistent with the Department's claimed policy, but in opposition to its practice. British immigrants should be deported as public charges if they had been and would continue to be a serious problem in Canada, or if they were anxious to go home and had friends and relatives to go to and the municipalities were urging deportation. But the Department should distinguish between those who were public charges solely because of unemployment and had no other problems, and those who otherwise had problems such as being ill or incapacitated, he said.[77] It is clear that there was no question of suspending the deportation of non-British public charge cases. Also left open was the option to continue to claim that there were other problems than unemployment to justify public charge deportations of Britons. Crerar may have cared about what was done to the unemployed, but he was told what his subordinates wanted him to know, in the time-honoured tradition of the

Department. There was no cleanup, no new broom; merely a confirmation that the more contentious of the Department's practices should be carried out more discreetly in politically acceptable ways.

Internal documents prepared to summarize Depression deportations refute the Department's claims that it was the unfit rather than the unemployed who were "shovelled out". In a report prepared in 1935, the Department attempted to analyse the number of deportations due to illness. There were 10,805 public charge deportations between 1 November 1931 and 31 January 1935 (those accompanying not included). Only 797 of these (7.4 per cent) were listed as related to illness. For the British the illness rate was 394 of 6,684 cases (5.7 per cent); for the non-British, 403 of 3,941 (10.2 per cent). Another analysis of public charge deportations for the calendar years 1932 and 1933 showed that of a total of 8,758 cases, 622 (7 per cent) involved illness; of the 5,578 British cases, 314 were illness related (5.6 per cent), while the rate for the 3,180 non-British cases was 308 (9.6 per cent).[78] Clearly illness was not a factor in most public charge deportations. Then what was meant by unfit? Was unemployability a matter of attitude rather than physical condition? The Department's records offer no satisfactory answers to these questions.

The extent of public charge deportations was considerable. According to unpublished Department figures, between the beginning of November 1931 and the end of January 1935, the Department deported 10,805 immigrants as public charges (not including accompanying). The published statistics of the Department from the annual reports show even greater numbers. Between fiscal 1929-30 and fiscal 1934-35, a total of 17,229 public charge deportations were carried out (not including accompanying).[79] There is every indication that the vast majority of these people were simply unemployed.

A sympathetic view would have it that the Department was caught in the middle during the Depression. If it had balked at deporting the unemployed, the municipalities would have been up in arms and the provincial governments could have used the issue to pressure the federal government to assume more of the costs of relief, especially for immigrants. On the other hand, if the Department openly and admittedly "shovelled out" the unemployed in the tradition of the British poor law and its own deportation policy, public protest would have added to political pressure that the Department and federal government could ill afford to increase. The Department either had to change its practice, or change what people could find out about its practice. It chose the latter course.

It began by trying to build airtight cases for public charge deportations, and to include other grounds, such as medical grounds, when possible. It also tried to purvey the claim that it did not deport the desirable unemployed. It made this claim to the municipalities, the transportation companies, Parliament, the press, prominent individuals, the left, and the general public. Further, it tried to sell the notion that most public charge deportations were "voluntary". The evidence on which it based these claims was questionable to say the least.

The general public did not have access to this information. Nonetheless, the files did not conceal the practice of having deports sign voluntary relief forms, whether done by the municipalities or by the Department (as it was done at various times for British and other immigrants). The case that the Department tried to build for public consumption was based on statistics which could be proved fallacious only by insiders. The Department created categories of evidence which it then used to produce statistics that were more or less technically correct but gave an essentially false picture of Departmental activities.

The Department's game of passing the buck on deportation requests from the municipalities was clever; it was literally true that the Department responded to municipal requests for deportation. Yet since 1906 the municipalities had been required to report deportable immigrants. While there was little the Department could do to enforce this provision, it is also clear that since 1906 it had been the practice of the Department to seek out deports actively, using the legal provisions for municipal reporting as a crucial part of the seeking-out mechanism.

The Department tried to escape being caught between conflicting interest groups (or more accurately, tried to avoid being caught) by the device of suspending some British public charge deportations. Ordering but not carrying out deportation was supposed to stop protest and calm public opinion. It had the opposite effect in some cases. If only the undesirable were deported, then ordering a deportation was tantamount to labelling someone as undesirable without allowing them to hear or refute the charge. This was a familiar tactic, used by the Department to manage its own employees.

In public charge deportations, the Department acted arbitrarily when it could, and retreated behind the smokescreen of lies and red tape when public or interest group pressure created political repercussions.

Deportation policy and practice during the 1930s served the interests of government (federal first, municipal last), and of corporations and employers. When cheap labour became redundant labour, the Department got rid of it. There was little humanity in its policy or its managers who went about Department business relatively unremarked, unobstructed, and uncontrolled.

"Purely Administrative Proceedings"

The Department of Immigration was arbitrary in the management of deportation. Curbs on this arbitrariness were few and ineffective. As J. F. Hodgetts points out, "There is a paradox in the fact that the administrative branch of the government is by far the largest of our public and private institutions and yet, even to the informed members of the general public, it is the least visible."[1]

The Department's immigration and deportation practices were not visible to, and therefore not controllable by, outsiders. A 1940 study by legal scholar C. F. Fraser comparing deportation in the U.K., Ireland, Northern Ireland, Canada, Australia, New Zealand, and South Africa, concluded that Canadian practices were the most arbitrary. Unchecked by an apathetic judiciary, the power of Canadian officials had grown dangerously, gone beyond its legislative authority, and continued to increase.[2]

The two likeliest sources of outside control over the deportation practices of the Department were Parliament and the courts.[3] Parliament was consistently uninformed or misinformed, and judicial review was severely limited by the Immigration Act. Neither chose to test the limits set upon their sphere of inquiry. Even the recurring and sometimes protracted debates in the 1920s about the repeal of the extraordinary powers added to Section 41 in 1919, revealed massive ignorance, and almost equally massive indifference in both Houses about deportation.

The mere expediency (rather than the principle) of the law was at issue, and Ministerial responsibility was easily shrugged off. The Senate especially made it clear that it did not disapprove of arbitrary proceedings against ''agitators''.

As Fraser's study commented, ''The most notable feature of deportation cases in Canada is the apparent desire to get agitators of any sort out of the country at all costs . . . .[T]he executive branch of the government, in its haste to carry out this policy . . . displayed a marked disregard for the niceties of procedure.''[4] The Department of Immigration for many years operated a clandestine and illegal immigration policy, established by executive fiat of the Minister, without benefit of Parliamentary debate. These decisions were carried out clandestinely by Ministerial action ''on account of the desire not to mention in any Order-in-Council that one country was preferred to another.'' This course of action had been decided at a conference with the transportation companies. In 1910, the Minister had ordered the admission of immigrants from ''preferred'' countries, in violation of the Immigration Act. Discrimination against the immigrants from Southern and Eastern European countries had been in practice ''all the time,'' Deputy Minister Egan testified in 1928 to the House Committee on Agriculture and Colonization. Asked by a surprised Committee member, ''How could the Minister go behind the Order-in-Council?'', Egan replied, ''It was a practice in vogue, and he did it, and not in any isolated cases at all, but in hundreds of cases it was done all the time.''

In 1922, an amendment to the legislation established a system of admission based on occupations. The Department continued its parallel illegal policy and practices. Egan described how the Department had evaded specific provisions such as landing-money, continuous voyage, and passport technicalities established by Orders-in-Council to exclude the unwanted and ill-equipped. When attractive immigrants from ''preferred'' countries did not meet these requirements, the Department illegally ''disregard[ed] the money test sometimes, or the passport regulations, particularly in connection with the countries of Northern Europe.''

Decisions like these determined who was admitted and who was deported. As Egan testified, these particular practices had been in effect for at least eighteen years. Parliament had known nothing about this powerful extralegal system that went beyond the legislated limits and procedures of Departmental actions. In reality, these decisions had neither been made, controlled, nor implemented by Parliament.[5] Subsequent years would bring no significant increase in Parliamentary knowledge of or control over the Department's practices.

The Senate displayed a marked tolerance for contradictory and unsupported claims from those responsible for the management of deportation. Tory Senator Gideon Robertson, who as Minister of Labour had been instrumental in breaking the Winnipeg General Strike, had insisted in 1920 that the added (Section 41) powers of 1919 had been used to clean out so many dissidents that they were now superfluous. In subsequent years, others were to claim that these powers, or even the original Section had never been misused. Senator Calder, who had been Minister of Immigration in 1919, and should have known what went on in his own Department, claimed in a 1926 debate on the 1919 Winnipeg General Strike that the deportation powers of the Department were neither arbitrarily nor summarily exercised. Immigration Secretary Blair promptly assured Bruce Walker, Director of European Emigration in London, that Calder's statement was "absolutely incorrect as a matter of law and the [Immigration Act] section as it stands does exactly what Mr. Calder said no Government would do, viz. put into the hands of any Board of Inquiry, even of one person, the power to order deportation." Like their counterparts in Cabinet, Senators were often little more than mouthpieces for the Department.[6] Debates were focused on policy rather than practice, on legalisms rather than reality.

Debates in the House were only slightly more critical, and not much better informed. Even those who pressed for deportation reform were uninformed and naive about the Department's practices. For instance, Woodsworth's 1920s campaign to repeal the extended 1919 powers of Section 41 was based on the complaint that these extended powers allowed deportation for political offences without trial by jury. In fact, jury trials had never been a part of deportation proceedings. Immigrants charged with crimes might be tried by juries in the courts, but deportation proceedings were separate and apart. Criminal proceedings took place in a court of law, and the accused had recourse to certain rights and a certain protection under that law, at least in theory. Deportation proceedings were conducted by a closed administrative tribunal. The Department wanted to avoid "purely technical and unwarrantable interference by pettifogging lawyers."[7] Woodsworth and his colleagues in both Houses remained apparently unaware of such practices and perhaps of such attitudes. It was Parliament which *passed* the laws relating to deportation, but the records of the Department make it clear that Parliament neither made those laws, nor knew, nor controlled how those laws were carried out.

As for the courts, their power to intervene in deportation matters was virtually nonexistent under the Immigration Act. The Act provided that "all matters pertaining to the detention and deportation of any rejected immigrant should be dealt with by the executive and not the judicial branch of the Government," as Mr. Justice Irwing explained. The Department had been careful to preserve its immunity from interference by the courts, arguing that the rights of deports were not jeopardized by such an exclusion. If the Department exceeded the law, then the courts could intervene; that was sufficient. The Department did not deny that its powers were increasingly broad; it argued that it should be trusted with these powers. Minister Calder on 14 May 1919 wrote in this vein to the Canadian Jewish Congress: "The Act . . . undoubtedly places large discretionary powers in the hands of the executive and its administrative officers . . . . I need scarcely assure you that every effort will be made to see that these powers are exercised sanely and reasonably."[8]

Given the exclusion of the judiciary from deportation matters, there was little the deport could do when the Department not infrequently failed to follow the path of sanity and reason. C. F. Fraser's study of 121 selected cases concluded that in Canada, "The earlier cases show a casual and unintentional rather than intentional disregard for the judiciary. The later cases indicated a premeditated intent to deprive the alien . . . of his right to judicial protection."[9]

There was almost no dissent from the courts. Typical was Mr. Judge Gibson's comment that Parliament intended and provided that all such questions should be dealt with "exclusively by the machinery of the Department of Immigration . . . subject only to an appeal to the Minister, and without any powers of review or control by the courts." Section 23 of the Immigration Act said that no court has jurisdiction to review, quash, reverse, restrain, or interfere with any proceeding, decision, or order of the Minister, Board of Inquiry, or Officer-in-Charge, concerning detention or deportation, "upon any ground whatsoever," except in the case of Canadian citizens or domiciled immigrants. He argued against the use of certiorari: the courts could not interfere with Boards of Inquiry even in cases of misunderstanding or misinterpretation of the law or regulations, or of illegal evidence, error, informality, or omission, "which may fairly be classed as a matter of procedure, or of departmental regulation."[10]

Such a position was not unusual; Canadian courts on the whole acquiesced to the informal and extralegal system of justice operated by the Department. As long as the Department was not caught exceeding the law or violating procedures laid down in the Act and regulations governing deportation, it had a virtual free hand insofar as the courts were concerned.

Judicial apathy or unwillingness to challenge this star chamber system, was clear in some cases: because deportation was not a criminal proceeding, the deport did not have the right to bail, to a speedy and fair trial by a jury of his or her peers, to know the evidence against him or her, or to confront his or her accuser, according to a series of Canadian court decisions. As Mr. Justice Mathers of Manitoba held, "Proceedings under the Immigration Act for the deportation of an undesirable alien are in no sense criminal and a person arrested and detained for such purpose is not committed for any crime . . . ." The Supreme Court of Canada confirmed this point of view on appeals by a group of radicals detained in Halifax awaiting deportation. Deportation was not a subject for the courts; it was "a purely administrative proceeding." In Fraser's view, "the most remarkable feature of the cases is that nowhere does there appear to be any appreciation on the part of judges of just how far their jurisdiction has been infringed by the executive without any apparent legislative authority for such infringement."[11]

The acquiescence of Canadian courts to the withholding of due process from deports may have been extreme compared to other Commonwealth countries, but it was similar to the actions of American courts. The U.S. Supreme Court ruled in 1893 that Congress could hand over the power to deport to administrative agencies, and that the courts were forbidden to interfere. Deportation was held not to be punishment for crime, so a deport was not entitled to the same protection as a criminal. A criminal under both American and Canadian law was presumed innocent; it was up to the prosecution to establish the guilt of the accused. But a deport was presumed guilty, and it was up to the accused to show why deportation should not take place. In 1932 William Van Vleck, Dean of the George Washington University Law School, pointed out, "There is a striking similarity in fact between the purposes and results of the expulsion process and those of a criminal trial. The courts have said, however, again and again that they are in legal theory entirely dissimilar."[12]

Some American judges argued against this interpretation. A dissenting opinion in the 1893 U.S. Supreme Court case had argued that deportation was punishment involving arrest, removal, and forcible expulsion from the country. Punishment implied a trial; according to common law, due process required a hearing before condemnation. The U.S. Immigration Act, in this opinion, "inflicts punishment without a judicial trial. It is, in effect, a legislative sentence of banishment."[13]

Such questions had become of even greater importance by the 1920s when, according to the U.S. Commissioner General of Immigration, deportation was "rapidly becoming one of the most important functions of the Immigration Service." American scholar Roscoe Pound, in his analysis of the development of administrative law from "delegated legislation", argued that the U.S. Immigration Bureau epitomized the practice of making law by administrative fiat. Protests about the actions of these officials came not from Congress or the courts but from "lawyers and humanitarians." U.S. courts "have confined within narrow limits the scope of their review of the administrative decisions of immigration officials."[14]

The similarities between the American and Canadian departments are striking. Lest it be thought that the United States was more arbitrary and more extreme, the somewhat wistful comment of the Dillingham Commission on the Canadian Immigration Act of 1910 is worth considering:

> The most striking feature of the Canadian immigration law, and the one in which it differs most widely from the United States law, is its flexibility, or adaptability to emergencies or changed conditions. The Canadian law confers almost unlimited power on the governor general in council in matters respecting immigration. In fact, it would seem under the terms of the law that the administration could, if deemed desirable, not only prohibit any particular class of immigration, but practically prohibit all immigration to Canada.[15]

The 1910 Act remained the legal basis of Canadian immigration practice until well after the Second World War. The 1919 Act merely increased ministerial discretion and thus increased flexibility.

After 1919, the Department's legal power to act arbitrarily was increased in degree, rather than modified in kind. The question was not of legality, but of practice. As long as deportation management remained an administrative matter and Department practice remained concealed from the public or Parliamentary eye, there was very little check on the power of the Department to do what it deemed appropriate. Efficiency, modernization, and rationalization of its procedures went hand in hand with increased arbitrariness and authoritarianism.

NOTES

CHAPTER ONE

1.   Dr. J. Halpenny of Winnipeg, writing in the October 1919 issue of *The Canadian Journal of Mental Hygiene*, cited by W. G. Smith, *A Study in Canadian Immigration*, Toronto, Ryerson, 1920, p. 226. See J. A. Stevenson, "The Problem of the Foreigner in Canada," *Westminster Review*, September 1913, for a sympathetic but typically racist discussion; Stevenson notes the importance of immigrant labour, the power of the corporations, and the involvement of the two major political parties in building a power base among "foreigners".
2.   Pat Thane, "Women and the Poor Law in Victorian and Edwardian England," *History Workshop Journal*, No. 6, Autumn 1978, p. 36. In Scotland, the situation was more or less similar. On this, see George Nicholls, *A History of the Scotch Poor Law in Connexion with the Condition of the People*, London, Murray, 1856.
3.   Dorothy George, *London Life Before the Eighteenth Century*, Evanston, Illinois, Harper and Row, [1925], 1964, p. 151; Dorothy Marshall, *The English Poor Law in the Eighteenth Century*, London, Routledge and Kegan Paul, [1926], 1969, p. 213. John Garraty, *Unemployment in History. Economic Thought and Public Policy*, New York, Harper and Row, 1978, pp. 24-59, describes the connections in several European countries between poor law development and attempts to control the poor, especially the use of vagrancy laws. See also Geoffry Oxley, *Poor Relief in England and Wales, 1601-1834*, London, David and Charles, 1974.
4.   See "Poor Laws Report," *Westminister Review*, 1834, in *Poverty in the Victorian Age. Debates on the Issue from 19th Century Critical Journals*, Vol. II, *English Poor Laws, 1834-70*, ed. E. W. Coats, London, Gregg, 1973, p. 475.
5.   Public Archives of Canada (PAC) Record Group (RG) 76, File 837, McNicholls to Department, 3 September 1895. All RG 76 files hereafter cited by "File" and number only.
6.   Ibid., Lowe's Testimony before The Select Standing Committee on Immigration and Colonization, 1877 Session; cited in Boardman to Fortier, 19 October 1894.
7.   Jane Perry Clark, ibid., pp. 132-3.

8. See E. Gibbon Wakefield, *Letters from Sydney and Other Writings*, London, Dent, 1929; Gary Teeple, "Land, Labour and Capital in Pre-Confederation Canada," in *Capitalism and the National Question in Canada*, Toronto, University of Toronto Press, 1972; see also the British House of Commons *Report on Agricultural Settlements in British Colonies*, 1906, British Parliamentary Papers (2978) LXXVI, 533.

9. See S. D. Clark, *The Position of the French Speaking Population in the Northern Industrial Community*, Report presented to the Royal Commission on Bilingualism and Biculturalism, 1966, for an analysis of the latter system at work. For an African comparison, see Bernard Magubane, "The 'Native Reserves' (Bantustans) and the Role of the Migrant Labour System in the Political Economy of South Africa," in A. Idris-Soven, E. Idris-Soven, and M. Vaughan, *The World as a Company Town. Multinational Corporations and Social Change*, The Hague, Mouton, 1978, p. 263. Magubane says that the South African system of intense exploitation of Africans as migrant workers developed because mine owners could not get a large and certain supply of imported cheap migrant workers. See also George Haythorne, *Labour in Canadian Agriculture*, Cambridge, Harvard University Press, 1960, pp. 22-32, 42. (At this time Haythorne was Canadian Assistant Deputy Minister of Labour.) See also his "Harvest Labour in Western Canada. An Episode in Economic Planning," *Quarterly Journal of Economics*, Vol. XLVII, August 1933.

10. Donald Avery, "Canadian Immigration Policy and the 'Foreign' Navvy, 1896-1916," Canadian Historical Association, *Historical Papers*, 1972; and *Dangerous Foreigners*, p. 9. See also Ernest Cashmore, "The Social Organization of Canadian Immigration Law," *Canadian Journal of Sociology*, Fall 1978, who says of the pre-World War II decades, "one could *almost* regard immigration policy during this period as a direct reflection of the CPR's and to a more limited extent, the Hudson's Bay Company's interest. When economic depression or war adversely affected those groups and unemployment and unrest ensued, legal innovation in imposing severe restrictions on entrance can be seen as an attempt to alleviate a condition defined by lawmakers as potentially dangerous. Consequently, an effort was made to force a reversal of a process which seemed under way, and curtail the incoming flow of labor in such a way as to minimize the possibility of political disruption and without jeopardizing the employers' decreased need for labor and investment."

11. D. Avery, *Dangerous Foreigners*, p. 12.

12. Ibid., see also Robert Harney, "Men Without Women: Italian Immigrants in Canada, 1885-1930," *The Italian Immigrant Women in North America*, Toronto, Multicultural Historical Society of Ontario, 1978, p. 82. As Harney points out, these came "intending brief sojourns, usually hoping for a summer's work in the railway, timbering and mining camps of the Canadian North."

13. George Haythorne, "Harvest Labor," pp. 536-7, 542; the majority of harvesters were Canadian but others constituted an important reserve. In 1928, 90 per cent of the British workers imported (in a particularly disastrous scheme involving unemployed industrial workers) returned home after the harvest was in.

14. D. Avery, *Dangerous Foreigners*, pp. 12, 29.

15. Michael Burawoy, "The Functions and Reproduction of Migrant Labour: Comparative Material from South Africa and the United States," *American Journal of Sociology*, Vol. 81, No. 5, March 1976, p. 1053. Also on the advantages to employers of "noncitizen" and undocumented workers, see Robert Thomas, "Citizenship and Gender in Work Organisation: Some Considerations for Theories of the Labor Process," *Marxist Inquiries*, American Journal of Sociology Supplement, Volume 88, 1982; see also S. Castles and G. Kosack, *Immigrant Workers and Class Structure in Western Europe*, London, Oxford University Press, 1973.

16.   Burawoy, ibid., pp. 1052-1063. See also P. C. Lloyd, *Africa in Social Change: Changing Traditional Societies in the Modern World*, Harmondsworth, Penguin, 1967, p. 94. "Migration does not create a wealthier category of men in the village." See also Y. M. Ivanov, *Agrarian Reforms and Hired Labour in Africa*, Moscow, Progress Publishers, English translation, 1979, pp. 10-32. On Canada, see for example Edmund Bradwin, *The Bunkhouse Man, A Study of Work and Pay in the Camps of Canada 1903-1914*, Toronto, University of Toronto Press, 1972; see also I. Abella and D. Millar, eds. *The Canadian Worker in the Twentieth Century*, Toronto, Oxford, 1978.

17.   Henry Drystek, "The Simplest and Cheapest Mode of Dealing With Them: Deportation from Canada before World War II," *Histoire Sociale*, November 1982, denies but does not refute this. For a more sophisticated discussion of the problems of providing social services, see Michael Katz, "Origins of the Institutional State," *Marxist Perspectives*, Winter 1978. On disposing of surplus labour, see B. Roberts, "Shovelling Out the Unemployed: Winnipeg City Council and Deportation, 1930-35." *Manitoba History*, Fall 1983, and B. Roberts, "Shovelling Out the 'Mutinous': Political Deportation from Canada before 1936," *Labour/Le travail*, Autumn 1986.

CHAPTER TWO

1.   Public Archives of Canada (PAC) Record Group (RG) 76, File 653, Chief Medical Officer Bryce to Medical Superintendent Hattie of Nova Scotia Hospital in Halifax, 22 August 1905. The proper name of the immigration service at this time was Immigration Branch of the Department of the Interior; it will be referred to as "the Department" or the Department of Immigration throughout for the sake of consistency; see Superintendent Scott to Minister Oliver, 28 March 1906; Scott to Harkin, 2 February 1907; See also File 837 on deportations from 1893-1906. For legal provisions see the Immigration Act of 1906.

2.   After 1906 a series of Orders-in-Council increasingly did so, limiting entry on racial, financial and occupational grounds. Because Orders-in-Council generally restricted entry rather than dealt with deportation, they are not germane to this discussion. See for example File 653, Privy Council report of 25 February 1908 on continuous voyage restrictions. Machinery necessary to carry out deportation of criminals was added by an amendment in 1907, Bill 143.

3.   File 653, Immigration Act of 1906.

4.   Ibid., 1910 Act (Bill 102), 22 March 1910.

5.   Ibid., Report of J. A. Coté for Acting Deputy Minister, 11 February 1904; U.S. law cited by William Van Vleck, *The Administrative Control of Aliens. A Study in Administrative Law and Procedure*, New York, The Commonwealth Fund, 1932, p. 9; see William Preston, *Aliens and Dissenters. Federal Suppression of Radicals 1903-1933*, New York, Harper, 1963, p. 32, and File 653.

6.   File 653, 1910 Immigration Act. The 1910 Canadian Act did not list anarchists among the classes prohibited to enter, relying instead on deportation after entry, because they believed that forbidden *entry* would be too hard to enforce, as shown by the American example. See House of Commons *Debates*, 1910, p. 5814 for Minister Oliver's explanation.

7.   File 653, no date but probably August 1900; Superintendent Scott to Staff, 20 January 1904; on U.S. Acts as models, see for example Bryce to Acting Deputy Minister of Justice, 23 July 1905; Scott to Minister Oliver, 28 March 1906.

8.   Ibid., Scott to Oliver, 28 March 1906, Scott to Deputy Minister of Justice, 18 May 1906; "Comparison between the American immigration law, old and new, and the

proposed new Canadian Act,'' 11 June 1906; see also Van Vleck, *Administrative Control*, p. 9.

9.   House of Commons *Debates*, 1909-1910, pp. 5813-6; File 653, Watchorn to Bryce, 13 June 1906.

10.   File 653, Obed Smith to Scott, 25 February 1906.

11.   Ibid., Memo for file, no date, January 1908; Fortier to Bryce, 1 January 1907 [sic]; Scott to all agents and Medical Officers, 7 January 1908; Memo for file, 12 December 1908; for the later draft see File 653, 22 March 1910.

12.   Ibid., Scott to McInnes, 8 March 1909.

13.   Ibid., McInnes to Scott, 8 March 1909; Scott to Oliver, 23 November 1909.

14.   Ibid., Secretary of Immigration Blair to Minister Calder, ''Memo regarding discussion with labour leaders concerning Section 41,'' 18 June 1919.

15.   Preston, *Aliens and Dissenters*, p. 32. The U.S. 1903 Act prohibited ''anarchists, or persons who believe in or advocate the overthrow by force and violence of the Government of the United States, or of all government, or of all forms of law, or the assassination of public officials'' or anyone who ''disbelieves in or who is opposed to all organized government, or who is a member of or affiliated with any organization entertaining and teaching such disbelief.'' The Canadian law of 1910 referred to those not Canadian citizens who advocated the overthrow by force or violence of the British, Canadian or other Imperial colonial governments, or of constituted law and authority, to the assassination of any public officials of government, or created riot or disorder in Canada by word or act. See File 653, Immigration Act as amended by Bill 102, 22 March 1910.

16.   File 653, 30 October 1918. The British Embassy in Washington sent the Department at Ottawa copies of the U.S. 1918 Act, and a memo to the Deputy Minister noted: ''place in file relating to proposed legislation.'' Another memo from Acting Deputy Minister Cory to Superintendent of Immigration Scott cross-referenced this file to dossiers on the IWW and other radicals, 12 November 1918. Subsequent internal correspondence identified specific provisions of the U.S. Act that Canada should adopt, Cory to Scott, 20 November 1918; and see also Scott to Cory, 21 November 1918, 19 November 1918, 20 July 1917. The U.S. 1918 Act was entitled ''An Act to Exclude and Expel from the United States Aliens Belonging to the Anarchist Classes,'' 16 October 1918.

17.   File 653, Memo to Deputy Minister, no date, March 1919; Senate *Debates*, 1920, p. 422.

18.   An Act to Amend an Act of the Present Session Entitled an Act to Amend the Immigration Act. *Statutes of Canada*, 1919.

19.   Senate *Debates*, 1919, p. 413.

20.   F. D. Millar, ''The Winnipeg General Strike, 1919: A Reinterpretation in the Light of Oral History and Pictorial Evidence,'' Unpublished M.A. thesis, Carleton University, 1970, Chapter 4. See also House of Commons *Debates*, 1919, p. 3041.

21.   See David Bercuson, *Fools and Wise Men: The Rise and Fall of the One Big Union*, Toronto, McGraw Hill Ryerson, 1978, p. 58; see also Edward Laine, ''Finnish Canadian Radicalism and Canadian Politics: The First Forty Years,'' in Jorgen Dahlie and Tissa Fernando, eds., *Ethnicity, Power and Politics in Canada*, Toronto, Methuen, 1981.

22.   F. D. Millar, John Bruce Interview, PAC Sound Division.

23.   File 653, Scott, ''Memo on Senate changes in Immigration Bill 52, passed by the Commons,'' 5 June 1919.

24.   Senate *Debates*, 1920, p. 500. See also File 653, Acting Deputy Minister to Minister, on plans to amend the Naturalization Act, 9 June 1919.

25.   File 653, Blair to Deputy Minister, 31 March 1926; Criminal Code Amendments 97A and 97B, Post Office Department Circular to Post-Masters, No. H-85, no date.
26.   Senate *Debates*, 1926, p. 275; see also Bill 153 to Amend the Criminal Code, 1926.
27.   Ibid., 1920, pp. 388, 419, 389.
28.   Bercuson, *Fools*, p. 101; Senate *Debates*, 1926, p. 276. "In Canada, the campaign against radicalism and Bolshevism was initiated, orchestrated, and executed by the federal government according to the laws on the books, or created especially for that purpose. The federal government never exceeded its legal authority, because it did not have to," Bercuson, *Fools*, p. 99. This is incorrect; the arrests and detention at Stoney Mountain Penitentiary of the strike leaders was admitted by Meighen himself to have been illegal. Even Bercuson's statement that there were no deportations under Section 41 is qualified; he says no British subjects were deported, although some of the aliens were secretly deported under Judge MacDonald's orders (p. 101). The Department claimed variously that (1) no British subjects were so deported, (2) no persons were so deported, (3) no one was ever deported under Section 41 either the 1910, 1919, or the amended 1919 version; Senate *Debates*, 1920, p. 389.
29.   File 653, An Act to Amend the Immigration Act, assented to 11 June 1928.
30.   Ibid., Commissioner Little to Featherstone, 20 June 1923, Blair to Minister, 19 April 1920.
31.   Ibid., Tom Moore to Minister Calder, 12 June 1919; Blair to Minister, 18 June 1919.
32.   Ibid., Acting Deputy Minister Cory to Secretary Blair, 19 April 1920; Bill X_2 was first read in the Senate 27 April 1920.
33.   Ibid., Blair to Minister Calder, 19 April 1920.
34.   Ibid., Blair to Calder, 23 April 1920.
35.   Senate *Debates*, 1920, pp. 388-9, 417, 422.
36.   Ibid., p. 587.
37.   File 653, Blair to Cory, 30 March 1921; Senate *Debates*, 1921, pp. 724-5; see also File 653, Blair's memo, for the file on "Efforts to amend Section 41," 1 June 1926.
38.   Montreal *Gazette*, 22 June 1922. See also Ottawa *Evening Journal*, 7 February 1922. This is a startling claim coming from Meighen, not only because it is unbelievable, but because he was the one who used it arbitrarily. Early on the morning of 17 June, eight strike leaders and four non-Anglo "New Canadians" were arrested and charged with seditious conspiracy and sent to Stoney Mountain Penitentiary, under the 6 June amendments. The wire sent to the RCMP by Minister of Immigration Calder to authorize the arrests did not arrive until after the fact. This was blatantly illegal and contravened the Immigration Act. Meighen's response was to wire, "Notwithstanding any doubt as to the technical legality of the arrest and detention at Stoney Mountain, I feel that rapid deportation is the best course now that the arrests are made, and later we can consider ratification." Roger Graham believes that the government's "willingness" to "overlook a technical illegality" shows that all were "abnormally excited." Roger Graham, *Arthur Meighen, Volume I. The Door of Opportunity*, Toronto, Clarke Irwin, 1960, p. 241. The Department calmly overlooked technical and other types of illegality quite consistently in its dealings with radicals and other deports. Graham might well have drawn a different conclusion had he been familiar with the inner workings of the Department.
39.   File 653, Bill 136; no date, early 1924.
40.   Ibid., Blair to Minister Robb, 20 June 1924; Blair, memo for file, "Efforts to amend Section 41," 1 June 1926, [Illegible] to Blair, 30 June 1924.
41.   Ibid., Blair to Mr. Throop, House of Commons, 10 March 1926, Blair to Deputy Minister, 31 March 1926, Blair to Deputy Minister, 29 April 1926, and Blair's memo for file regarding his discussion with Woodsworth, 29 March 1926.

42.   Ibid., Memo to Deputy Minister, 23 April 1926, Blair to Deputy Minister, 30 March 1926.
43.   Ibid., 30 March 1926; see also Memo to Deputy Minister, 23 April 1926.
44.   Ibid., Blair to Deputy Minister, "Discussion with Deputy Minister of Justice concerning amendments to the Criminal Code," 23 March 1926.
45.   Ibid., Blair to Deputy Minister, 1 June 1926.
46.   Ibid., Blair to Deputy Minister, 7 June 1926, and 31 March 1926.
47.   Ibid., Blair to Minister, "Memo prepared for the Minister to use in the House," 29 April 1926.
48.   Ibid., An Act to Amend the Immigration Act, 1926; Blair to Dandurand, 14 June 1926.
49.   Senate *Debates*, 1926, pp. 239, 242, 244; Senate *Debates*, 1920, pp. 422, 417, 389.
50.   Ibid., 1926, McMeans from Winnipeg, 244-5, Dandurand pp. 179-80, 267.
51.   Ibid., pp. 249, 281-2 for Aylesworth, p. 244 for Dandurand, and Belcourt pp. 249-50.
52.   Ibid., p. 247.
53.   Ibid., p. 281. Calder's comment is consistent with some of his other statements about Section 41. In 1909 and 1910 when the Section was being debated, Calder had said that it was not right to declare people members of the anarchist classes and so on, until there was proof that they really were in those groups. For that reason, he opposed exclusion of anarchists. "When we undertake to interfere with the right of expression of opinion, the right of personal liberty, to question the right of men to say what they please, we should only take action where we have it within our power to establish the facts." See House of Commons *Debates*, 1909-1910, p. 5870. Calder's role in the anti-radical activities of the Department needs further examination. Was he misinformed by his staff about what his department was doing? Did he not know of the procedures used in deportation cases? What did Meighen tell him about Winnipeg? How did Calder assess the events of June 1919, in retrospect? In 1926 Liberal Minister of Labour Peter Heenan had opened the 1919 correspondence files for the House of Commons. Perhaps Calder felt it necessary to put a good face on the illegal deportation proceedings.
54.   File 653, Blair to Bruce Walker, 17 June 1926.
55.   House of Commons *Debates*, 1928, pp. 1868, 2484; Senate *Debates*, 1928, pp. 421, 522, 612; File 653, Act to Amend the Immigration Act, 1928; Blair to Tom Moore of the TLC, 31 August 1928.
56.   File 653, no date, March 1930; Bill 44, first reading 11 May 1931; Commissioner of Immigration to Minister, 13 May 1931 and 9 March 1933; Commissioner to Minister Gordon, 19 February 1934.
57.   References are to the Act as published in 1929 in pamphlet form by the Department, found in ibid.

CHAPTER THREE

1.   Department of Immigration and Colonization, *Annual Report*, 1933-34, p. 85. All calculations in this chapter are based on this source.
2.   Computations by B. Roberts and D. Millar. All calculations are by Roberts and Millar, unless otherwise noted.
3.   Computer graphs were produced with the assistance of David Millar and Greg Smith.

4.   Domicile was no absolute bar against deportation; immigrants who could be shown to belong to the prohibited classes, for example, could be deported after many years' residence. Legal categories were constructed to make it possible to fit immigrants' circumstances into the necessary configuration. As legal and political criteria changed, so did the likelihood of deportation. See Ernest Cashmore, ''The Social Organization of Canadian Immigration Law,'' *Canadian Journal of Sociology*, Fall 1978, p. 427: ''those groups controlling Canada's economic resources, also determine the content and form of immigration law and the implementation of this law reflects the concerns of those groups. On this view it is easy to see how the criminal category of ''illegal immigrant'' is a *creation* of law, rather than a cause of it. Additionally, it follows that the same groups affecting the development of law also have a determining influence on the provision of meaning and problems for both criminals and non-criminals and on legislative interpretations of order and popular conceptions of rule-breaking. The category of ''illegal immigrant'' has become a legislative construction, designed to serve the imperatives of private resource-holding enterprises.'' But following the law was less important than being seen to do so: for examples of illegal deportations of Canadian-born children under the accompanying category, for example, see Public Archives of Canada (PAC) Record Group (RG) 76, file 351406, ''Statements and lists of deportations 1926-32'' passim.
5.   See Colin Sumner, ''The Ideological Nature of Law,'' in Piers Beirne and Richard Quinney, eds., *Marxism and Law*, New York, John Wiley, 1982.
6.   Elizabeth Comack, ''The Origins of Canadian Drug Legislation,'' in Thomas Fleming, ed., *The New Criminologies in Canada. State, Crime, and Control*, Toronto, Oxford, 1985, pp. 82-3.
7.   Donald Avery, *Dangerous Foreigners*, Toronto, McClelland and Stewart, 1979; for a U.S. example see William Preston, *Aliens and Dissenters. Federal Suppression of Radicals, 1903-1933*, New York, Harper, 1963.
8.   Jason Ditton, *Controlology. Beyond the New Criminology*, London, Macmillan, 1979. See chapter two on statistics.
9.   John Kitsuse and Aaran Cicorel, ''A Note on the Uses of Official Statistics,'' *Social Problems*, Fall 1963, pp. 136-8.
10.   For an early modern European example, the development of the poor laws and the use of ''vagrancy'' see John Garraty, *Unemployment in History. Economic Thought and Public Policy*, New York, Harper and Row, 1978, pp. 24-59. On present-day Britain see Stuart Hall et al., *Policing the Crisis. Mugging, the State, and Law and Order*, London, Macmillan, 1978.
11.   John McMullan, ''Law, Order and Power: Theory, Questions, and Some Limits to Social History of Crime in Early Modern England,'' [np], 1985; Victor Gatrell et al., eds., *Crime and the Law Since 1550*, London, Europa, 1980.
12.   Richard Quinney, *Class, State, and Crime. On the Theory and Practice of Criminal Justice*, New York, Longmans, 1977, pp. 131-39.

CHAPTER FOUR

1.   Public Archives of Canada (PAC) Record Group (RG) 76, File 837, titled ''Pauper, insane and otherwise undesirable immigrants to be returned,'' see 10 March 1896, Cloutier to Dominion Lands Secretary, concerning arrangements for the care of Louis Rauserot.
2.   Ibid., Department to Canadian Pacific Railway Agent McNicholl, 9 March 1895; see correspondence Autumn, 1894 and Memo, no date, February 1894.

3.   Ibid., See correspondence from Montreal Immigration Agent Hoolahan, concerning the Lea family. Mr. Lea finally got a job as a printer at the Montreal Gazette at a wage of $10 per week. Hoolahan had sheltered them in the Agency and advanced the family $5, before Mr. Lea became employed; passim, Autumn, 1894.

4.   Ibid., See correspondence passim, Summer 1895.

5.   Ibid., CPR Agent McNicholl to Department, 9 March 1895. The unfortunate Dane was eventually sent home at CPR expense, after the government brought persuasion to bear. See ibid., 12 March 1895.

6.   Ibid., Montreal Agent to Ottawa, 10 August 1903, and see correspondence, Hoolahan to Ottawa, passim, October 1903.

7.   Ibid., Hoolahan, 7 November 1903; Ottawa to Hoolahan, 22 November 1903; Hoolahan to Ottawa, 3 December 1903.

8.   See B.A. Roberts, "A Work of Empire: Canadian Reformers and British Female Immigration" in L. Kealey, ed., *A Not Unreasonable Claim: Women and Reform in Canada, 1880's-1920's*, Toronto, Women's Press, 1979; "Sex, Politics and Religion: Controversies in Female Immigration Work in Montreal, 1880-1920," *Atlantis, A Journal of Women's Studies*, Fall 1980. This practice (as did deportation) originated in the poor law system in the British Isles in the sixteenth and later centuries. See G. Nicholls, *A History of the Irish Poor Law*, New York, Augustus Kelley, 1967 [London, J. Murray 1856]. As part of provisions added in 1715 to assist servants to collect wages owed to them, servants were required upon leaving a position to obtain a certificate attesting to their good character. Such a certificate was supposed to be necessary to get another job. It came to be called simply a "character".

9.   See *Women at Work, Ontario, 1850-1930*, Toronto, Women's Press, 1974.

10.   File 563236, Bryce to Medical Superintendents of Asylums, 4 October 1906; Bryce to Southworth, Director of Colonisation for Ontario, 4 October 1906. On the medical outlook, see Peter Bryce, "Immigration in Relation to the Public Health," *The Canadian Journal of Medicine and Surgery*, April 1906; C. K. Clarke, "The Defective and Insane Immigrant," University of Toronto *University Monthly*, Vol. 8, 1907-8. For doctors' assumptions about desirability, see Leon Kamin, *The Science and Politics of IQ*, Potomac Maryland, Lawrence Erlbaum Associates, 1974, especially chapter 2, "Psychology and the Immigrant." For a glimpse of day-to-day immigration medical work, see Allan McLaughlin, "How Immigrants are Inspected," *Popular Science Monthly*, February 1905. On the role and work of Canadian doctors in the Immigration Branch, see Barbara Roberts, "Doctors and Deports: The Role of the Medical Profession in Canadian Deportation Policy and Practice, 1900-1935," *Canadian Ethnic Studies*, January 1987.

11.   File 563236, Bryce to Southworth, 25 October 1906. It is not clear why Blanchet was appointed to scour Quebec, but perhaps patronage was partly responsible. There would seem to be no compelling necessity for personal contacts by an officer of the Department. File 567097, Scott to Blanchet, 11 October 1906; Blanchet to Scott, 15 October 1906; Memo, 16 October 1906; Scott to all Wardens etc., 16 October 1906. For Ontario, see File 563236, passim; see for example Ontario Inspector of Asylums and Prisons, Armstrong to Bryce, advocating rounding up inmates and shipping them back in a group. The problem was to assure their reception on the other side. This sort of thing was commonly done by New York State, according to Armstrong, 23 November 1906. See also Armstrong's letters of 1 May 1907, and Dr. Clarke's letters of 11 May 1907 and 23 March 1908. Dr. Clarke, head of the Toronto Asylum, wanted to deport British inmates who had gained Canadian citizenship by many years of residence in Canada. This was not legal in 1908, although it soon would be. See also Bryce's lengthy discussions in his Annual Reports, in the Annual Reports of the Department. See Chuen-Yan David Lai,

"A 'Prison' for Chinese Immigrants," *Asianadian*, Vol. 2, No. 4, 1980, on the conditions for Chinese immigrants in the Victoria Detention Hospital.

12.   File 563236, Scott to Southworth, 7 November 1906; Scott to Warden of Dorchester Penitentiary, 7 November 1906; Scott to Provincial Governments, 17 November 1906; Scott to Premier of Saskatchewan, 20 November 1906.

13.   Ibid., Scott to Provincial Secretary of Quebec, 14 September 1908; Blanchet to Scott, 19 September 1908; Scott to Southworth, Ontario Director of Colonization, 7 October 1908; Scott to R. H. Lane, Secretary of Charity Organization Society, Montreal, 1 October 1908.

14.   Ibid., Scott to R. H. Lane, 12 October 1908.

15.   Ibid., Scott to Mayor of Englehart, Ontario, Dr. R. C. Lowney, 13 October 1908.

16.   Ibid.

17.   Ibid., Scott to City Clerk of Toronto, 30 October 1908; Scott to Montreal Agent Hoolahan, 30 October 1908.

18.   Ibid., Scott to Lane, Charity Organization Society. Montreal, 6 November 1908; Scott to Town Clerk of Deseronto, Ontario, 16 November 1908.

19.   Michael Piva, *The Condition of the Working Class in Toronto, 1900-1921*, Ottawa, University of Ottawa Press, 1979. See pp. 66-7, on the 1908 and 1913 depressions. File 563236, Scott to Alfred Coyell, Relief Officer of the City of Toronto, 19 June 1913.

20.   File 837, Ottawa to CPR Agent McNicholl, 9 March 1895; File 563236, Scott to Winnipeg Commissioner of Immigration, 17 March 1908, and, passim, Scott to various municipalities, for example, 16 November 1908.

21.   Ibid., Memo, "Minister's ruling concerning undesirables in the different towns and cities," 30 December 1908.

22.   Ibid., Scott to Lane, Charity Organization Society, 22 January 1909; numerous memos, passim, February 1909.

23.   Ibid., Deputy Minister of Justice to Scott, 3 June 1908; Ottawa to Winnipeg, 7 May 1908. "Smoothly" meant no official or public outcry would be raised, on either side of the Atlantic. Another amendment passed 4 April 1911 specified that the first two years of this residence must take place immediately following landing. See ibid., Assistant Superintendent of Immigration to Deputy Minister of Justice, 26 November 1913; Scott to Edmonton Agent Clegg, 15 April 1914; Scott to Medical Superintendent of Battleford Asylum, 27 April 1914.

24.   Ibid., Memo, 7 March 1913; see for instance the "Report of the Interview with Robert Rogers" (then Minister), Inspector of Prisons and Public Charities for Ontario to Scott, 8 October 1913; MacGill to Scott, 6 October 1911. MacGill shortly thereafter left the Department. Scott's reply: 25 October 1911.

25.   Ibid., Vancouver Agent Malcolm Reid to Scott, 9 June 1912; Scott to Reid, 22 June 1912.

26.   See for example, File 961162, Secretary Blair to Agent, 18 December 1919, concerning suspect Nicholas Babyn. Blair noted that Babyn was registered as an Austrian. If he had been interned he would have been very easy to deport, "as a matter of course and without any further examination or difficulty." Babyn was an OBU sympathiser. Blair suggested attempting to deport him under Section 41, but was afraid that Babyn might be "prepared to fight for his supposed principles." The Department was not eager to be "in the position of having to put a man on the witness stand without first being able to establish that we have a case against him" under Section 41. Because he was domiciled, deportation for other causes (such as criminal conviction) was not possible. Concluded Blair, "I think, however, if it is desired to get rid of him, the best plan is to have him interned and then his deportation is very simple." Or see ibid., memo regarding

"Minister's comments on examinations of aliens under Section 41," 27 April 1920. Else Saborecki was a German national, who arrived here 1 June 1914. She was "associating with enemy subjects," was a Communist Party member, a "revolutionist of a pronounced type." Her deportation was ordered under Section 41 but not carried out since she could not be sent to Germany during the War. She was interned and "repatriated" as a "prisoner of war" on 27 February 1920. See also Donald Avery, "Continental European Immigrant Workers in Canada, 1896-1919: From 'Stalwart Peasants' to Radical Proletariat," *Canadian Review of Sociology and Anthropology*, Vol. 12, 1975, pp. 60-4.

27.   File 803230, Winnipeg Commissioner of Immigration to Scott, 18 September 1914; Scott to Winnipeg, 15 September 1914. File 563236, Assistant Superintendent of Immigration Robertson to Department Officers, 11 September 1914; Scott to Winnipeg Office, 6 October 1914.

28.   File 563236, Scott to Inspector of Prisons and Public Charities for Ontario, 5 November 1915; copies to other municipalities and institutions.

29.   Ibid., Scott to Belleville Ontario City Clerk, 24 March 1915.

30.   Ibid., Scott to Mssrs. Smoke and Sanders, Paris, Ontario, 26 May 1915. "Foreigners" were not protected by any patriotic concern for their countries' welfare during the war, and feared deportation for unemployment. See Roseline Usiskin, "Toward a Theoretical Reformulation of the Relationship Between Political Ideology, Social Class, and Ethnicity: A Case Study of the Winnipeg Jewish Radical Community, 1905-1920," unpublished M.A. thesis, University of Manitoba, 1978, pp. 213-220 about fear of deportation in the Jewish community, and the Social Democratic Party of Canada's organizing around this issue. See also File 563236, Winnipeg Office to Scott, 8 January 1917. The use of vagrancy convictions for political or other forms of deportation was made easier by the passage of the 1918 Order-in-Council known as the "anti-loafing" law, requiring "every man in Canada from the age of 16 to 60 . . . regardless of his financial position . . . [to be] engaged in some useful occupation." Borden described it as "a very good law in time of war . . . [and] a pretty good law in time of peace." Quoted by R. C. Brown, "Whither Are We Being Shoved? Political Leadership in Canada During World War I" in J. L. Granatstein and R. Cuff, eds., *War and Society in North America*, Toronto, Thomas Nelson, 1971, p. 108. Enforcement was in the hands of municipal authorities.

31.   File 563236, Scott to Windsor, Ontario Inspector, 13 July 1917; Windsor to Scott, 18 July 1917.

32.   Ibid., Scott to Hoolahan, 14 October 1915; Scott to Inspector of Prisons and Public Charities for Ontario, 5 November 1915; Scott to Deputy Minister of Justice, 28 October 1914.

33.   Ibid., Scott to heads of institutions, etc. May 1, 1915.

34.   Ibid., Scott to Inspector of Prisons and Public Charities for Ontario, 20 February 1918 and 5 July 1919.

35.   On using wartime conditions to get rid of agitators, see File 912791, Secretary Blair to Commandant of the Vernon Internment Camp, 11 October 1919. For camps, see Desmond Morton, "Sir William Otter and Internment Operations in Canada During the First World War," *Canadian Historical Review*, March 1974. See also File 563236, Deputy Minister of Justice to Scott, 21 July 1919. See also note 26 above.

36.   Ibid., Scott to Fred Wilson, New Liskeard, Ontario, 7 March 1916, and File 912971, Scott to Lt. Colonel MacPherson, Internment Operations Office, Ottawa, 21 November 1916.

37. File 912971, Scott to Director of Internment Operations, 26 November 1918, Director to Scott, 26 November 1918 and 6 February 1918, and Privy Council of Canada Report, 23 January 1919. See also Desmond Morton, "Sir William Otter," Ibid.
38. Ibid., Scott to Director of Internment Operations, 25 April 1919, 7 May 1919; Director to Scott, 16 May 1919; Scott to Director of Internment Operations, 15 May 1919 and 17 May 1919.
39. Ibid., Scott to Director of Internment Operations, 16 May 1919. File 563236, Deputy Minister of Justice to Blair, 12 October 1919. In File 912971, see for example Scott to Director of Internment Operations, 26 August 1919, and Superintendent of Verdun Asylum to Secretary of Immigration, 17 November 1919. It is unclear if these people were sent over on later sailings.

CHAPTER FIVE

1. Public Archives of Canada (PAC) Record Group (RG) 76, File 900111, see Mayor of Winnipeg to Minister Oliver, 9 April 1908; Superintendent Scott to Department of Justice, 15 April 1908; Justice to Scott, 4 May 1908. In a memo to the Minister of Immigration, Scott suggested that "we might perhaps debar her on the grounds of insanity if she attempts to come across the boundary." Oliver decided against this plan; 15 December 1908. See also File 817610, Vancouver Agent to Scott, 15 February 1912. On the strike, see A. R. McCormack, *Reformers, Rebels and Revolutionaries. The Western Canadian Radical Movements, 1899-1919*, Toronto, University of Toronto Press, 1979, pp. 106-9. See also I. Abella and D. Millar, eds., *The Canadian Worker in the Twentieth Century*, Toronto, Oxford University Press, 1978, pp. 59-72.
2. File 563236, Deputy Minister of Justice to Acting Minister of Justice, 6 November 1913. This omission was deliberate; see Minister of Interior Oliver, House of Commons *Debates*, 1909-10, p. 5814. Canada did not include the provision because it was not effective in the U.S. See also ibid., p. 5870, Calder, on exclusion of alleged anarchists without proper proof of such beliefs.
3. On the former, see McCormack, *Reformers*, p. 130; see also D. Bercuson, *Fools and Wise Men. The Rise and Fall of the One Big Union*, Toronto, McGraw-Hill Ryerson, 1978, p. 58. On the last, see McCormack, ibid., Bercuson, ibid., and Edward Laine, "Finnish Canadian Radicalism and Canadian Politics: The First Forty Years," in Jorgen Dahlie and Tissa Fernando, eds., *Ethnicity, Power and Politics in Canada*, Toronto, Methuen, 1981. On the U.S. scene see William Preston, *Aliens and Dissenters. Federal Suppression of Radicals, 1903-1933*, New York, Harper, 1963. See also Joyce Kornbluth, ed., *Rebel Voices: An IWW Anthology*, Ann Arbor, University of Michigan Press, 1964, for an account of the Chicago trial, pp. 319-320; for persecution and prison conditions, pp. 320-322; raids, 324-325.
4. Bercuson, *Fools*, p. 99.
5. Ibid., pp. 101-3.
6. PAC MG 26 HI(a) V 104-OC519(1), Militia Department Records, Leonard, St. Catherine's, to Captain Coventry, DIO, Camp Borden Ontario, 30 July 1917.
7. Ibid., 13 August 1917, and RG 76, File 917093, 4 October 1917.
8. File 917093, Scott to Harvey, McCarter, Macdonald and Nesbitt, Cranbrook, British Columbia, 1 May 1917; Scott to Minnesota Commissioner of Public Safety, Minneapolis, 16 July 1917.
9. Ibid., Minister of Labour to Scott, 16 July 1917; Scott to Minister of Labour, 17 July 1917.

10.   Ibid., Scott to Minister of Labour, 28 July 1918.

11.   Ibid., 24 July 1917.

12.   Ibid., Scott to Travelling Inspector for Alberta and British Columbia, 25 July 1917 and 2 August 1917 and Winnipeg Commissioner of Immigration to Scott, 27 October 1917. RCMP Report on P. Lintz, MacLeod, Alberta, 31 July 1917. See also RCMP Special Agent's Report of 3 August 1917, for an explicit reference to illegal interception of correspondence.

13.   Ibid., 11 August 1917.

14.   Ibid., Scott to Winnipeg Commissioner of Immigration, 17 August 1917, my emphasis.

15.   Ibid., Winnipeg to Ottawa, 16 August 1917; Commissioner of Immigration at Winnipeg to Scott, 18 September 1917.

16.   Ibid., Vancouver Agent to Scott, 10 April 1918.

17.   Ibid., Inspector Jolliffe, Vancouver, to Scott, 3 September 1918, and 5 September 1918.

18.   McCormack, ibid., pp. 149-152.

19.   Militia Department Records, Cahan to Minister of Justice Doherty, 26 September 1918.

20.   RG 24, Vol. 2543 File 2051, 14 October 1918, 16 January 1919. See Ian Angus, *Canadian Bolsheviks. The Early Years of the Communist Party of Canada*, Montreal, Vanguard, 1981, p. 26.

21.   RG 76, File 917093, Scott to Deputy Minister of the Department of Militia and Defence, 6 September 1918.

22.   Ibid., Deputy Minister of Jutice to Scott, 9 September 1918. Based on F. D. Millar, ''Labour and Welfare Law in Ontario, 1867-1977,'' np, nd, and Ed Laine, ibid., p. 28. See also File 917093, Scott to Agents, 18 October 1918; Acting Winnipeg Commissioner of Immigration to Scott, 5 June 1919; RCMP to Scott, 3 July 1919.

23.   On spies see RG 24 Vol. 2544 File 2051, for example 29 April 1919, McLean to Davis (enclosing a thirteen-page memo on the extent of spying and nature of conclusions); 30 April 1919, McLean to Davis (enclosing Winnipeg detectives' report on the One Big Union); 3 May 1919, secret memo passed to Lt. Governor of Manitoba, Inspector General for Western Canada, etc. See also RG 18 B2 Vol. 68 File 18, RNWMP Commander to Superintendent Starnes, Winnipeg, 15 February 1919; on secret agents in various unions, see 15, 17, 20, 24, 27 February 1919; Secret Agent 32's memo, 15 April 1919. On generally held views see William Byron, ''The Menace of the Alien,'' *Maclean's* Vol. 32, No. 10, 1919.

24.   RG 76 File 961162, ''Report on a conference between Ireland and Blair, Canadian Department of Immigration, and United States Commissioner of Immigration Caminetti,'' 24 November 1919. File 917093, Percy Reid, Chief Immigration Inspector, to Minister of Immigration, 12 December 1919. See also Blair to Caminetti, 17 December 1919. Ron Adams, ''The anti-communist role of the RCMP in the Depression,'' Canadian Historical Association, 1978, says he found no evidence the RCMP and the U.S. exchanged intelligence data in the interwar period. Yet Immigration records show that such practices were well established by the end of the First World War. See for example Blair's memo about preparing an index to list radicals whose names were sent by U.S. authorities. These names were given by Ottawa to Canadian immigration officials at ports of entry: File 961162, 21 June 1920.

25.   Bercuson, *Fools and Wise Men*, pp. 88, 89; RG 24 Vol. 2543 File 2051, Cahan to General Gwatkin of the Militia, 3 January 1919.

26.   RG 76 File 917093, Blair to Ireland, 28 November 1919.

27.   Preston, ibid., pp. 216-8.

28.   File 917093, Blair to Caminetti, 23 December 1919.

29.   File 961162, Blair to Immigration Agent, 18 December 1919. A wartime Order-in-Council ordered the deportation of all interned enemy aliens who were "dangerous, hostile or undesirable" under order of the Minister of Justice. (The order applied to those interned at the time the armistice was signed, not to those previously interned.) On this see Calder, House of Commons *Debates*, 1919, p. 1977. According to Joseph Boudreau, "The Enemy Alien Problem in Canada, 1914-21," unpublished Ph.D. thesis, University of California, 1964, 1,644 Germans, about half from British colonies in the West Indies and elsewhere, and 302 "Austrians" (i.e., Eastern Europeans) were deported as enemy aliens after the First World War. Some of these were deported because of nationality despite the fact that they were established immigrants. Radicals were particularly liable to deportation by this method, especially after 1919. There were 106 "prisoners" sent to asylums during the war and 103 subsequently deported. See also Desmond Morton, "Sir William Otter and Internment Operations in Canada during the First World War," *Canadian Historical Review*, March 1974. The Department of Immigration said there were over 8,000 still legally classed as internees as of 1 May 1919, 6,130 of whom were paroled, 100 being deported. Over 81,000 were still reporting monthly or quarterly: File 884866, Scott to Calder, 1 May 1919. For illegal deportations see RG 18 A2 Vol. 137 (Comptroller McLean's Letterbook, 27 February – 14 April 1919), letter to Scott discussing Thomas Tasckent's deportation, 6 March 1919.

30.   Ibid., Blair to Colonel Margeson, Pensions Board, Ottawa, 5 January 1920.

31.   For the blind spot, see ibid.; also see F. D. Millar, "The Winnipeg General Strike, 1919: A Reinterpretation in the Light of Oral History and Pictorial Evidence," unpublished M.A. thesis, Carleton University, 1970. Roger Graham claims that the real reason that deportation proceedings were never begun against the 17 June 1919 strikers was that the strike had collapsed. So it was decided by Cabinet to go to the courts for criminal trials under the new Section 97A and 97B. Of course, deportation would have been impossible in some cases; George Armstrong, for example, was Canadian-born. The Criminal Code amendments had been recommended by a special Parliamentary committee on sedition and seditious propaganda, appointed before the Winnipeg Strike started, Graham points out. But the June 1919 changes to both the Criminal Code and Immigration Act were "obviously designed" to deal with Winnipeg. Roger Graham, *Arthur Meighen, Volume I. The Door of Opportunity*, Toronto, Clarke, Irwin, 1960, pp. 242-3. For pertinent correspondence, File 961162, Blair to Margeson, 5 January 1920 and especially 8 October and 24 December 1919; 13, 15, 29 January, 4 February, 28 May, and 2 June 1920. See also B. Roberts, "Shovelling Out the 'Mutinous': Political Deportation from Canada before 1936," *Labour/Le travail*, January 1987. On prevention, see File 961162, Blair to Undersecretary of State Mulvey, 9 January 1920.

32.   Ibid., Gelley to Blair, 10 January 1920, and Blair to Gelley, 12 January 1920, and passim, January 1920.

33.   Ibid., U.S. Department of Justice to RCMP, 22 January 1920; Commissioner of Immigration Little to Travelling Inspectors, 9 February 1920.

34.   File 961162, passim, January 1920.

35.   Ibid., Acting Deputy Minister of Immigration to Sir Joseph Pope, Undersecretary of State for External Affairs, 26 May 1920.

36.   Record Group 13, Volume 241, File 2321, Pt. Arthur T.L.C. to Department of Justice, 17 September 1919; File 2374, Secretary of Immigration Blair to Acting Deputy Minister of Justice, 11 September 1919 and 23 September 1919.

37. Record Group 76, File 917093, Assistant Vancouver RCMP Commissioner Wroughton to Vancouver Commissioner of Immigration Jolliffe, 11 April 1921; RCMP Superintendent for Manitoba District to RCMP Commissioner, Ottawa, 9 September 1921, for example. See File 817510, Vancouver Agent to Secretary of Immigration, 21 September 1921 and Secretary of Immigration to Winnipeg Commissioner of Immigration, 29 December 1922. See also File 917093, Gelley, Winnipeg, to Travelling Investigating Officer George, Calgary, 13 October 1923; RCMP to Deputy Minister of Immigration, 23 June 1923, warning of IWW activity in Vancouver; Jolliffe of Vancouver, to Gelley of Winnipeg, 6 August 1923, concerning rumours of plans for an IWW organizing drive among wheat harvest workers; RCMP memo to officers in Saskatchewan districts, 5 September 1923; Gelley to RCMP Commanding Officer, Regina, 12 September 1923; memo to Travelling Officer George, 13 October 1923.

38. File 917093, Gelley to RCMP Commanding Officer, Regina, 12 September 1923.

39. Ibid., Munroe to Gelley, 30 October 1923, Ottawa to Gelley, 30 October 1923.

40. Ibid., Calgary *Herald*, to Minister of Public Works, 23 January 1924; Minister of Labour to Calgary *Herald*, 23 January 1924; Vancouver Board of Trade to King, 23 February 1924.

41. Ibid., 13 March 1924.

42. Ibid., Jolliffe to Reid, 26 March 1924.

43. Ibid., Reid to Vancouver RCMP, 14 May 1923 [sic, but internal evidence dates this letter in 1924].

44. File 267931, Immigration to Deputy Minister of Justice, 7 August 1924. File 563236, Justice to Immigration, 24 August 1924; Ottawa to Vancouver, 2 September 1924. See also Preston, ibid., pp. 145-51.

45. File 917093, Blair to Minister of Immigration, "Memo: Appeal of Sam Scarlett," 24 September 1924. File 563236, Acting Minister of Justice to Deputy Minister of Immigration, 24 August 1924. File 917093, Commissioner of Immigration, Winnipeg, to RCMP, Regina, 12 September 1924, and to Minister, "Memo: Appeal of Sam Scarlett," 24 September 1924, copy of the appeal attached to Blair's memo. File 961162, Immigration to Justice, 24 September 1924, and Justice to Immigration, 24 September 1924. File 917093, Blair's pencilled note on margin of letter from Justice to Immigration, 24 September 1924.

46. File 917093, Blair's memo re: the appeal, 24 September 1924 and passim, September 1924.

47. File 267931, Commissioner Jolliffe, Ottawa, to Winnipeg Division Commissioner, 23 July 1925. See also Donald Avery, "Sam Scarlett," *Canadian Ethnic Studies*, Vol. 10, No. 2, 1978.

48. File 961162, 7 March 1925. See Kenneth McNaught, "Political Trials and the Canadian Political Tradition," *University of Toronto Law Review*, 1975, p. 151.

49. File 961162, Blair to Egan, 7 March 1925.

50. Record Group 13, Vol. 237, file 1432, entitled "Deportation of persons coming under Section 41 of the Immigration Act," Scott to Deputy Minister of Justice, 23 May 1919.

51. Record Group 76, File 917093, Winnipeg Commissioner of Immigration to Scott, 5 October 1917, and 11 October 1917.

52. File 961162, "Comments by the Minister on examination of aliens under Section 41," 27 April 1920. In these cases as well as others, other Sections of the Act may finally have been used on the deportation order, although the charge for which they were examined was political offences, Section 41.

53.   See Henry Trachtenberg, ''The Winnipeg Jewish Community and Politics: The Inter-
war Years 1919-1939,'' *Manitoba Historical and Scientific Society Transactions*, Vol 35,
1978/79-1979/80, pp. 119-20, 143. On 1 July 1919 the RCMP raided homes of various
Jewish activists including Charitonoff, Boris Daviotkin, Max Tassler, Yude Austin, and
Henry Geller. Trachtenberg comments that ''many Jews lived under the fear of . . .
possible arrest and deportation,'' ibid., p. 120. Almazov later moved to Toronto.
Blumenberg was freed on appeal and left Canada, possibly to avoid further deportation
attempts. On this see Lyle Dick, ''Deportation under the Immigration Act and the Canadian
Criminal Code, 1919-1936,'' unpublished M.A. thesis, University of Manitoba, 1978.
Transcripts of the Blumenberg, Almazoff and Charitonoff Boards of Inquiry are in RG 18
Vol. 3314 File HV-1(4), 14 July 1919, 16 July 1919, 16 July, 14 and 15 August 1919,
respectively. On the presence of Noble on the Board see RG 76 File 653, Blair to Bruce
Walker, 17 June 1926.
54.   Record Group 13, Vol. 241, File 2241, Deputy Minister of Immigration Cory to
Deputy Minister of Justice, 10 September 1919; memo for Deputy Minister of Justice,
12 September 1919.
55.   See Donald Avery, *Dangerous Foreigners: European Immigrant Workers and Labour
Radicalism in Canada, 1896-1932*, Toronto, McClelland and Stewart, 1979, pp. 85-6.
The Schoppelrei case was not as clear cut as the cause for deportation might suggest.
He had ''illegally entered'' by coming in as a recruit for the military forces. According
to the record, a recruiting officer had told the men to say they were Canadian-born, but
Schoppelrei's counsel was not allowed to say so at the deportation hearings. Another
black mark against Schoppelrei was his refusal to inform on his friends, when asked
questions at the Board of Inquiry. See RG 18 HI Vol. 4, 17 July 1919. See also RG 76,
File 912971, Murray to Calder, 30 October 1919; as cited by Avery. See also F. D. Millar,
''The Winnipeg Strike,'' chapter 5.
56.   Millar, ibid..
57.   Bercuson, *Fools and Wise Men*, p. 101.

CHAPTER SIX

1.   Public Archives of Canada (PAC) Record Group (RG) 76, File 563236, Blair to
Winnipeg Commissioner, 18 November 1920; Blair to Gelley, 21 December 1920; Blair
to Minister Calder, 6 December 1920.
2.   Ibid., 18 November 1920.
3.   Ibid., 6 December 1920.
4.   Ibid., Vancouver Agent to Secretary Blair, 6 October 1921; Blair to Minister,
9 December 1922.
5.   Ibid., Blair to Colonel Dennis, 10 May 1927.
6.   Ibid., Commissioner to Fraser, 5 February 1929; Assistant Deputy Minister to
Badgley, 15 September 1927.
7.   Ibid., Deputy Attorney General to Vancouver Commissioner of Immigration, 6 January
1923; Deputy Minister of Immigration to Deputy Minister of Justice, 6 November 1923;
Justice to Immigration, 10 November 1923.
8.   Ibid., Winnipeg Commissioner of Immigration to Blair, 19 September 1922; Blair
to Winnipeg, 22 September 1922.
9.   Ibid., Blair to Vancouver Commissioner Jolliffe, 30 January 1924.
10.   Ibid., Ottawa to Winnipeg Commissioner of Immigration, 8 November 1922; Blair
to Director of Department of Soldiers, Civil Re-establishment, 29 December 1922.

11.   Ibid., Blair to Amyot, 7 May 1921; Amyot to Blair, 10 May 1921.
12.   Ibid., Memo to Blair, 17 May 1923 (my emphasis).
13.   Ibid., Blair to staff, 21 May 1923.
14.   Ibid., Commissioner of Immigration to Dr. D. A. Clarke, Assistant Deputy Minister, Department of Health.
15.   Ibid., Division Commissioner Fraser to Jolliffe, "Memo, regarding cause of deportation," 21 June 1928.
16.   Ibid., Commissioner Jolliffe to Deputy Minister Egan, 26 June 1928.
17.   Department of Immigration and Colonization, Annual Report, 1924; File 563236, Blair to Consul General of Poland, 13 February 1923.
18.   Annual Report, ibid., 1924.
19.   File 563236, Little to Montreal Agent, 2 November 1922; Blair, "Memo concerning conference with Department of Health re: deportation costs," 13 November 1922. Health had agreed to advance funds to Immigration because the latter had not yet gotten an appropriation to pay for deportations done outside the provisions of the general Immigration Act. This was a temporary, makeshift measure, quite without significance here.
20.   Ibid., Reid to Agent Regimbal, 4 January 1923.
21.   From Annual Reports, 1925, 1926, and 1928, respectively.
22.   See for example the 1924 Annual Report, p.44. That year from the Pacific Division there were 123 Chinese deported, and 116 deportations under the ONDA, only one of whom went to the U.S., the rest to "other countries". The Division said that the OND was used to deport "undesirable chinamen" who had acquired Canadian domicile. There were 39,587 Chinese in Canada in 1921, according to the census; 23,533 in British Columbia (out of a total B.C. population of 524,582). See J. Morton, In the Sea of Sterile Mountains: A History of the Chinese in British Columbia, Vancouver, J.J. Douglas, 1974, pp. 237-241 for an account of the passage and implications of, and B.C. reactions to, the 1923 Chinese Immigration Act.
23.   File 563236, Winnipeg to Commissioner Little, Ottawa, 14 March 1923.
24.   Ibid., Whitton to Deputy Minister Egan, 15 July 1929; Egan to Whitton, 16 August 1929 and 4 September 1929; Whitton to Egan, 2 October 1929.
25.   See Emily Murphy's The Black Candle (1921), on the prejudices of the latter group. On the OND see Elizabeth Comack, "The Origins of Canadian Drug Legislation," in Thomas Fleming, ed., The New Criminologies in Canada. State, Crime, and Control, Toronto, Oxford, 1985.
26.   File 563236, Scott to Winnipeg Office, 24 September 1915.
27.   Ibid., Walker to Scott, 27 September 1915.
28.   Mrs. K. A. Chiman, "State Guardianship of Young People," Report of the International Congress of Women, Toronto, June 24-30, 1909, Vol. II, Toronto, National Council of Women of Canada, 1910, p. 362-3.
29.   PAC Manuscript Group (MG) 281, Volume 13, "Reports of the Y.W.C.A. Immigration Committee, 1912-1916," Report of June 11, 1914; Volume 37, Miss Falconer, "On Immigration in Canada," "Our Unfolding Purpose". Report of the World's Y.W.C.A., Stockholm, 1914, pp. 137-9.
30.   Ibid., Volume XIII, No. 1, January 1914, pp. 53-5, 56. See also Suzann Buckley, "British Female Immigration and Imperial Development," Hecate: Women's Interdisciplinary Journal, January 1977, and Barbara Roberts, "A Work of Empire: Canadian Reformers and British Female Immigration," in L. Kealey, ed., A Not Unreasonable Claim: Women and Reform in Canada, 1880's-1920's, Toronto, Women's Press, 1979.

31.   Roberts, "A Work of Empire," passim; see also Barbara Roberts, "Sex, Politics, and Religion: Female Immigration Workers in Conflict, Montreal 1880's-1920's," *Atlantis, A Journal of Women's Studies*, Fall 1980; MG 281, Volume 14, "Immigration and Travellers' Aid Committee Papers," Meeting of the Y Immigration Committee, 23 February 1925, and Miss Burnham to Y worker, 20 March 1923. The Y decided that only trained workers could do follow-up work for purposes of "protection and prevention of exploitation," so it was not practical to institute this system on a large scale. 10 April 1923.
32.   Ibid., Meeting of the Y Immigration and Travellers' Aid Committee, 2 February 1925; Burnham to Committee, 11 January 1926, 5 May 1926, and 10 September 1926; Committee Minutes, 4 October 1926 and 2 November 1927.
33.   Roberts, "Sex, Politics and Religion," and Buckley, "British Female Immigration." See MG 281, ibid., Committee Minutes, 4 April 1927, 9 May 1927, and 10-11 October 1927.
34.   RG 76, File 563236, Blair to Superintendent of Immigration for Canada, London, England, 7 December 1922; Report of Investigating Officer Munroe, Regina, 12 December 1922 and 12 January 1923.
35.   Ibid., Blair to Accountant, 19 January 1923.
36.   Ibid., Memo, 2 December 1927. The Calgary Agent went too far. He raided a bawdy house with the police, and "assumed the duties of a police constable." He was criticized for being overzealous. The Winnipeg Commissioner complained to Ottawa that Department Officials should neither be "expected" nor "permitted" nor "encouraged" to do this sort of thing. Ibid., 3 March 1921.
37.   File 434173, passim; Memo, 19 February 1937.
38.   Ibid., "Report on minor problems under the Aftercare Agreement," not dated, 1932; "Report on unmarried mother cases under the Empire Settlement Scheme," not dated, 1933.
39.   File 563236, Memo, Assistant Deputy Minister to Jolliffe, 29 June 1926; Macnaghten to Secretary Blair, 18 June 1928.
40.   Ibid., Commissioner to Little, 7 July 1928.
41.   Ibid., Blair to Macnaghten, 17 July 1928 and 18 July 1928.
42.   Ibid., Macnaghten to Blair, 3 November 1928.
43.   File 434173, "Report on unmarried mother cases . . . ," 1933; "Analysis of major problem cases coming to attention up to 31 December 1932 under the Aftercare Agreement," not dated.
44.   "Analysis of major problem cases coming to attention up to 31 December 1932 under the Aftercare Agreement," not dated.
45.   Ibid., "Causes for deportation of Empire Settlement women showing the contributing factors which necessitated deportation, to the end of March 1934," not dated.
46.   Ibid., "Non-Empire Settlement major problems dealt with between 1 January 1921 and March 31, 1934, for British women." Not dated.
47.   Ibid., "Statement showing year of arrival of Empire Settlement problem cases which arose during the fiscal year ending 31 March 1932," not dated.
48.   Ibid., "Aftercare Report from 1 January 1926 to 31 March 1933," not dated; this report includes those who had arrived in January, February and March of 1926, after the advent of the Aftercare Agreement but before the beginning of fiscal 1926-27. This study differed from the one cited before in two respects: the latter included 262 immigrants and 18 "problems" from the January through March 1926 arrivals (out of the total of 1,885, and was based on problems arising for a period twelve months longer than the first study.

49.   Ibid., "Major problem cases coming to the attention of the Department between 1 January 1926 and 31 March 1936," not dated. By this date, all who had remained here would have satisfied the requirements for domicile (five years) and therefore could probably not be deported, unless perhaps it were shown that they had never been legally landed because they belonged to prohibited classes. Presumably the bulk of these immigrants deportable under these (in effect) retroactive exclusionary clauses of the Immigration Act had been deported by this date. See also "Standing of above problems as of 31 March 1936," not dated.

50.   Ibid., The following computations are based on the figures in this report.

51.   "Bad conduct" cases listed in 1934 gave these behaviours as examples: "Attempted suicide, petty theft, incorrigible, refused to accept employment, etc." Ibid., "Causes for deportation of Empire Settlement women to the end of March 1934, showing the contributing factors which necessitated deportation."

CHAPTER SEVEN

1.   William Beeching and Phyllis Clarke, eds., *Yours in the Struggle: The Reminiscences of Tim Buck*, Toronto, NC Press, 1977, p. 161; hereafter Buck, *Yours*. Ian Angus claims the CP itself was partly to blame for not responding effectively in court; it had lost most of its members and isolated itself from the broader left movement, and the Buck group were so focused on sectarianism and adventurism and a suicidal clash with the authorities (which they called revolutionary) that it almost invited persecution. On internal splits within the Party during the thirties, see Ian Angus, *Canadian Bolsheviks. The Early Years of the Communist Party of Canada*, Montreal, Vanguard, 1981. For 1930s political deportation from Canada, see Barbara Roberts, "Shovelling Out the 'Mutinous': Political Deportation from Canada before 1936," *Labour/Le travail*, Autumn 1986.

2.   In 1930 the absolute minimum upon which a worker's family could live with some degree of health and decency, although certainly not in comfort, was $20 weekly. This figure is based on unpublished research by F. D. Millar, "Real incomes in Manitoba"; see also Barbara Roberts, "Social Policy, Female Dependence and the Living Wage," paper to the Canadian Women's Studies Association, Learned Societies, 9 June 1982, Ottawa, and Roberts and Millar, "Living with less," Western Association of Sociology and Anthropology, Regina, 1984. For an account of such activities see J. Petryshyn, "R. B. Bennett and the Communists," *Journal of Canadian Studies*, November 1974, and "Class Conflict and Civil Liberties: The Origins and Activities of the Canadian Labor Defense League, 1925-1940," *Labour/Le travailleur*, Autumn 1982. See also Merrily Weisbord, *The Strangest Dream*, Toronto, Lester and Orpen Dennys, 1983, pp. 10-48.

3.   Michiel Horn, "Keeping Canada Canadian: Anticommunism in Toronto, 1928-29," *Canada. An Historical Magazine*, September 1975, and "Free Speech within the Law: The Letter of the 68 Toronto Professors, 1931," *Ontario History*, March 1980; the *Canadian Labor Defender* (CLD) 1930-1934 *passim* describes many such campaigns. Weisbord's brief account of the 1931 sedition trials in Montreal is illuminating: pp. 35-7. She notes that one of the Montreal sedition prisoners, David Chalmers, was deported to Scotland after he served his one-year prison term at Bordeaux: p. 39.

4.   City of Winnipeg Archives, Winnipeg City Council Papers, File 15141, Sudbury City Clerk to Winnipeg City Clerk, 11 May 1931; Barbara Roberts, "Shovelling Out the Unemployed: Winnipeg City Council and Deportation, 1930-35," *Manitoba History*, Fall 1983; Lyle Dick, "Deportation under the Immigration Act and the Canadian Criminal

Code, 1919-1936," unpublished M.A. thesis, Department of History, University of Manitoba, 1978, p. 118.

5. Public Archives of Canada (PAC) Manuscript Group (MG) 26K, (Bennett papers), File C-650, "Communists, 1931, S98", Webb to Bennett, 29 May 1931; Webb to Robertson, 9 July 1931, cited by Michiel Horn, ed., *The Dirty Thirties*, Toronto, Copp Clark, 1972, pp. 457-8. The Bennett papers are an excellent source of examples. PAC Record Group (RG) 76, File 95027, Winnipeg Commissioner of Immigration Gelley to Commissioner of Immigration Jolliffe, 25 June 1931. All RG 76 files will hereafter be cited only by file number.

6. Henry Trachtenberg, "The Winnipeg Jewish Community and Politics: The Inter-war Years, 1919-1939," *Manitoba Historical and Scientific Society Transactions*, Vol. 35 (1978/9-1979/80), p. 131.

7. Ron Adams, "The 1931 Arrest and Trial of the Leaders of the Communist Party of Canada," Canadian Historical Association, 1977; Lita Rose Betcherman, *The Little Band*, Ottawa, Deneau, 1983, chapters 15-17, is the best published account, especially when read with Tim Buck, *Yours*.

8. Public Archives of Ontario (PAO) Attorney-General's Department, Record Group 4, Series D-1-1-, File 3188/1931, Justice Minister Guthrie to Ontario AG Colonel Price, 18 March 1931 and 1 April 1931. See also Petryshyn, "Bennett", Betcherman, *Band*, Buck, *Yours*. Weisbord describes the problems with the indictment, which Chief Justice Rose refused to accept as initially written. He did not accept the view that mere membership in an illegal organization was an offence as provided in Section 98; he believed the accused had to be an officer of the organization *and* commit the illegal actions laid out in the Section, to be indictable. The prosecutors had to negotiate with Justice officials in Ottawa, and eventually change the wording of the indictment: see her discussion pp. 36-9.

9. For biographical sketches see CLD December 1931, pp. 4-5; William Rodney, *Soldiers of the International*, Toronto, University of Toronto Press, 1968, pp. 161-70; Anthony Rasporitch, "Tomo Cacic: Rebel without a Country," *Canadian Ethnic Studies*, Vol. 10 No. 2, 1978; and Files 513173 part 2 and 531057.

10. Frank Scott, "The Trial of the Toronto Communists," *Queen's Quarterly*, August 1932; Adams, "1931 trial," Betcherman, *Band*, have details. The transcript can be found in Rex v Buck et al., Ontario Court of Appeals, Mulock CJO, *Dominion Law Reports* (1932)3.

11. Petryshyn, "Bennett", p. 45; Rasporich, "Cacic"; Dick, "Deportation", pp. 124-5 citing Sedgewick to Price, 17 October 1931, "it would establish the unlawfulness of the association, and future proceedings could be taken against those who are mere members of the association, as was always intended." Ontario AG papers, File 3188/1931.

12. Lorne and Caroline Browne, *An Unauthorized History of the RCMP*, Toronto, Lorimer, 1978, p. 64 citing McNaughton papers, Vol. 10 File 46, Secret memo of Chief of General Staff to Adjutant General, 14 October 1931.

13. File 563235, Memo from the Assistant Deputy Minister, 26 June 1931; see also Shin Imai, "Deportation in the Depression," *Queen's Law Journal*, Vol. 7, No. 1, 1981, p. 89; he points out that in the fiscal year ending March 1932, there were 239 certificates revoked, a six times greater rate than average. He also mistakenly claims the Department did not resort to illegalities: on this see B. Roberts, "Purely Administrative Proceedings: The Management of Canadian Deportation, Montreal 1900-35," unpublished Ph.D. dissertation, Department of History, University of Ottawa, 1980, and "Shovelling Out the Unemployed." File 513157, Jolliffe to Mulvey, 18 November 1931, Mulvey to Jolliffe, 24 November 1931. File 513057, RCMP Commissioner J. H. MacBrien to Jolliffe,

16 November 1931. Bennett had appointed MacBrien to succeed Starnes. According to Sawatsky, MacBrien was "an even greater anti-Communist fanatic" than Starnes: John Sawatsky, *Men in the Shadows: The RCMP Security Service*, Toronto, Totem, 1980, p. 65.
14. The order to tell Mulvey etc. was underlined in ink on the original typed memo: File 513057, Department memo, 19 November 1931. Radicals were not infrequently warned not to apply, or rejected for citizenship in the 1930s. See "Branded as a Communist in 1930s," Toronto *Globe*, 17 June 1974, p. 8, about Nick Urkewich who was told by the RCMP not to apply, after a 1932 strike in Crowsnest Pass; when he finally did apply in 1972, he was rejected, presumably on the basis of his involvement in left and other labour causes in the 1930s. Others in the area were in a similar situation and it took intervention by their MP to get citizenship, after 40 years. See also comments on citizenship refusals by Shin Imai, "Deportation", pp. 70-1.
15. The list of 82 is in RG 26, Vol. 16, "Deportation of Communist Agitators, 1931-1937."
16. File 513047, Mulvery to Jolliffe, 24 November 1931. File 513116 (Arvo Vaara) Memo, Immigration to RCMP, 21 November 1931.
17. File 513057, Memo for file, 17 June 1932, and see also RG 26 Vol. 16.
18. File 513057. Deputy Minister of Immigration to Secretary of State Skelton, External Affairs, 20 June 1932. They were Tekla Ogrodnuk (Mrs. Pete Sarakopas), Anna Schurbatz (Mrs. Tony Zingle), and Anton Pysanuk.
19. "Deportation Abuses," Winnipeg *Tribune*, 26 October 1931.
20. Oscar Ryan, *Deported!*, Canadian Labor Defense League, Toronto, nd [1932], p. 10, and RG 26 Vol. 16.
21. Satu Repo, "Lakehead in the 1930s – A Labour Militant Remembers" [Einar Nordstrom], *This Magazine*, July/August 1979.
22. File 563236, Department memo requested by High Commissioner for Canada Ferguson, London, 4 March 1931.
23. File 274485, Memo for Mr. Jolliffe, 23 July 1927. Three-page RCMP spy report included. Similar cases are discussed passim.
24. Personal communication, John Ferris, Sault Ste. Marie, 19 August 1981; see also CLD June 1930.
25. Discussion about his research with Mauri Jalava, 27 July 1981. At the time he was researching an M.A. thesis on leftwing Finns in Sudbury, for Laurentian University.
26. For examples of deportation after vagrancy convictions, see file 563236, Commissioner of Immigration to Divisions, 26 June 1931; Leslie Morris, "Labour Defense and the Vagrancy Laws," CLD September 1930.
27. See for example discussion of the need to hire legal counsel for the Department if the Poles detained in Winnipeg had been charged under Section 41: File 817510, Winnipeg to Ottawa, 3 September 1931. File 563236, Winnipeg Commissioner to Ottawa, 5 September 1931, Ottawa to Winnipeg, 2 October 1931, and 6 November 1931. File 817510, Winnipeg Commissioner to Ottawa, 3 September 1931. The Poles had refused to sign passport applications but the Department ingeniously found their photographs and other necessary documentation on their entry cards, as they had come in under the Railway Agreements, a series of 1920s agreements permitting the transportation companies to bring in agricultural immigrants.
28. File 513057, Memo for file, 17 June 1932; names on RG 26 Vol. 16 list. File 513057, memo to Jolliffe, 17 June 1932; CLD November 1932; eight names appear on the RG 26 list, for the Rouyn deports: Mathias Ruhinski, Lauri Renko, Emile Suorsa, Kalle Simola (all domiciled Finns), Steve Garich, Mitar Mrdic, Steve Pavletich (Yugoslavs, Pavletich domiciled), Byll Semergo (Pole, here since 1913). For Timmins, the following

were listed: Arvi Tielinen, Thomas Pollare (aka Tom Blaren), Viljo Piispa, Emil Maki (Makynen), (all Finns, none domiciled). File 513057, memos 17 June 1932. CLD January 1931, January 1932, May 1933; Hautamakki is on the RG 26 list; so is Karpenkower, whose case is mentioned in CLD September 1931. Jacobsen is on the RG 26 list, and is mentioned in the CLD of February 1931. For Panjata see *Canadian Forum*, May 1931, pp. 284-5.

29.   For Hymie Sparaga see CLD January 1931 and May 1931; *Canadian Forum* May 1931, p. 284; Louise Watson, *She Never Was Afraid. The Biography of Annie Buller*, Toronto, Progress, 1976, p. 111. See also Stanley Hanson, "Estevan 1931," in Irving Abella, ed., *On Strike*, Toronto, James Lewis and Samuel, 1974, p. 57. Gryciuk and Revay are on the RG 26 list. Relief camp strikers also risked deportation as radicals. See Ralph Pimlotte's account of the May 1933 "riot" in Saskatoon: "Closing Relief Camps Sparks Riot," *Briarpatch*, January-February 1983; several of his fellow 'rioters' were deported for their pains, p. 29. See Glen Makahonuk, "The Saskatoon Relief Camp Workers' Riot of May 8, 1933: An Expression of Class Conflict," *Saskatchewan History*, Spring 1984. Thomas O'Hara, convicted of unlawful assembly and sentenced to nine months' hard labour, plus three months for assaulting police, was deported 10 August 1934; Patrick O'Dare was also deported for his part in the riot: see Makahonuk pp. 67-9, and the RG 26 list. James Forrest was also deported: see Makahonuk, p. 70, and RG 76 File 563236 Saskatoon Workers Defence League to Minister of Immigration, demanding the release of 21 men from the Prince Albert gaol (some of these were from the riot), and protesting the deportation of Forrest, Furlong, and Sutton, 6 January 1934. See also ibid., Women's Labour League Saskatoon Branch to Minister of Immigration, 14 March 1934, protesting the deportation of prisoners upon completion of sentences; this likely refers to some of the rioters.

30.   See "They're Killing Sophie in Jail," CLD June 1932; see also CLD December 1931, November 1932; she is on the RG 26 list.

31.   File 244957, Secretary of Immigration to Prime Minister's Secretary, 6 October 1932; see also Ryan, *Deported!*; RG 26 Vol. 16; CLD November 1932.

32.   Photographs of Reinkanen's and a Mrs. Morton's bruises in CLD August 1931; jail and deportation information, CLD November 1931. He is on the RG 26 list. For Langley and Farley see CLD January 1932, RG 26 Vol. 16, and Betcherman, *Band*, pp. 44-50. For Zepkar see CLD October/November 1934; he is on the RG 26 list.

33.   Personal communication, Ferris to Roberts, 19 August 1981.

34.   See Roberts, "Shovelling Out the Unemployed," for a discussion of reaction to the deportation of the unemployed.

35.   All information from File 530021, "Kluchnik, Sam, Undesirable, Winnipeg, 1932-52"; includes Board of Inquiry transcript, 21 July 1932.

36.   File 513116, memo, Immigration to RCMP, 24 November 1931; Secretary of State to Commissioner of Immigration, 24 November 1931; warrant for the arrest of Dan Chomicki sent by Minister to Jolliffe, 4 December 1931. Subsequent testimony in Orton Wade's case revealed that his warrant had been issued at about the same time.

37.   File 513111, warrant to search Dan Chomicki's residence.

38.   House of Commons *Debates*, 6 May 1932, pp. 2658-9.

39.   Account taken from Frank Scott, "Immigration Act: False Arrest, Illegal Treatment of Arrested Person," *Canadian Bar Review*, January 1936; see also Wade v Egan et al., Manitoba Court of Appeal, Prendergast CJM, *Canadian Criminal Cases* 193 Vol. 54.

40.   The Halifax Agent pointed out the danger of using only Section 41 in such cases, suggesting that Section 3 be used as well or instead. Under S3 when membership in the prohibited classes was established, persons were illegally in the country, no matter how long they had resided here. File 513057, Personal to Munroe, 9 June 1932. For Cessinger, File 513057, Assistant Commissioner of Immigration Munroe to Commissioner Jolliffe, 11 May 1932. See also File 513111 containing his Board of Inquiry transcript and other documents relating to the case.

41.   File 513057, Memo on Sembaj, 10 May 1932. The spy was Secret Agent #125 J. M. Tatko.

42.   File 513057, Munroe to Jolliffe, 16 May 1932.

43.   File 513057, Munroe to Jolliffe, 14 May 1932.

44.   *Canadian Forum*, February 1934, p. 165; File 513057, 13 May 1932.

45.   For earlier details on Vaara's "criminal" activities, see File 513116, passim; Betcherman, *Band*, pp. 30-41; File 513057, Munroe to Jolliffe, 16 May 1932.

46.   File 513057, Memo, Halifax Inspector in Charge to Commissioner, 26 May 1932.

47.   File 513057, Munroe to Jolliffe, 25 May 1932.

48.   File 513057, 6 May 1932.

49.   RG 26 Vol. 172 File 3-10-111, "Communist name cases . . . Robinson, Reid, Carr etc.," Memo from V. J. LaChance, Chief, Bureau of Records, on Parker et al. appeals, 15 October 1932. See also Arvo Vaara and others v the King, *Canadian Law Reports*, Supreme Court of Canada, (1932) 37-43, and File 513057, R. B. Curry to Brother Stanislaus, 24 February 1966.

50.   For the CLD see Petryshyn, "Class Conflict" and "Bennett"; see also Rodney, "Soldiers," p. 122.

51.   Buck, *Yours*, pp. 162-4 and Betcherman, *Band*, p. 177.

52.   Horn, "Free Speech". Several of the founders of the League for Social Reconstruction, which arose in part out of this experience, were among the 68. See also Kenneth McNaught, *A Prophet in Politics. A Biography of J. S. Woodsworth*, Toronto, University of Toronto Press, 1959, pp. 256-60.

53.   McNaught, *Prophet*, pp. 242-5. Woodsworth did not support the CLDL; not surprising given CP attacks on the CCF as a "fascist" organization. See ibid., pp. 266-70. For efforts in Parliament see for example House of Commons *Debates*, 22 February 1932, pp. 380-4 and 7 March 1932, pp. 842-5.

54.   Ryan, *Deported!*; the pamphlet discusses several specific cases, providing some details not given in the CLD and other sources.

55.   Contrast this view to Donald Avery's discussion of the existence of a hidden system of importing industrial workers, hidden under Canada's ostensible policy of promoting permanent agricultural settlement: *Dangerous Foreigners*, Toronto, McClelland and Stewart, 1979, chapter 1. See also B. Roberts, "Shovelling Out the 'Mutinous'" and Oscar Ryan, *Deported!*, pp. 7-10.

56.   CLD, September 1932; Ryan, *Deported!*, p. 12; for evidence that deporting radicals as public charges was a long standing practice of both the U.S. and Canada, see File 961162, "Report on Conference between Ireland and Blair, Canadian Department of Immigration, and United States Commissioner of Immigration Caminetti," 24 November 1919.

57.   Petryshyn, "Bennett", pp. 46-52, and "Class Conflict", p. 63.

58.   On Cacic, see Rasporich, "Tomo Cacic", passim; case records on File 513173-2. Also see Rasporich, *For a Better Life. A History of the Croatians in Canada*, Toronto, McClelland and Stewart, 1982, pp. 136-44 and especially 142, for a clear and perceptive discussion of conditions causing radicalism, the risks of militant activity, and the threat of political deportation for Croats and other immigrant industrial workers. Rasporich incorrectly cites RG 26 Vol. 16 as RG 76 Vol. 16; see his footnote 27, p. 163 for example.

59.   See File 513109, memo from Assistant Commissioner to Jolliffe, 27 August 1932: "You will remember there was a question as to whether we would take action against those men under Section 41 . . . The majority of those concerned are either Canadian-born, British subjects with Canadian domicile, or have the protection of their Canadian naturalization certificates." He noted that the State Department did not seem happy about the proposal to cancel the naturalization certificates in this case, and suggested that although it might be a good idea to have Boards of Inquiry for all of them, a Ministerial Order had to be issued soon for Cacic's Board. See also ibid., Munroe to Officer Reynolds, "Memo for guidance in Board of Inquiry," 1 February 1933.

60.   See ibid., Fall 1933 passim.

61.   Ibid., Minister of Immigration Gordon to Jolliffe, 15 November 1933; Yugoslav Consul General, Montreal, to Department of Immigration, Ottawa, 17 October 1933; Roberts, "Shovelling Out the Unemployed," particularly discussion of letter from several European consuls; the letter had to be answered but it certainly had little impact. File 513173-2, Department to Consul, 24 October 1933.

62.   Ibid., to Minister of Justice, 10 November 1933. See also N. Dreisziger et al., *Struggle and Hope. The Hungarian-Canadian Experience*, Toronto, McClelland and Stewart, 1982. Deportations are discussed pp. 141-2 only in terms of economic causes (public charge). A brief note on the attractions of communism for Hungarians is found pp. 151-2, and some information on the Hungarian Workers' Club[s], pp. 158-9.

63.   File 513173-2, Gordon to Jolliffe, 15 November 1933.

64.   Ibid., Jolliffe to Guthrie, 14 November 1933, Assistant Commissioner of Immigration, Memo for file, 14 November 1933.

65.   Ibid., Acting Deputy Minister of Justice to Immigration, 2 December 1933.

66.   Ibid., 5 December 1933, 11 December 1933; transcript of Board of Inquiry, December 14-18 1933.

67.   Ibid., Guthrie to Jolliffe, 10 December 1933. One wonders if Immigration would have reacted as nervously as Justice, had the telegram been differently addressed. Immigration tended to be more blasé. On the other hand, Bennett was pulling the strings.

68.   In his first Board of Inquiry, he had stated he would not appeal; he saw it as an expensive and useless formality. For a transcript of his first Board, see ibid., 2 February 1933; Assistant Commissioner of Immigration to Warden of Kingston Penitentiary, 19 December 1933; Deputy Minister of Justice Edwards to Minister of Immigration Gordon, 19 December 1933.

69.   Ibid., Onie Brown to Minister of Immigration, 19 December 1933; Stewart Edwards to General Ormond, 20 December 1933.

70.   Ibid., passim, December 1933; Assistant Commissioner Munroe to Deportation Officer Howell, 22 December 1933.

71.   Ibid., David Goldstick, CLDL lawyer, to Gordon, 25 December 1933; see also Ottawa *Citizen*, 28 December 1933; File 513173-2, Halifax Agent to Munroe, 2 January 1934. Cacic escaped en route and got to Moscow. Later he fought in Spain and was held in a French concentration camp after leading a group of refugees out of Spain. He escaped the camp in 1941 and fled to Yugoslavia where he fought with the Partisans. He died in 1969. See Rasporich, "Tomo Cacic" for details. On the deportation, see also *Canadian Forum*, February 1934, p. 165.

72.   File 95027, Starnes to Jolliffe, 15 August 1930. See also Becky Buhay, "Bennett's Answer to the Unemployed: Deportation," CLD June 1931, especially her comment about Don Evanov of Toronto and the consequences of his deportation to Bulgaria. There is a further mention of Evanov in "Facing Bulgarian Gallows," CLD July 1931. See as well discussion of the case of Peter Zepkar, a Croat arrested in a Ft. Frances lumberworkers' strike in January 1934 and ordered deported to Yugoslavia: CLD October/November 1934. Other cases include Ted Merino of Vancouver, ordered deported to Japan, CLD January 1935, and Nick Stitch of Pt. Arthur ordered deported to Hungary, *Labor Defender*, April 1935.

73.   Irving Abella and Harold Troper, *None is Too Many: Canada and the Jews of Europe, 1933-1948*, Toronto, Lester and Orpen Dennys, 1982, pp. 7-9. The Reds and the Jews not infrequently (but not necessarily admittedly) were linked as twin demons in the official mind: see a rare instance of such views in print, from the RCMP quarterly magazine quoted by Merrily Weisbord, *The Strangest Dream*, p. 30: "tearing the camouflage from the Red beast," destroying "the ugly cancer gnawing at the vitals of the Dominion," and confronting the "dark Jewish conspiracy."

74.   File 513057, 1 December 1932, 3 December 1932; Immigration to RCMP, 15 December 1932.

75.   Ibid., Minister Gordon to CLDL, 17 December 1932. A. Upton, *The Communist Parties of Scandinavia and Finland*, London, Weidenfeld and Nicholson, 1973. He points out that in 1918 about 20,000 Reds were killed directly or died in prison camps as a result of repression by the Whites: p. 119. By the late 1920s, communists in Finland were being arrested for political activities. By 1930, fascist vigilantes were terrorising communists with the approval of the government. In October 1930 anti-communist laws were passed and during the 1930s there was very little communist or communist front activity in Finland: it simply was unsafe. See pp. 153-5, 178-93. For a brief mention of the anti-communist regime in Hungary, see Dreiszinger et al., *Struggle*, pp. 16-18. See also File 513057, Ottawa to London office, 20 December 1932; House of Commons *Debates*, 14 February 1933, pp. 2101-2.

76.   File 95027, Starnes to Deputy Minister of Immigration, 22 November 1926; 31 July 1928.

77.   Ibid., Commissioner of Immigration to Commissioner of RCMP, 29 January 1932; Commissioner of Immigration to Department of Immigration Inspectors, 24 March 1934. For an account of the experiences of some Canadian Finns in Karelia, see Larry Warwaruk, *Red Finns on the Coteau*, Saskatoon, Core Communications, 1984, pp. 65-83.

78.   File 961162, RCMP to Immigration, 21 August 1933, for example; Immigration Branch, Home Office, U.K., to Canadian Immigration, passim 1934; Canadian External Affairs to Canadian Immigration, 5 January 1935.

79.   For example, File 969713, Windsor Agent to Ottawa, 9 March 1932, enclosing a clipping on the Ford Motor Company "riots" where four "rioters" were killed. Some names such as that of Foster, remained on the "lookout" list for years, all through the twenties and thirties.

80.   File 513057, RCMP Commander Wood, E Division, Vancouver, to RCMP Commissioner, Ottawa, 14 May 1933.

81.   On this point see memos re: appeals from the Halifax Ten, File 513057, May 1932 passim; R. Curtis, "Demand the Release of Campbell," CLD June 1931; A. E. Smith, "Terrorism – Capitalism's Secret Weapon Against the Workers," CLD July 1931 mentions Campbell's sentence to Oakalla. See also Betcherman, *Band*, pp. 92, 94-95, 154-5 on Campbell.

82.   Betcherman, *Band*, pp. 29-33. Vaara was not Jones' only target. See File 95027, Jolliffe to Starnes, 23 April 1930, re: Jones' letter informing on Hannes Sula, another Red Finn returning to Sudbury after a visit to the U.S.S.R. Jolliffe ordered his officers to take "any action possible under the circumstances."

83.   Petryshyn, "Class Conflict," pp. 50-3: Justice Minister Guthrie's comment that in the repeal campaign "the CLDL had managed to build up a huge protest movement with even the churches committing themselves." See the Regina Manifesto, Section 12, Freedom, in McNaught, *Prophet*.
84.   File 563236, Ottawa to Winnipeg Commissioner, 1 April 1933.
85.   Betcherman, *Band*, p. 124.
86.   Justice Minister Guthrie gave credence to such accusations later when he said that the eleven shots had been fired at Buck "to frighten him." Winnipeg *Free Press*, 27 June 1934, cited by Betcherman, *Band*, p. 215.
87.   Petryshyn, "Class Conflict," pp. 53-9. See also Buck, *Yours*, pp. 247-8.
88.   File 513057, Division Commissioner of Immigration at Vancouver to Commissioner at Ottawa, 11 February 1935; Ottawa to Vancouver, 19 February 1935.

CHAPTER EIGHT

1.   Public Archives of Canada (PAC), Record Group (RG) 76, File 563236, Eastern Division Commissioner of Immigration to Mr. Munroe, 22 October 1929.
2.   Ibid., Eastern Division Commissioner to Mr. Munroe, 22 October 1929, 25 October 1929. Much of this unemployment was the result of the great 1929 drive to bring out British unskilled labour for farms. Most of these were city men. Discontented, they flooded Toronto and went on relief, according to the Province. Ontario Department of Labour *Report*, Special Paper No. 23, 1930, p. 37.
3.   File 563236, Ottawa to Western Division Commissioner at Winnipeg, 27 May 1930.
4.   Ibid., 10 June 1930.
5.   "Minutes of an interview of representatives from certain municipalities in Ontario, Manitoba, Alberta, Saskatchewan and British Columbia, and of the Provincial Governments of Manitoba, Saskatchewan, Alberta and British Columbia with the Cabinet, 26 February 1930 to 1 March 1930, Ottawa," as cited by Donald Avery, *Dangerous Foreigners*, p. 113.
6.   File 563236, telegram from Egan to Charles Stewart, then at the Royal Alexander Hotel in Winnipeg, 18 June 1930. The Ottawa Commissioner of Immigration had only the previous month ordered a stop to the practice of requesting Ministerial Orders in bulk by wiring lists of names. Adopted as an emergency measure to expedite large numbers of public charge deportations from the West in the fall of 1929, the practice was "not in keeping with the requirements of our regulations."
7.   File 563236, Memo to Mr. Little, 18 August 1930.
8.   Ibid., Winnipeg to Ottawa, 6 July 1931; Ottawa to Winnipeg 18 July 1931.
9.   See Avery's discussion of these conflicting interests, *Dangerous Foreigners*, Chapter 4. See also File 563236, Memo 16 February 1931.
10.   *Montreal Star*, 29 October 1930; File 563236, Egan to Jolliffe, 4 November 1930. Such deportations continued less conspicuously until February 1932, when the Department of Health informed the Department of Immigration that, although it would continue to report such cases, it would not press for deportation. Ibid., confidential memo, Immigration to Health, 9 February 1932. The Department of Immigration lied about this type of deportation, too. For example, it wrote to the YWCA that deportation was "never" carried out after ten years' residence and only very rarely after five years' in the cases of immigrants who were members of the prohibited classes. Ibid., 19 June 1931. Yet cases like this continued. For example, Sofia Fekete had come to Canada in 1909. In 1932, a public charge patient at the Ontario Hospital, Hamilton, she was ordered deported. After unsuccessful attempts to get the parish priest to intervene, the CLDL was called in.

They argued for a stay of proceedings based on the position that when her husband had applied for and been granted citizenship in 1932, she, as his wife, had automatically been naturalized along with him. The new law ending such practice, which had gone into effect in January 1933, did not affect her status. She was a citizen, and not deportable, the CLDL claimed. The CLDL won a month's stay; it is unclear if she was eventually deported. *The Worker*, 10 October 1935, p. 2.

11.   File 563236, Egan to Vernon, 19 December 1930. Egan pointed out that "mental" and "criminal" cases were not classified as "public charge" deportations.

12.   *Montreal Gazette*, 6 February 1931, in File 563236.

13.   Ibid. Memo on the S. S. *Ascania* deportation, 26 January 1931; on using vagrancy convictions, Memo to Division Commissioners, 26 June 1931; on denials concerning unemployment as cause for *Ascania* deportations, *Winnipeg Free Press* in ibid., 12 February 1931.

14.   In File 563236, 14 February 1931, by editor Charles Bowman.

15.   Ibid., Commissioner of Immigration to Division Commissioner, 9 March 1931; Memo to Deputy Minister from Secretary, 25 February 1931.

16.   File 563236, Commissioner to Agents and Officers Conducting Boards of Inquiry, 16 February 1931. "Becoming established" usually meant sticking it out in the hope that things would improve. For a description of the distress, misery, generally awful conditions and occasional starvation experienced by some of the British settlers who tried to stick it out near Tracadie, New Brunswick in the 1930s, see David Millar's interview with John Bruce, Sound Archives, PAC. Also on Empire Settlement immigrants in New Brunswick see File 563236, Memo, 7 March 1933. See also Deputy Minister to German Consul General, 27 March 1931.

17.   Ibid., Ottawa to Winnipeg Commissioner of Immigration, 9 May 1931; copies to all Divisions. The practice persisted and was sufficiently widespread to create protest and become an issue for the left. See the protest letter sent to the Department by the September 1931 "United Front" Conference of fourteen "workers' organisations" held in Hamilton. They demanded "that the municipalities forcing men to sign 'voluntary deportation' pledges cease." MG 26K, File 92730, 1931.

18.   RG 76, File 563236, Ottawa to Toronto office, copies sent to all ports and major centres, 13 November 1931.

19.   MG 26K, File 150484, letter from J. H. Thomas of the British Secretary of State for External Affairs to Bennett, 2 December 1931. See also ibid., Files 150477-150481 inclusive. For windows, RG 76, File 563236, ADM to Secretary, 7 December 1931.

20.   Ibid., 20 June 1932.

21.   Ibid.

22.   File 156271, 1 December 1926; File 563236, Memo, 2 March 1932; File 156271, Memo, 2 March 1933.

23.   File 563236, Memo, 2 March 1932, for example.

24.   E. G. Higgins and F. A. Peake, *Sudbury Then and Now: A Pictorial History 1883-1973*, Sudbury, Chamber of Commerce, 197[-].

25.   File 563236, Immigration Inspector-in-Charge Langlois, Montreal to Ottawa, 23 August 1932; Oscar Ryan, *Deported!*, Canadian Labour Defense League, 1932, p. 4; Personal communication, John Ferris, 19 August 1981, Sault Ste. Marie.

26.   T. Peterson, "Ethnic and Class Politics in Manitoba," in Martin Robin, ed., *Canadian Provincial Politics*, Toronto, Prentice Hall, 1972, p. 90; Winnipeg City Council, Minutes of Council, 9 June 1930.

27.   T. Peterson, ibid.; *Minutes of Council*, 18 January 1932; and Winnipeg City Council, Council Papers, File 15357, Council to Honoré Parent, 19 January 1932.

28.   See Ed Rea, "The Politics of Class: Winnipeg City Council 1919-1943" in C. Berger and R. Cook, eds., *The West and the Nation*, Toronto, McClelland and Stewart, 1976; Ed Rea, "The Rea Report," City of Winnipeg, 1976; Barbara Roberts, "Shovelling Out Paupers: Winnipeg City Council and Deportation of the Unemployed, 1930-35," *Manitoba History*, Summer 1983.

29.   Provincial Archives of Manitoba (PAM), MG 13I2, File 892, Box 85, Assistant DM to Unemployment Relief Committee, 19 February 1932 (hereafter cited as Bracken papers).

30.   *Minutes of Council*, 29 March 1932, is virtually incomprehensible. See Winnipeg *Tribune* 30 March 1932 for a clearer account. The Unemployment Relief Committee was a tripartite body with federal, provincial and municipal representation. As Louise Carpenter points out, it "supposedly exerted control over recommendations for the deportation of public charges." ("Supposedly" is the operative word here.) See Louise Carpenter, "Deportation of immigrants during the depression," unpublished paper, University of Manitoba, 1973, p. 20. Copy supplied by Ed Rea. On Simpkin's resolution, Yeas were Andrews, Cuddy, Flye, Bardal, Simpkin, Simpson, Gray, Blumberg and Ferley. *Minutes of Council*, ibid. On deportation rates see Carpenter, ibid., p. 15.

31.   *Minutes of Council*, 4 July 1932, p. 597.

32.   The memo in Council papers is headed *to* Fraser. But it was treated as if it *were* Fraser's. Relief Department papers were unavailable, apparently secreted, lost or destroyed. I was unable to determine the origin of the memo. The 1983 head of Winnipeg's social welfare services described Fraser to me as a "miserable old bastard who" should never have been allowed to wield such power over people. The head's father, a 1930s official in a neighbouring municipality, detested Fraser and brought home anecdotes about him. Based on my research, I have concluded that Fraser consistently lied to the Unemployment Relief Committee. For example in the Committee's *Minutes* of 23 November 1933:
> Mr. Fraser: "We do not report them for deportation. Our information is given in accordance with the [Immigration] Act."

See also Roberts, "Shovelling Out the Unemployed."

33.   Council Papers, File 15488, "Memo to J. D. Fraser," 27 June 1932. For paying transportation costs see Unemployment Relief Committee *Minutes* 1932-35 passim. Such requests appear to have been routinely granted. See also Council Papers, ibid., Fraser to Council, 4 July 1932. Louise Carpenter interviewed G. V. O'Brien about his job as a typist in the Relief Department during this period. O'Brien told her he had spent most of his first few weeks on the job typing up reports on how much relief had been given to various immigrants eligible for deportation (ostensibly to keep Department records for later repayment). O'Brien said he did not realize the "implications" of the task, at the time. Carpenter, ibid., p. 23. I was unable to find evidence that the Unemployment Relief Committee knew about these lists. Carpenter also believes that Councillors remained ignorant of the extent of deportation.

34.   Council Papers ibid. Preudhomme to Ryley, then Chair of the "Special Committee on Unemployment Relief" [sic] variously titled in the records, 29 June 1932.

35.   Some of MacNamara's proposals are startling. For instance, he drew up a draft proposal for 1933-34 unemployment relief, suggesting that the federal government should pass laws to commit men who refused work to military-run prison camps. These laws "could also be made to apply to agitators." Leftwingers on the Relief Committee were upset and insisted their opposition be recorded in the minutes. MacNamara, as author of offending Clause 7, modestly abstained. The vote was Yea, four Citizens, Nay, four

Labourites. URC *Minutes,* nd [mid-to-late April 1933]. See also Roberts, "Shovelling Out the Unemployed," note 22 on anti-Fraser complaints. Reliefers who complained ("agitators") were usually cut off relief.
36.   Council Papers, File 15488, dated 11 July 1932, signed by the City Clerk.
37.   RG 76, File 563236, Toronto Agent to Eastern Division Commissioner Fraser, 13 March 1931; Fraser to Toronto Agent, 9 April 1931. Fraser said reporting was required by law. See City Council Scrapbook, 16 January 1932. The vote was 11-6 along general party lines, 26 January 1932.
38.   Council Papers, File 15488, copy of form.
39.   Ibid., Preudhomme to J. D. Fraser; Preudhomme's unpublished memoirs "Winnipeg as seen by a City Solicitor" do not mention deportation. The manuscript is in the Provincial Archives of Manitoba.
40.   *Minutes of Council* show no reference. URC *Minutes* for 16 February 1933 note receipt of the communication and record a decision to continue to request repayment but without resorting to legal action. There is no indication of extensive discussion or the slightest controversy.
41.   RG 76, File 563236, Winnipeg Commissioner of Immigration to Ottawa, 26 July 1933 and 18 December 1933; City Council Scrapbook 19 December 1933, 11 September 1934 and 25 May 1933.
42.   File 563236, Memo from Winnipeg to Ottawa office, 27 June 1933; Joint Committee of Winnipeg to Winnipeg Immigration Office, 6 July 1933. The Winnipeg Immigration official estimated there were 1,000-2,000 demonstrators.
43.   Ibid., Commissioner of Immigration to Winnipeg Immigration Office, 6 July 1933; reply, 14 July 1933.
44.   Ibid., 26 July 1933; see Preudhomme's letter of 1 February 1933 cited above; see also URC *Minutes* of 4 May and 16 May 1932, and passim 1933 and 1934.
45.   File 563236, Winnipeg to Ottawa, 18 December 1933.
46.   Winnipeg *Tribune,* 15 and 19 December 1933; Winnipeg *Free Press* 18 December 1933, "Deportation procedures," described in detail the official steps in deportation proceedings. A careful reader would realize that these proceedings were arbitrary. "Underlying causes" could easily be found or manufactured. Councillor Simonite said in an interview by Louise Carpenter that someone with good moral character who went on relief had no worries about deportation. According to him, only someone with some "fault, some failure in their behaviour" was at risk of being deported. "That was generally the reason for deportation." He continued, "In some cases, I used to think that was made up for the excuse of having a case against the person." Simonite claimed to Carpenter that he was opposed to deportation. Louise Carpenter, ibid., p. 17.
47.   File 563236, Memo, nd [January 1934]; Winnipeg to Ottawa, 26 April 1932; Memo to Minister of Immigration Crerar, 18 November 1935.
48.   There are accounts in the Winnipeg *Tribune,* 21 and 22 December 1933. Louise Carpenter cites other examples of immigrants going off relief to avoid deportation, even though they faced virtual starvation. Carpenter, ibid., p. 22.
49.   The Winnipeg *Tribune* and *Free Press* described the meeting, 19 December 1933. See also City Council Scrapbooks; *Minutes of Council* 18 December 1933; RG 76, File 563236, December 1933 passim. The City Solicitor had said they were legally bound to report: *Minutes of Council* 18 December 1933.
50.   File 563236, ADM to McClintock at Toronto, 31 October 1933; "Deportation work, calendar years 1932 and 1933," nd.
51.   Ibid., Memo, nd [January 1934].

52.   Ibid., "Immigrants deported as public charges during calendar years 1932 and 1933," nd.

53.   Ibid., Copies to all Divisions. Example of Department's false statements in appeal memos: Sam Kluchnik of Winnipeg. His file (530021) includes the transcript, dated 21 July 1933 (in RG 76).

54.   *Minutes of Council*, 2 and 15 January 1934. RG 76, File 563236, Winnipeg Commissioner of Immigration to Minister of Immigration, 12 January 1934.

55.   For a hard-luck story see Winnipeg *Free Press*, 20 January 1934, "The Futorski Case." On embarrassing questions, see ibid., 27 January 1934, and 31 January 1934. On the balance of power in Council see Brian McKillop, "The Communist as Conscience: Jacob Penner and Winnipeg Civic Politics, 1934-35" in R. McCormack and I. MacPherson, eds., *Cities in the West*, Ottawa, Mercury Series, Museum of Man, 1975. Because of the crossing of party lines on the deportation issue, partisan power blocs are not as central a consideration here as on other issues. For example, Andrews, relatively a hard liner on unemployment and relief issues, who had at first publicised Ottawa's spurious claims on deportation, by December 1933 was in the anti-deportation camp (albeit only briefly). Ed Rea suggested that partisan politics may have been a factor; the Liberals (such as Andrews) may have used the occasion to strike a blow at Bennett's Tories: personal communication, 15 December 1981. My hunch is that Andrews must have been angry at being lied to by Ottawa, and worse, at being made a fool of by not only believing but repeating those lies – surely a motive for revenge. I do not doubt his sincere outrage at the situation, nor do I doubt that he was acting on principle. At the risk of sounding naive, I think the Councillors did act on principle, at least in December and January.

56.   *Minutes of Council*, 29 January 1934. See also Winnipeg *Tribune*, 30 January 1934.

57.   File 563236, Winnipeg Immigration Office to Ottawa, 9 February 1934.

58.   Ibid., Minister to Ottawa Legion Headquarters, 22 June 1932.

59.   File 81829, Memo re: Duties under the Immigration Act, Blair to D. R. Cansell, 30 September 1931; *Saturday Night*, 3 March 1934. After many years' research, I am prepared to say flatly that Gordon was lying; he did not, and he *could* not, personally authorize all such deportations. He was probably only vaguely aware of policy and procedures.

60.   Winnipeg *Free Press*, 23 February 1934. Some municipalities were reporting selectively. Brandon, Manitoba refused to report public charges in cases where relief was the sole cause: File 563236, Departmental memo, 14 March 1934. *Saturday Night*, ibid.

61.   My grandfather, Charles Bowman, was skeptical of many government claims of the period; *Citizen*, 14 February 1931. Former Relief Department worker O'Brien pointed out to Carpenter that the number of deportations was greatly diminished when the Relief Department could no longer report: Carpenter, ibid.

62.   *Minutes* of the URC, 8 February 1934, 22 February 1934; *Minutes of Council*, 26 February 1934, and 27 February 1934.

63.   *Minutes* of the URC, 8 March 1934; File 563236, City of Winnipeg Social Welfare Council to Winnipeg Division Commissioner of Immigration, 15 March 1934; Commissioner to Mrs. Stewart-Hay, 16 March 1934; Commissioner to Ottawa, 19 March 1934.

64.   *Minutes of Council*, 27 March 1934, 9 April 1934, 4 July 1934. For the vote see Roberts, "Shovelling Out the Unemployed."

65.   File 563236, Winnipeg Commissioner of Immigration to Ottawa, 17 July 1934, 10 August 1934, 20 September 1934; Ottawa to Commissioner, 3 August 1934; *Minutes of Council*, 10 September 1934, URC *Minutes*, 17 July 1934, 2 August 1934, 6 September 1934, 13 September 1934, 20 September 1934, 11 October 1934 and later.

66. See *Minutes of Council*, 10 September 1934, 9 October 1934. In September, Avery, *Dangerous Foreigners*, p. 114. The timing is curious; the rates had been falling anyway. See Roberts, ''Shovelling Out the Unemployed,'' and especially Mike Goeres' M. A. thesis, ''Disorder, Dependency and Fiscal Responsibility: Unemployment Relief in Winnipeg, 1907-42,'' University of Manitoba, 1981, p. 284.

67. File 563236, 11 February 1933; drunkenness was a recurring issue. There are complaints of a drunken deport officer scaring children on the train: File C1599, 28 May 1930. The Montreal Agent during this period was apparently often drunk and was eventually fired on that account. Ibid., Commissioner of Immigration to ADM, 4 February 1930 ff.

68. Ibid., Division Commissioner to Deputy Minister, 31 July 1931.

69. Ibid., Commissioner to ADM, 4 February 1930; Acting Agent Beard to DPW-Montreal, 14 February 1930; ADM Jolliffe to DPW-Montreal, 10 April 1930; Commissioner to Deputy Minister, 28 August 1931, 27 January 1932, 22 April 1932, 22 October 1932; Toronto *Star* exposé, discussed ibid., Division Commissioner Fraser to ADM, 4 January 1932.

70. Ibid., Dr. Helen MacMurchy, Chief, Division of Child Welfare, Department of Health, to Miss Burnham, Supervisor of Women's Branch; ADM's memo, 22 April 1932. See also 29 May 1928, 5 April 1928, 22 May 1930, 28 May 1930, 2 June 1930. Dr. Gurd to Dr. Pagé, Chief of Immigration Medical Service, Department of Health, 10 October 1929; Montreal Agent Moquin to Commissioner of Eastern Division, 22 October 1929; Agent Beard to Fraser, 21 November 1930; Division Commissioner to Deputy Minister, 31 July 1931.

71. Ibid., 10 February 1932; Miss Burnham to Deputy Minister, 17 November 1932; Division Commissioner to ADM, 4 January 1932.

72. Ibid., Division Commissioner to ADM, 4 January 1932; the Deputy Minister agreed; Division Commissioner to Deputy Minister, 31 July 1931; Commissioner to DM, 28 August 1931.

73. Ibid., 1930-35 passim.

74. File 563236, Memo to Crerar, 18 November 1935; 13 February 1934. Memo discussing 1932-33 public charge deportations, nd [January 1934]; Memo from Ottawa to Divisions, 23 August 1934.

75. Ibid., Memo from Ottawa to Divisions, 23 August 1934.

76. RG 26, Vol. 16, file on 1930s public charge deportations. The total cases by nationality were 8, 1, 2, 1, 5, 3, 5, 1, 1 respectively.

77. RG 76, File 156271, Memo, 18 November 1935; File 563236, Memo to Minister, 18 November 1935.

78. RG 26, Vol. 16, ''Summary of public charge deportations 1 November 1931 to 31 January 1935,'' nd; RG 76, File 563236, ''Immigrants deported as public charges during calendar years 1932 and 1933,'' nd.

79. Figures from *Annual Report* of the Department of Immigration and Colonization, 1936.

CHAPTER NINE

1. J. F. Hodgetts, *The Canadian Public Service. A Physiology of Government, 1867-1970*, Toronto, University of Toronto Press, 1973, p. 341.

2. C. F. Fraser, *Control of Aliens in the British Commonwealth of Nations*, London, Hogarth, 1940. See pp. 104, 106, 111, 114.

3.   The third, and least likely, was public opinion. The invisibility of what the Department did was an important barrier against public opinion. Only in isolated instances did
public opinion prove influential – partly because the Department masked its practices
so well, and partly, as Hodgetts points out (in the context of staff management and other
internal concerns) because ministers and cabinets have protected their flanks, and partly
due to complexity.
4.   C. F. Fraser, ibid., p. 114.
5.   Report of the Select Standing Committee on Agriculture and Colonization, Minutes
of Proceedings and Evidence and Report, Appendix Number Eight of Select Committee,
Sessional Papers, House of Commons, 1928. Testimony of Deputy Minister Egan. There
is no indication that Parliament was disturbed by Egan's revelations. On this, see Blair
Fraser, "The Built-in Lie Behind Our Search for Immigrants," *Maclean's* Vol. 78, 19 June
1965. Blair Fraser says, "Canadian immigration policies and practice are a monument
to Canadian hypocrisy."
6.   Public Archives of Canada (PAC) Record Group (RG) 76, File 653, 17 June 1926.
RG 76 files hereafter cited by "File" and number only. The power to deport had been
given to Boards of Inquiry, or to one officer acting as a Board, by the 1906 Act. Subsequent
changes had merely increased the paperwork, rather than decreased the power, of such
Boards or officers. Blair to Dandurand, 14 June 1926. (Compare this with the Senate
Debates). See also, "Memo prepared for the Minister to use in the House," File 653,
29 April 1926.
7.   Ibid., Percy Reid to Cory, 19 December 1918.
8.   In re: Munshi Singh, 1914, cited by C. F. Fraser, p. 100; File 653, Reid to Cory,
19 December 1918, 14 May 1919.
9.   C. F. Fraser, ibid., p. 114.
10.   File 563236, Law Reports of Quebec, Mr. Justice Gibson, Quebec, Mr. Justice
Gibson, Quebec Superior Court, commenting on re: Tershinsky vs. Moquin, 1928.
11.   Cited by C. F. Fraser, Rex vs. Almazoff, p. 102; Arvo Vaaro case, p. 109. See
also File 513116, on Vaaro, and File 513111, on Dan Chomicki, for information on their
case in the Nova Scotia courts and their ultimate deportations. Case of Rex vs. Almazoff,
1919, in Manitoba Superior Court, cited by Fraser, p. 102; Nova Scotia Supreme Court
decision cited by Fraser, p. 109. For the case, see *1933 Dominion Law Reports*, Second
Volume, p. 348.
12.   M. R. Konvitz, *Civil Rights in Immigration*, Ithaca, Cornell University Press, 1953,
pp. 97-98; William Van Vleck, *The Administrative Control of Aliens. A Study in Administrative Law and Procedure*, New York, The Commonwealth Fund, 1932, pp. 48-49, 206.
13.   On the U.S. side, see Jane Perry Clark's description of U.S. law and practice, in
Deportation of Aliens From the United States to Europe, New York, AMS Press, [1931]
1968, p. 116. This was done as part of their Columbia University Studies in the Social
Sciences Series (number 351). For Canada, see File 653, passim.
14.   U.S. deportations cited by Perry Clark, p. 30. Roscoe Pound, "Social and Economic
Problems of the Law," *Annals of the American Society of Political and Social Science*,
Volume 137, Number 225, March 1928, pp. 6-9.
15.   See the Report of the Immigration Commission, *The Immigration Situation in Canada*,
Washington, Government Printing Office, 1910, p. 45. See also William Preston, *Aliens
and Dissenters*; John Higham, *Strangers in the Land. Patterns of American Nativism,
1860-1925*, New York, Atheneum, 1971; and especially Van Vleck on judicial review,
pp. 149-207.

APPENDIX

Ministers Responsible for Immigration, 1867-1936

1867-1869	Jean-Charles Chapais *Agriculture*	1905-1911	Frank Oliver *Interior*
1869-1871	Christopher Dunkin *Agriculture*	1911-1912	Robert Rogers *Interior*
1871-1873	John Henry Pope *Agriculture*	1912-1917	William J. Roche *Interior*
1873-1876	Luc L. de St.-Just *Agriculture*	1917-1921	James A. Calder *Immigration and Colonization*
1876-1877	Isaac Burpee (Acting) *Agriculture*	1921	John W. Edwards *Immigration and Colonization*
1877-1878	Charles A. P. Pelletier *Agriculture*		
1878-1885	John Henry Pope *Agriculture*	1922	Hewitt Bostock (Acting) *Immigration and Colonization*
1885-1892	John Carling *Agriculture*	1922-1923	Charles Stewart (Acting) *Immigration and Colonization*
1892	Edgar Dewdney *Interior*	1923-1925	James A. Robb *Immigration and Colonization*
1892-1896	T. Mayne Daly *Interior*		
1896	Hugh John MacDonald *Interior*	1925	George N. Gordon *Immigration and Colonization*
1896	Richard W. Scott (Acting) *Interior*	1925-1926	Charles Stewart (Acting) *Immigration and Colonization*
1896-1905	Clifford Sifton *Interior*		
1905	Wilfrid Laurier (Acting) *Interior*	1926	Robert J. Manion (Acting) *Immigration and Colonization*

1926	Henry Drayton (Acting) *Immigration and* *Colonization*	1930-1932	Wesley A. Gordon *Immigration and* *Colonization*
1926-1929	Robert Forke *Immigration and* *Colonization*	1932	Wesley A. Gordon (Acting) *Immigration and* *Colonization*
1929-1930	Charles Stewart (Acting) *Immigration and* *Colonization*	1932-1936	Thomas Crerar *Immigration and* *Colonization*
1930	Ian A. McKenzie *Immigration and* *Colonization*		

Deputy Ministers for Immigration, 1867-1936

1867-1888	Joseph C. Taché *Agriculture*	1921-1923	Frederick C. Blair (Acting) *Immigration and* *Colonization*
1888-1893	John Lowe *Agriculture*	1923	William D. Scott (Acting) *Immigration and* *Colonization*
1893-1897	Alexander M. Burgess *Interior*	1923-1934	William J. Egan *Immigration and* *Colonization*
1897-1904	James A. Smart *Interior*		
1904-1917	William W. Cory *Interior*	1934-1936	T. Magladery *Immigration and* *Colonization*
1918	Joseph A. Coté (Acting) *Immigration and* *Colonization*		
1918-1921	William W. Cory *Immigration and* *Colonization*		

BIBLIOGRAPHY

PRIMARY SOURCES

Public Archives of Canada, Ottawa

Interviews
Bauer, Martin, F. D. Millar, Sound Division.
Bruce, John, F. D. Millar, Sound Division.
Rees, David, F. D. Millar, Sound Division.

Manuscripts
R. B. Bennett Papers, MG 26K.
Young Women's Christian Association Papers, MG 28I.

Public Records
Department of Justice, RG 13.
Royal Canadian Mounted Police, RG 18.
Department of National Defence, RG 24.
Department of Citizenship and Immigration, RG 26.
Department of Interior, Department of Immigration and Colonization, RG 76.

Published Reports

Canada
Department of Interior, *Annual Reports*, 1892-1919.
Department of Immigration and Colonization, *Annual Reports*, 1919-1935.
House of Commons *Debates*, 1900-1938.
Senate *Debates*, 1900-1938.

Ontario
Department of Labour, *Report*, Special Paper Number 23, 1930.

Great Britain
Parliamentary Papers.

United States
The Immigration Commission, *The Immigration Situation in Canada*, presented by Mr. Dillingham, 61st Congress, 2d Session, Senate Document No. 469, Washington, U.S. Government Printing Office, 1910.

Provincial Archives of Manitoba

Manuscript Group 1312, Bracken papers.

Provincial Archives of Ontario

Attorney-General's Department, Record Group 4.

Winnipeg City Archives

Winnipeg City Council, *Minutes of Council*, 1929-1936.
Winnipeg City Council, Council Papers, 1929-1936.
Winnipeg Unemployment Relief Committee, *Minutes*, 1932-35.

Winnipeg Free Press Archives

Winnipeg City Council Scrapbooks, 1929-1935.

Newspapers and Periodicals

Canadian Forum, 1931-34; *Canadian Labor Defender*, 1930-1935; *Labor Defender*, 1935; Montreal *Gazette*, 1922-31; Ottawa *Citizen*, 1933; Ottawa *Evening Journal*, 1922; *Saturday Night*, 1934; Toronto *Globe*, 1974; Winnipeg *Free Press*, 1931-33; Winnipeg *Tribune*, 1933.

Published Articles

Bryce, Peter. "Social Ethics as Influenced by Immigration." *Papers and Reports of the American Public Health Association*, Vol. XXXIII, Part I, 1906.

Bryce, Peter. "Immigration in Relation to the Public Health". *Canadian Journal of Medicine and Surgery*, April 1906.

Byron, William. "The Menace of the Alien". *Maclean's*, Vol. 32, No. 10, 1919.

Clarke, C. K. "The Defective and Insane Immigrant". University of Toronto *University Monthly*, Vol. 8, 1907-08.

McLaughlin, Allan. "How Immigrants are Inspected". *Popular Science Monthly*, February 1905.

Pimlotte, Ralph. "Closing Relief Camp Sparks Riot". *Briarpatch*, January-February 1983.

Pimlotte, Ralph. "Life in Saskatoon during the 'Hard Times'". *Briarpatch*, March 1983.

Pound, Roscoe. "Social and Economic Problems of the Law". *Annals of the American Society of Political and Social Sciences*, Volume 137, Number 225, March 1928.

Rex v Buck et al., Ontario Court of Appeals, Mulock CJO. *Dominion Law Reports* (1932)3.

Scott, Frank. "Immigration Act: False Arrest, Illegal Treatment of Arrested Person". *Canadian Bar Review*, January 1936.

Scott, Frank. "The Trial of the Toronto Communists". *Queen's Quarterly*, August 1932.

Stevenson, J. A. "The Problem of the Foreigner in Canada". *Westminster Review*, September 1913.

Wade v Egan et al., Manitoba Court of Appeal, Prendergast CJM. *Canadian Criminal Cases* 193 Vol. 54.

Published Books

Abella, Irving, and David Millar, eds. *The Canadian Worker in the Twentieth Century*. Toronto: Oxford University Press, 1978.

Beeching, William, and Phyllis Clarke, eds. *Yours in the Struggle: The Reminiscences of Tim Buck*, Toronto: NC Press, 1977.

Blais, Hervé. *Les Tendances Eugenistes au Canada*. Montréal: L'Institut familial, 1942.

Bradwin, Edmund. *The Bunkhouse Man. A Study of Work and Pay in the Camps of Canada, 1903-1914*. Toronto: University of Toronto Press, 1972.

Clark, Jane Perry. *Deportation of Aliens From the United States to Europe*. New York: AMS Press, [1931], 1968.

Coats, E. W., ed. *Poverty in the Victorian Age: Debates on the Issues from 19th Century Critical Journals. Volume II. English Poor Laws, 1834-70*. London: Gregg, 1973.

Fraser, C. F. *Control of Aliens in the British Commonwealth of Nations*. London: Hogarth, 1940.

Haythorne, George and L. C. Marsh. *Land and Labour. A Social Survey of Agriculture and the Farm Labour Market in Central Canada*. Toronto: Oxford University Press, 1941.

Horn, Michiel, ed. *The Dirty Thirties*. Toronto: Copp Clark, 1972.

Magrath, C. A. *Canada's Growth and Some Problems Affecting It*. Ottawa: Mortimer, 1910.

Murphy, Emily. *The Black Candle*. [Toronto: Thomas Allen, 1922] Toronto: Coles, 1973.

National Council of Women of Canada. *Report of the International Congress of Women, Toronto, June 24-30, 1909*, Volume II. Toronto: National Council of Women, 1910.

Nicholls, George. *A History of the Irish Poor Law*. [London: John Murray, 1856] New York: Augustus Kelley, 1967.

Nicholls, George. *A History of the Scotch Poor Law in Connexion With the Condition of the People*. London: Murray, 1856.

Ryan, Oscar. *Deported!* Canadian Labour Defense League, 1932.

Smith, W. G. *A Study in Canadian Immigration*. Toronto: Ryerson, 1920.

Van Vleck, William. *The Administrative Control of Aliens. A Study in Administrative Law and Procedure*. New York: The Commonwealth Fund, 1932.

Wakefield, E. Gibbon. *Letters from Sydney and Other Writings*. London: Dent, 1929.

Young Women's Christian Association. *Our Unfolding Purpose. Report of the World's Y.W.C.A.* Stockholm: Y.W.C.A., 1914.

SECONDARY SOURCES

Unpublished Graduate Theses and Essays

Bacchi, Carol. "Liberation Deferred. The Ideas of English Canadian Suffragists, 1877-1918." Unpublished Ph.D. thesis, McGill University, 1976.

Boudreau, Joseph. "The Enemy Alien Problem in Canada, 1914-1921." Unpublished Ph.D. thesis, University of California at Los Angeles, 1964.

Dick, Lyle. "Deportation under the Immigration Act and the Canadian Criminal Code, 1919-1936." Unpublished M.A. thesis, University of Manitoba, 1978.

Drysteck, Henry. "Deportation of European Immigrants during the Administration of R. B. Bennett." Unpublished M.A. essay, Carleton University, 1976.

Goeres, Michael. "Disorder, Dependency and Fiscal Responsibility: Unemployment Relief in Winnipeg, 1907-42." Unpublished M.A. thesis, University of Manitoba, 1981.

Millar, F. David. "Shapes of Power. The Ontario Labour Relations Board, 1930-1970." Unpublished Ph.D. thesis, York University, 1981.

Millar, F. David. "The Winnipeg General Strike, 1919: A Reinterpretation in the Light of Oral History and Pictorial Evidence." Unpublished M.A. thesis, Carleton University, 1970.

Usiskin, Roseline. "Toward a Theoretical Reformulation of the Relationship Between Political Ideology, Social Class, and Ethnicity: A Case Study of the Winnipeg Jewish Radical Community, 1905-1920." Unpublished M.A. thesis, University of Manitoba, 1978.

Unpublished Articles and Papers

Adams, Ron. "The Anticommunist Role of the RCMP in the Depression." Unpublished paper presented to the Annual Meeting of the Canadian Historical Association, London, 1978.

Buckley, Suzann. "The Impact of World War I upon Canadian Public Health Reform." Paper presented to the conference of the Canadian Association for American Studies, McMaster University, October 1977.

Carpenter, Louise. "Deportation of Immigrants during the Depression." Unpublished paper, University of Manitoba, 1973.

McMullan, John. "Law, Order and Power: Theory, Questions, and Some Limits to Social History of Crime in Early Modern England." [np], 1985.

Millar, F. David. "Chronology of Labour and Welfare Law in Ontario, 1867-1977." Not published, 1977.

Millar, F. David. "Real Incomes in Manitoba." Not published, 1984.

Roberts, Barbara. "Social Policy, Female Dependence and the Living Wage." Paper presented to the Annual Meeting of the Canadian Women's Studies Association, Learned Societies, Ottawa, 1982.

Roberts, Barbara and David Millar. "Living with Less: Trends in Women's Earnings." Paper presented to the Annual Meeting of the Western Association of Sociology and Anthropology, Regina, 1984.

Published Articles

Adams, Ron. "The 1931 Arrest and Trial of the Leaders of the Communist Party of Canada". Canadian Historical Association, 1977.

Avery, Donald. "Canadian Immigration Policy and the 'Foreign' Navvy, 1896-1916". *Historical Papers*, 1972.

Avery, Donald. "Continental European Immigrant Workers in Canada, 1896-1919: From Stalwart Peasants to Radical Proletariat". *Canadian Review of Sociology and Anthropology*, Vol. 12, 1975.

Avery, Donald. "Sam Scarlett". *Canadian Ethnic Studies*, Vol. 10, No. 2, 1978.

Boudreau, Joseph. "The Enemy Alien Problem in World War I". *Alberta Historical Review*, Winter 1964.

Brown, R. C. "Whither Are We Being Shoved? Political Leadership in Canada during World War I". In J. L. Granatstein and R. Cuff, eds. *War and Society in North America*. Toronto: Thomas Nelson, 1971.

Buckley, Suzann. "British Female Immigration and Imperial Development". *Hecate: Women's Interdisciplinary Journal*, January 1977.

Burawoy, Michael. "The Functions and Reproduction of Migrant Labour: Comparative Material from South Africa and the United States". *American Journal of Sociology*, Vol. 81, No. 5, March 1976.

Cashmore, Ernest. "The Social Organization of Canadian Immigration Law". *Canadian Journal of Sociology*, Fall 1978.

Comack, Elizabeth. "The Origins of Canadian Drug Legislation". In Thomas Fleming, ed. *The New Criminologies in Canada. State, Crime, and Control*. Toronto: Oxford University Press, 1985.

Drystek, Henry. "The Simplest and Cheapest Mode of Dealing with Them: Deportation from Canada before World War II". *Histoire sociale*, November 1982.

Fraser, Blair. "The Built-in Lie behind Canada's Search for Immigrants". *Maclean's*, Vol. 78, 19 June 1965.

Godler, Zlata. "Doctors and the New Immigrants". *Canadian Ethnic Studies*, Vol. XI, No. 1, 1977.

Haythorne, George. "Harvest Labor in Western Canada: An Episode in Economic Planning". *Quarterly Journal in Economics*, Vol. XLVII, August 1973.

Horn, Michiel. "Keeping Canada Canadian: Anticommunism in Toronto, 1928-29". *Canada. An Historical Magazine*, September 1975.

Horn, Michiel. "Free Speech within the Law: The Letter of the 68 Toronto Professors, 1931". *Ontario History*, March 1980.

Imai, Shin. "Deportation in the Depression". *Queen's Law Journal*, Vol. 7, No. 1, 1981.

Katz, Leslie. "Some Legal Consequences of the Winnipeg General Strike". *Manitoba Law Journal*, Vol. 4, 1970.

Katz, Michael. "Origins of the Institutional State". *Marxist Perspectives*, Winter 1978.

Kitsuse, John and Aaran Cicorel. "A Note on the Uses of Official Statistics". *Social Problems*, Fall 1963.

Lai, Chuen-Yan David. "A 'Prison' for Chinese Immigrants". *Asianadian*, Vol. 2, No. 4, 1980.

Laine, Edward. "Finnish Canadian Radicalism and Canadian Politics: The First Forty Years, 1900-1940". In Jurgen Dahlie and Tissa Fernando, eds. *Ethnicity, Power and Politics in Canada*. Toronto: Methuen, 1981.

MacKenzie, J. B. "Section 98, Criminal Code and Freedom of Expression in Canada". *Queen's Law Journal*, Vol. 4, No. 11, 1972.

Magubane, Bernard. "The 'Native Reserves' (Bantustans) and the Role of the Migrant Labour System in The Political Economy of South Africa". In A. Idris-Soven, E. Idris-Soven, and M. Vaughan. *The World as a Company Town. Multinational Corporations and Social Change*. The Hague: Mouton, 1978.

Makahonuk, Glen. "The Saskatoon Relief Camp Workers' Riot of May 8, 1933: An Expression of Class Conflict". *Saskatchewan History*, Spring 1984.

Makahonuk, Glen. "The Saskatchewan Coal Strikes of 1932: A Study in Class Relations". *Prairie Forum*, Vol. 8, No. 1, 1984.

Makahonuk, Glen. "Class Conflict in Saskatoon during the 'Red Decade'". *Briarpatch*, May 1983.

McKillop, Brian. "The Communist as Conscience: Jacob Penner and Winnipeg Civic Politics, 1934-35". In R. McCormack and I. MacPherson, eds. *Cities in the West*. Ottawa: Mercury Series, Museum of Man, 1975.

McNaught, Kenneth. "Political Trials and the Canadian Political Tradition". *University of Toronto Law Review*, 1975.

Morton, Desmond. "Sir William Otter and Internment Operations in Canada During the First World War". *Canadian Historical Review*, March 1974.

Peterson, T. "Ethnic and Class Politics in Manitoba". In Martin Robin, ed. *Canadian Provincial Politics*. Toronto: Prentice Hall, 1972.

Petryshyn, J. "R. B. Bennett and the Communists". *Journal of Canadian Studies*, November 1974.

Petryshyn, J. "Class Conflict and Civil Liberties: The Origins and Activities of the Canadian Labor Defense League, 1925-1940". *Labour/Le travailleur*, Autumn 1982.

Rasporitch, Anthony. "Tomo Cacic: Rebel without a Country". *Canadian Ethnic Studies*, Vol. 10, No. 2, 1978.

Rea, Ed. "The Politics of Class: Winnipeg City Council 1919-1943". In C. Berger and R. Cook, eds. *The West and the Nation*. Toronto: McClelland and Stewart, 1976.

Repo, Satu. "Lakehead in the 1930s – A Labour Militant Remembers" [Einar Nordstrom]. *This Magazine*, July/August 1979.

Roberts, Barbara. "A Work of Empire: Canadian Reformers and British Female Immigration". In L. Kealey, ed. *A Not Unreasonable Claim: Women and Reform in Canada, 1880s-1920s*. Toronto: Women's Press, 1979.

Roberts, Barbara. "Doctors and Deports: The Role of the Medical Profession in Deportation Policy and Practice, 1900-1936". *Canadian Ethnic Studies*, January 1987.

Roberts, Barbara. "Ladies, Women and the State: Managing Female Immigration, 1880-1920". In Jacob Muller, Roxana Ng and Gillian Walker, eds. *Management of Dissent: Community Organizing and the State*. Forthcoming, 1988.

Roberts, Barbara. "Sex, Politics and Religion: Controversies in Female Immigration Work in Montreal, 1880-1920". *Atlantis. A Journal of Women's Studies*, Fall 1980.

Roberts, Barbara. "Shovelling Out the Unemployed: Winnipeg City Council and Deportation, 1930-35". *Manitoba History*, Fall 1983.

Roberts, Barbara. "Shovelling Out the 'Mutinous': Political Deportation from Canada before 1936". *Labour/Le travail*, Autumn 1986.

Smith, David Edward. "Emergency Government in Canada". *Canadian Historical Review*, December 1969.

Smith, Dorothy. "The Social Construction of Documentary Reality". *Sociology Inquiry*, Vol. IV, No. 4, 1975.

Sumner, Colin. "The Ideological Nature of Law". In Piers Beirne and Richard Quinney, eds. *Marxism and Law*. New York: John Wiley, 1982.

Thane, Pat. "Women and the Poor Law in Victorian and Edwardian England". *History Workshop Journal*, No. 6, Autumn 1978.

Thomas, Robert. "Citizenship and Gender in Work Organisation: Some Considerations for Theories of the Labor Process". *Marxist Inquiries, American Journal of Sociology* Supplement, Volume 88, 1982.

Thompson, John. "The Political Career of Ralph H. Webb". *Red River Valley Historian*, Summer 1976.

Trachtenberg, Henry. "The Winnipeg Jewish Community and Politics: The Inter-war Years, 1919-1939". *Manitoba Historical and Scientific Society Transactions*, Vol. 35, 1978/79-1979/80.

Published Books

Abella, Irving and Harold Troper. *None is Too Many: Canada and the Jews of Europe, 1933-1948*. Toronto: Lester and Orpen Dennys, 1982.

Angus, Ian. *Canadian Bolsheviks. The Early Years of the Communist Party of Canada*. Montreal: Vanguard, 1981.

Avakuvomic, Ivan. *The Communist Party in Canada. A History*. Toronto: McClelland and Stewart, 1975.

Avery, Donald. *Dangerous Foreigners: European Immigrant Workers and Labour Radicalism in Canada, 1896-1932*. Toronto: McClelland and Stewart, 1979.

Bercuson, David. *Confrontation at Winnipeg: Labour, Industrial Relations, and the General Strike*. Montreal: McGill-Queen's, 1974.

Bercuson, David. *Fools and Wise Men: The Rise and Fall of the One Big Union*. Toronto: McGraw Hill Ryerson, 1978.

Berger, Carl, and Ramsay Cook, eds. *The West and the Nation. Essays in Honour of W. L. Morton*. Toronto: McClelland and Stewart, 1976.

Betcherman, Lita Rose. *The Little Band*. Ottawa: Deneau, 1983.

Braverman, Harry. *Labor and Monopoly Capital. The Degradation of Work in the Twentieth Century*. New York: Monthly Review, 1974.

Browne, Lorne and Caroline. *An Unauthorized History of the RCMP*. Toronto: Lorimer, 1978.

Castles, S. and G. Kosack. *Immigrant Workers and Class Structures in Western Europe*. London: Oxford University Press, 1973.

Clark, S. D. *The Position of the French-Speaking Population in the Northern Industrial Community*. Report to the Royal Commission on Bilingualism and Biculturalism, 1966.

Dahlie, Jurgen and Tissa Fernando, eds. *Ethnicity, Power and Politics in Canada*. Toronto: Methuen, 1981.

Ditton, Jason. *Controlology. Beyond the New Criminology*. London: Macmillan, 1979.

Dreisziger, N. et al. *Struggle and Hope. The Hungarian-Canadian Experience*. Toronto: McClelland and Stewart, 1982.

Fleming, Thomas, ed. *The New Criminologies in Canada. State, Crime, and Control*. Toronto: Oxford University Press, 1985.

Garraty, John. *Unemployment in History. Economic Thought and Public Policy*. New York: Harper and Row, 1978.

Gatrell, Victor et al., eds. *Crime and the Law Since 1550*. London: Europa, 1980.

George, Dorothy. *London Life Before the Eighteenth Century*. Evanston, Illinois: Harper and Row, [1925] 1964.

Graham, Roger. *Arthur Meighen. Volume I. The Door of Opportunity*. Toronto: Clarke, Irwin, 1960.

Hall, Stuart et al. *Policing the Crisis. Mugging, the State, and Law and Order*. London: Macmillan, 1978.

Harney, Robert et al., eds. *The Italian Immigrant Woman in North America*. Toronto: Multicultural History Society of Ontario, 1978.

Haythorne, George. *Labor in Canadian Agriculture*. Cambridge: Harvard University Press, 1960.

Higgins, E. G. and F. A. Peake. *Sudbury Then and Now: A Pictorial History 1883-1973*. Sudbury: Chamber of Commerce, 197[-].

Higham, John. *Strangers in the Land. Patterns of American Nativism, 1860-1925*. New York: Atheneum, 1971.

Hodgetts, J. F. *The Canadian Public Service. A Physiology of Government, 1867-1970.* Toronto: University of Toronto Press, 1973.

Idris-Soven, A. et al. *The World as Company Town. Multinational Corporations and Social Change.* The Hague: Mouton, 1978.

Ivanov, Y. M. *Agrarian Reform and Hired Labour in Africa.* Moscow: Progress Publishers, 1979.

Kamin, Leon. *The Science and Politics of I.Q.* Potomac, Maryland: Lawrence Erlbaum Associates, 1974.

Kealey, Linda, ed. *A Not Unreasonable Claim. Women and Reform in Canada, 1880s-1920s.* Toronto: Women's Press, 1979.

Konvitz, C. R. *Civil Rights in Immigration.* Ithaca: Cornell University Press, 1953.

Kornbluth, Joyce, ed. *Rebel Voices: An IWW Anthology.* Ann Arbor: University of Michigan Press, 1964.

The Labour Collective. *Women at Work. Ontario, 1850-1939.* Toronto: Women's Press, 1974.

Lindstrom-Best, Varpu, ed. *Finns in Ontario,* Special Issue of *Polyphony: Bulletin of the Multicultural History Society of Ontario,* Fall 1981.

Lloyd, P. C. *Africa in Social Change. Changing Traditional Societies in the Modern World.* Harmondsworth: Penguin, 1967.

Marshall, Dorothy. *The English Poor Law in the Eighteenth Century.* London: Routledge and Kegan Paul, [1926] 1969.

McCormack, A. R. *Reformers, Rebels, and Revolutionaries. Western Canadian Radical Movements, 1899-1919.* Toronto: University of Toronto Press, 1979.

McNaught, Kenneth. *A Prophet in Politics. A Biography of J. S. Woodsworth.* Toronto: University of Toronto Press, 1959.

Morton, J. *In the Sea of Sterile Mountains: A History of the Chinese in British Columbia.* Vancouver: J. J. Douglas, 1974.

Oxley, Geoffrey. *Poor Relief in England and Wales, 1601-1834.* London: David and Charles, 1974.

Palmer, Bryan. *A Culture in Conflict. Skilled Workers and Industrial Capitalism in Hamilton, Ontario, 1860-1914.* Montreal: McGill-Queen's, 1979.

Piva, Michael. *The Condition of the Working Class in Toronto, 1900-1921.* Ottawa: University of Ottawa Press, 1979.

Preston, William. *Aliens and Dissenters. Federal Suppression of Radicals, 1903-1933.* New York: Harper, 1963.

Quinney, Richard. *Class, State, and Crime. On the Theory and Practice of Criminal Justice.* New York: Longmans, 1977.

Rasporich, Anthony. *For a Better Life. A History of the Croatians in Canada.* Toronto: McClelland and Stewart, 1982.

Rea, Ed. *Parties and Power: An Analysis of Winnipeg City Council, 1919-1975*. Winnipeg: City of Winnipeg, 1976.

Rodney, William. *Soldiers of the International*. Toronto: University of Toronto Press, 1968.

Sawatsky, John. *Men in the Shadows: The RCMP Security Service*. Toronto: Totem, 1980.

Teeple, Gary, ed. *Capitalism and the National Question in Canada*. Toronto: University of Toronto Press, 1972.

Therborn, Goran. *What Does the Ruling Class Do When It Rules? State Apparatuses and State Power under Feudalism, Capitalism and Socialism*. London: N.L.B., 1978.

Thompson, E. P. *The Making of the English Working Class*. Harmondsworth: Penguin, 1968.

Upton, A. *The Communist Parties of Scandinavia and Finland*. London: Weidenfeld and Nicholson, 1973.

Warwaruk, Larry. *Red Finns on the Coteau*. Saskatoon: Core Communications, 1984.

Watson, Louise. *She Never Was Afraid. The Biography of Annie Buller*. Toronto: Progress, 1976.

Weisbord, Merrily. *The Strangest Dream*. Toronto: Lester and Orpen Dennys, 1983.